PRAISE FOR *FOR BROWN GIRLS WITH SHARP EDGES AND TENDER HEARTS*

"Required reading.... A celebration of brownness at a vital moment [and] a manual for tapping into brown girls' power.... Mojica Rodríguez's electrifying debut channels mesmeric prose to heal the wounds of white supremacy."

—Jean Guerrero, *Los Angeles Times*

"Searing and revolutionary, this book blazes a trail towards liberation."

—Diane Guerrero, author of *In the Country We Love*

"Anyone who has ever felt stepped on or pushed aside could benefit from reading [this book].... in her manual for fighting generations of sexism, racism and classism, Mojica Rodriguez pushes readers to step outside their comfort zone, sit in someone else's seat and understand the struggle."

—CNBC.com

"This is the Brown girl manifesto I've been waiting for my whole life."

—Erika L. Sánchez, author of *I Am Not Your Perfect Mexican Daughter*

"Through her intimate storytelling and warm embrace of the Black and brown girls she writes for, [Mojica] Rodríguez also gently holds the reader as she invites them on the painful path toward freedom."

—*POPSUGAR Latina*

"Thought-provoking and enlightening.... beautifully and earnestly written to reach the hearts of women of color working toward justice and equity. The book may also be instructional for non-Latinx folks: it offers a valuable lesson in decentering our world view, so we may humbly listen and understand."

—*Seattle Book Review*

"I wish I had found this book as a sixteen-year-old, then as a twenty-six-year-old, and again now. Prisca writes with the familiar voice of an older prima that wants to teach you everything she's learned. This book is beyond a love letter. It a reckoning and an affirmation that there is power beyond the fear of our fearlessness. This book has fed me what I did not know I hungered for."
—Yesika Salgado, author of *Corazón*

"Impassioned and accessible....Aiming to redistribute knowledge she gained during her graduate studies to young women who may not have access to higher education, Mojica Rodríguez interweaves her life story with primers on such concepts as colonialism, the myth of meritocracy, the male gaze, and intersectionality...this is an inspiring and well-informed call to action."
—*Publishers Weekly*

"Rodriguez's life has been challenging, which is why, she says, she wrote this powerful book: to connect to other BIPOC women and girls who understand her background and to show those readers that they are seen and important....Highly recommended."
—*Library Journal*

"Prisca has crafted a fierce and vibrant book that brings to life the secret fears and profound hopes of so many brown girls, across so many communities of color. She is a brilliant storyteller with a stunning voice. This is a book for brown girls to hold close."
—Sonalee Rashatwar, LCSW MEd, co-owner, Radical Therapy Center

"Prisca Dorcas Mojica Rodriguez writes about her own life story, colonialism, imposter syndrome, colorism, meritocracy, intersectionality, and how women can break free from systemic oppressions that hold them back. Part memoir, part empowering guide."
—*People en Español*, September Issue

"Prisca Dorcas Mojica Rodríguez perfectly balances the art of memoir with a biting critical eye, offering an understanding of Latina womanhood bursting with intellect, but grounded in real-life experience. With her carefully chosen words, she invites readers into a deeper relationship with themselves, their communities, and the world at large."
—Melissa A. Fabello, PhD, author of *Appetite*

"Prisca works to empower women of color by sharing her own experiences and stories of decolonizing her mentality. With vulnerable insight into her hopes and fears, her words will undoubtedly motivate you to fight for your own voice."

—BE Latina

"This memoir/guide/educational resource is ultimately a love letter to brown girls that's also a testament to the power of reclaiming your identity in the face of white supremacy."

—HipLatina

"In this book, Prisca Dorcas Mojica Rodriguez shares truths with precision and unapologetic vulnerability, and teaches us through her stories and insights. Her book is a deep and profound gift for her readers. A necessary and treasured read for generations to come."

—Johanna Toruño, Salvadoran multimedia artist and founder, The Unapologetic Street Series

"Tackles racism, colorism, classism, the immigrant experience, and more in ways that are honest, relatable, refreshing, and inspiring"

—Reader's Digest

"Prisca is a Latinx voice who calls for accountability, healing, and growth in her book. Her writing will connect with our communities, who are seeing themselves represented for the first time. A breath of fresh air."

—Curly Velasquez, queer actor and writer

"Prisca Dorcas Mojica Rodríguez is among the most brilliant Latina thinkers of our generation.... Here, she explores the inequalities of race, class and gender, discussing issues of code-switching, colorism, intersectional feminism, decolonization and more."

—Mitu

"I will never forget when Prisca sent me the kindest of messages about the outlet I had founded in 2011 and how it inspired her to set her own course as an influential writer, voice and author. Prisca has the unique talent to speak to her generation with honesty, fearlessness and truth. Her latest work is foundational in understanding what it means to be a Brown girl today."

—Julio Ricardo Varela, award-winning journalist and founder, Latino Rebels

FOR
BR♥WN
GIRLS
WITH
SHARP EDGES
AND TENDER
HEARTS

PRISCA DORCAS MOJICA RODRÍGUEZ

FOR BR♥WN GIRLS

GIRLS

WITH SHARP EDGES AND TENDER HEARTS

A LOVE LETTER TO WOMEN OF COLOR

SEAL PRESS

New York

Copyright © 2021 by Prisca Dorcas Mojica Rodríguez

Cover design by Ann Kirchner
Cover images © Bibadash / Shutterstock.com; © Mary Long / Shutterstock.com
Cover copyright © 2022 Hachette Book Group, Inc.

Seal Press
Hachette Book Group
1290 Avenue of the Americas, New York, NY 10104
www.sealpress.com
@sealpress

Printed in the United States of America

Originally published in hardcover and e-book by Seal Press in September 2021
First Trade Paperback Edition: October 2022

Published by Seal Press, an imprint of Perseus Books, LLC, a subsidiary of Hachette Book Group, Inc. The Seal Press name and logo is a trademark of the Hachette Book Group.

The Hachette Speakers Bureau provides a wide range of authors for speaking events. To find out more, go to www.hachettespeakersbureau.com or call (866) 376-6591.

The publisher is not responsible for websites (or their content) that are not owned by the publisher.

Print book interior design by Amy Quinn.

Library of Congress Cataloging-in-Publication Data
Names: Mojica Rodríguez, Prisca Dorcas, 1985- author.
Title: For brown girls with sharp edges and tender hearts: a love letter to women of color / Prisca Dorcas Mojica Rodriguez.
Description: New York: Seal Press, 2021. | Includes bibliographical references. |
Identifiers: LCCN 2021016112 | ISBN 9781541674875 (hardcover) | ISBN 9781541674868 (ebook)
Subjects: LCSH: Mojica Rodríguez, Prisca Dorcas, 1985- | Nicaraguan American women—Biography. | Racism—United States. | United States—Race relations | Minority women—United States—Conduct of life. | Nicaraguan Americans—Race identity. | Indigenous peoples—Ethnic identity. | Immigrant students—United States—Biography. | Christian women—United States—Biography. | Coming of age.
Classification: LCC E184.N53 M65 2021 | DDC 305.48/8073—dc23
LC record available at https://lccn.loc.gov/2021016112

ISBNs: 9781541674875 (hardcover), 9781541674868 (ebook), 9781541674882 (trade paperback)

LSC-C

Printing 3, 2024

For the difficult daughters.

CONTENTS

DEAR BROWN GIRL...

You are eternal. You have a fire burning inside you, and it comes from your mami's side. Protect your fire, protect that flame. You feel everything and feel nothing. You carry your pain, the pain that comes from asking too many questions, because once you've heard your chains rattle, you cannot unhear them. You persevere for yourself, but also for your mami and your papi, and for your little hermanita who is only now beginning to understand the limitations that our cultura has placed on her.

You are neither here nor there, but everywhere. You carry your cultura in your veins and academia in your heart. You have not forgotten where you come from, but you have learned and earned and maybe even forced your way into spaces not meant for you. You are poderosa like that. You defy the expectations of respectability and you do not seem to care—do you, Brown girl.

Your vocabulary is vast and your wit is sharp. You are unstoppable.

You are going places that no one in your family has ever been and you are fearful of your fearlessness. You belong to no one but are accountable to many. We depend on you. Do not let anyone else tell you differently.

You are groundbreaking. Your parents brag about your brilliance all while exhorting you to be more like their friends' daughters, the good obedient daughters who did what they were told. Your parents say this because they do not know what to do with their Brown girl. They have not been able to hold your fire for some time now. But you must hold your parents in your heart as you dismantle the systems that have kept people like them down. They were kept down, but not you, Brown girl. You owe it to them to keep fighting.

Partners have tried to pin you down, they have tried to claim you, but you have resisted because you are not meant to belong to anyone. You belong entirely to yourself.

Your laugh carries liberation in it.

Brown girl, do not let them take away your passion. Because they will try, without any compassion, to keep you down. But remember that without passion you will extinguish, and so to be safe, make sure that you keep others nearby who can pick you up and light you up again.

Because, Brown girl, we need each other.

INTRODUCTION

This book is my way of democratizing knowledge. Those in power maintain their status by gatekeeping. The halls of power have always been intended for some and locked away from many. You cannot find most of the books that changed my life in a public library; you have to search for them in university libraries. And once you get your hands on those books, they are not meant to be understood by people without at least a college degree. The jargon and verbosity that is admired by academics is intentionally inaccessible. That inaccessibility is gatekeeping at its finest. If academics make all their theories readily available to you, then how can they stay relevant? If they give you all the resources, they lose power. If they make their sources and vast knowledge easily available to oppressed communities, they lose power. Accessibility is about power, gatekeeping is founded on the protection of power, and to all that I say: fuck that, because information that can change lives should never be hoarded.

This book is a map, and it can lead to many destinations—internally, interpersonally, and far beyond. This book is my little kernel of knowledge for you. May it heal you, may it challenge you, may it make you laugh, but most importantly, may it lead you back to you.

Now, before we run this marathon together, let's be sure we begin on the same starting line.

I utilize the word Latinx, instead of Hispanic or the gendered male Latino, to talk about my communities. Hispanic does not include people without Spanish ancestry, and it does not include non-Spanish speakers. I am not utilizing the word Hispanic since it does exclude so many people from Latin America and the Caribbean, including Indigenous communities and Portuguese-speaking folks. On the other hand, Latino is a gendered term, and like many romance languages, the plural of many of our nouns defaults to a male use of that noun, which centers men. With a positioning like mine, where I am trying to explicitly denounce patriarchy, to then turn around and use a plural term that is male feels contradictory. I use Latinx to encompass the complexities of our countries, and to include women and other genders.

I do not italicize Spanish. Spanish is my first language, and though I am a highly proficient English speaker, to italicize Spanish would denote it as foreign, and that is simply not the case. I have been in conversations, attended classes, and read books where I was outside the assumed circle of common knowledge, and I had to go out alone and find that privileged information for myself. So, I implore my readers: for those of you who cannot grasp what I am saying, fully sit in the experience of what it feels like to be an outsider. Allow the moments that do not include you to inform how you read this text.

I do not believe in true objectivity. What I do believe is that that term is used by people in power, people who are usually white, to give them authority over topics they have only ever read about. Society has weaponized objectivity to silence us, to kill us, and to oppress us. So, since all perspectives are subjective, I will start by letting my readers know how this text will be informed by me and my own foundations. This is a living, breathing text that reflects my politics and my lived experiences.

I do not write for white people; there are an endless number of books written for them. I write for BIWOC, I write for immigrants, I write for those of us who have been harmed by toxic theologies, I write for those of us whose hearts were first broken by our dads, I write so that you can feel seen and held. But this book is not for everyone. No book should be, despite how much white people will advocate for their universal appeal. Every book comes from a person whose life dictated how they wrote it and why they wrote it. There is no universal perspective that can inform everything for everyone. William Shakespeare was a white British playwright, Jane Austen a white English novelist, and Sandra Cisneros a Mexican-American storyteller. Take note of who gets to become relatable to everyone and who is niche, and then deconstruct that.

The idea of democratizing knowledge has always felt important to me. I do not come from folks who were great students, I come from raw talent and a skill to make magic happen out of nothing. I do not want to be a voice for the voiceless, I want to eliminate the barriers that keep people without fancy degrees out of important conversations.

I do not believe that everyone needs to get a college education and a subsequent graduate degree. Meritocracy is a myth, and working hard for these artificial accolades is not a predictor of success—or intelligence. At the same time, when it comes to my own story, I would not have had the access to the knowledge I gained without those institutions. I was very insulated by my conservative Christian upbringing. I needed schooling to learn theory and gain a necessary perspective shift, and to meet people who were focused on this type of learning. Slowly this knowledge resonated for me, helped nourish me and helped me grow.

Senior year in high school, I was walking through the school library and saw this tiny blue book, and I pulled it out and began reading it. I was merely intrigued by its slimness; it looked just different enough to stand out and spark my interest. That book was a collection of poems by Langston Hughes, and the first poem I read was "Let America be America Again." There is a specific line repeated throughout his poem that struck me: *America never was America to me.*

Those lines felt different than anything I had encountered in the canon up to that point; the writing felt intimate, and I understood them not as a Black person living in the United States dealing with the history of slavery, but as a Brown immigrant and a noncitizen. I felt seen through some of those lines, which were not even meant for me. But glimpses of this life-changing knowledge would otherwise elude me. I had no one around me to acknowledge my struggle with Americanness. As an immigrant, I was constantly reminded that I did not belong and I felt like I was always fighting America. America was like this abusive girlfriend: she said she was here to provide opportunities across the board, but on the ground and in my life, everything felt harder to accomplish. When I failed at becoming the American Dream, I was blamed for not working hard enough. America never was America to me, because America was never the America she said she was. I convinced mi mami to buy me that Langston Hughes poetry collection, which I still own. Each time I revisited those words, it felt like I was fanning a fire inside of me that would otherwise have faded.

In graduate school, a network of Black queer women began to recommend books to me. I think these women saw my hunger for learning, and they blessed me with more than I could ever have received outside of the ivory tower of academia. I was familiar with the term feminism, but when I was first introduced to womanism it felt more personal to me. Alice Walker has this famous line, "Womanist is to feminist as purple is to lavender." They're related terms, but womanist is specific to Black women's experiences. Same tree, different branches. My mami's favorite movie is *The Color*

Purple. She sees herself in these women and in their relationships to the men in their lives. I saw it too. It would be Jennifer Bailey who would inform me that my own term existed. She is an ordained reverend of the African Methodist Episcopal Church and now the executive director of Faith Matters, and she sent me to google the term mujerista. Mujerista is a non-Black Latina feminist liberation theology, and part of this theory prioritizes the poor and disenfranchised above anyone else. I remember her gentle and knowing glances at me, saying something along the lines of, *Womanism is not for you, but there is something out there that is meant for you.*

I remember when Carlin Rushing, a grassroots organizer and Black Lives Matter activist in Nashville, handed me the book *Indecent Theology* by Marcella Althaus-Reid and said, "You need to read this." I remember these gifts, which led me down trails of knowledge about our gente. I remember needing those guiding voices, more than I could ever vocalize. For a woman with my background, attending seminary was in itself an act of resistance. But learning through these books how to completely free myself from toxic theologies that had shaped me was a revolutionary act of self-preservation.

My graduate program taught me life-changing terminology that finally freed my worldview from internalized sexism, classism, racism, ableism, xenophobia, and so on. I needed that knowledge, but the exchange almost killed me. I suffered tremendously because I hated how I was seen and treated in those spaces.

I do not think that we should be required to give up our dignity in order to access life-changing knowledge. No one should have to prove to the privileged that you are one of the "good" Brown people. With this book I am attempting to bring this access to you, without having to endure racist standardized testing, prohibitive tuition, the "universal" dead-white-men canon, and the dominating white gaze.

I wanted to write a book that I could have used. I wanted to write the book that would have sparked a fire within me. With this book, I want you to then do whatever you are ready to do with the information you are given. This is your life, and self-determination is a beautiful gift that not many of us have the privilege to truly experience. So I want you to read this book and if something sticks, keep it like I kept my Langston Hughes poems—to fan the fire within you.

My method for this type of knowledge redistribution is called an autoethnography. This is not a memoir, rather a curation of my lived experiences. I am attempting to explain big theory terms by personalizing them, contextualizing. I am not going to define tone policing strictly within academic jargon, instead I will share my own experiences with microaggressions. I will tell you about respectability politics through my own struggles with respectability politics. I will explain decolonization by speaking about my own liberation. These isms do not exist for philosophical salon conversations among the academic elites; these are real lived experiences and will be written about as such.

I will warn you that this work is not pretty and that you might lose a lot of friends and even family along the way, but it is good work because it has the ability to set us free from everything that we have internalized about Blackness, Brownness, Indigeneity, hard work, respect, purity, masculinity, and femininity.

I identify as Brown because I am Brown. This was not always how I identified. As a non-Black and also a non-white person, I am often prompted to pick a race category that does not include me. I am either given a white or black box to check, and I did not always understand where I belonged. I do not read as white, I am not presumed to be white-until-I-speak, nor do people ever get surprised to hear that I am not a white American, in fact I am often asked upon an introduction to explain what type of non-white person I am, with the ever so casual, "where are you really from?" I am not given access to whiteness. When I say I am Brown, I am referring to the color of my skin. It is a beautiful shade of caramel, it is a distant memory of my Indigenous ancestors, and it is a skin that I've had to learn to love. Being Brown skinned is not a metaphor, and not all non-Black Latinxs are Brown. When I say that I am Brown, I am claiming myself. I am reminding myself that all the times I thought something was wrong with me were times when there was actually something wrong with them. When I say that I am Brown, I am referring to a slew of experiences that marked me, kept my head low, made me apologize, convinced me to wear colored contacts—you name it. When I say that I am Brown, I am standing in the pain and disowning it.

I use the term BIPOC to mean Black, Indigenous, and people of color. This acronym replaces the POC acronym to highlight the unique histories of Black and Indigenous people. While many people of color are diminished for being immigrants, they or their ancestors still often had the privilege of choosing to come to America. In contrast, white Americans founded the nation by murdering Indigenous people and forcing survivors off their own land. White Americans built their economy and wealth by kidnapping and enslaving Black people. And white Americans violently continue these legacies today. BIPOC is not a perfect term, and it might evolve further, but for this book this particular term felt the most accurate in reflecting my own politics.

I have Indigenous ancestors, and I identify as someone in the Indigenous diaspora, but I realize that when my birth country talks about its people, that includes me, for better or for worse. My immigrant identity is tied to a nation of origin, Nicaragua, whether I like it or not. I do not experience what Indigenous people experience today, in my country and around the world, because I speak the language of my colonizers and have adopted colonizer posturing through generations of forced self-erasure. But I see myself in Indigenous people, and I stand firmly with them. May they not experience that lack of connection to their roots like I do. My oppression and subjugation are not in competition with

Black and Indigenous people. Rather, I hope to fight alongside these communities.

White supremacy is global, and whether you acknowledge it or not, it exists. This book will not attempt to convince you of the existence of global white supremacy. It is a given. Pretending it does not exist does nothing but promote white supremacy.

I utilize the word "girl" to refer to myself and my audience, because there are aspects of my childhood, my girlhood, that were robbed from me by isms. Sexism was the first system of oppression I knew intimately, and I actively saw it destroy my ties with the men in my family. In my family, it became more about upholding sexism than about loving and supporting one another. Patriarchy is a system that is maintained by everyone, and we all participate in it. It is often the first encounter with systems of oppression that many BIWOC experience, and it is common to experience it violently through our dads, brothers, and even mothers. The patriarchy was my initiation into becoming desensitized to my own constant oppression.

We first need to name the forces that are set against us, because we cannot become free of things we cannot understand. And once we understand systemic oppressions and their violence, then we can begin to fight together against them. This book will give you the names, so you can clearly see all the ways power is locked away from us. This book will give you all the forbidden keys.

Liberation starts with knowledge. And it takes painful work. Freedom is not a destination; it is a communal journey. This book is for you, by someone like you. Through storytelling, I hope to give you more tools for your own liberation.

CHAPTER 1

VOLUNTOURISM

What you hear in my voice is fury, not suffering. Anger, not moral authority. There is a difference.

—Audre Lorde

As a child growing up in Nicaragua, I had some experiences with white doctors and dentists, and I have a soft spot for those people. Access to medical care, good medical care, is expensive for poor folks in many Latin American countries and the Caribbean. White doctors and dentists would travel from the United States or Europe to serve communities that most will not, not even the voluntourists. In fact, my first tooth was pulled by a white American dentist, and I remember the care and attention I received. Another time I had a rough fall off my bike, and a white American doctor gave me the stitches I needed. He was staying in our home, and I still have my scar to always remember that day. I also want to note that I do not remember these doctors asking me for pictures. They were too busy helping people. I hold these people who come to our countries and do that kind of work in high regard. But voluntourists are another story.

Voluntourism is violent. Voluntourism disguises itself as a good deed to hide that it is an exploitative act of voyeurism. Voluntourists seem to forget history or strategically ignore it. Either way, we cannot reward ignorance, even if it comes dressed in the semblance of goodness.

I know this from my own experiences as the assigned beneficiary of voluntourists and missionaries. I was born in Managua, Nicaragua. Many of my childhood toys, clothes, and meals came from ships that were stocked with charity from an organization called Gospel Outreach. I recall walking onto those boats and seeing piles of toys and boxes upon boxes of three-minute soups. These much-needed supplies were crucial to my childhood.

Now, the people sending this very important stuff decided that they needed to see the faces of the people whose lives they were changing. They not only expected our gratitude, but they also wanted time with us. I do not have very many Nicaraguan childhood memories that do not include voluntourists, or as they like to benevolently call themselves, missionaries. I call short-term white "helpers" voluntourists because that is what they were doing: touring our country and our people and disguising their tourism with the "good deeds" of helping us. Do not let them fool you into believing otherwise.

After hearing about a series of devastating natural disasters and a massively traumatic civil war, a white American church sent missionaries to Nicaragua. They offered aid, along with their agenda to "save" us. These were Christians seeking to "save" our spiritual souls; Protestants aiming to convert Catholics. When my Catholic parents converted to this Protestantism, our new church required that we become hosts and often guides to the hordes of missionary groups that came to visit our home country.

I think back on that time and recall that they were really kind, almost too kind. It was the sort of kindness where they did not ask for our mailing addresses or phone numbers, because it was not about becoming lifelong friends. It was and continues to be about the feeling we gave them about themselves. They had feelings about my poverty, my Brownness, and they seemed to feel good about saving me. They loved seeing how little we had, as it helped them appreciate how much they had back at home. They often would say we changed their lives. They were so grateful not to be us. While we remained poor and struggling, waiting for the next shipment of goods, they got to go home feeling safer in their distance from our poverty.

In exchange for life-giving goods we had to give them a life-changing experience.

We had to welcome them to our lands with our arms wide open, as though their country had no role in causing our distress. As if their country had not gained power and wealth when their government stole our resources and brought war to our lands. As if their comfort and safety didn't come from our suffering and endangerment.

They wanted us to say mil gracias to their smiling faces, as if reparations are not due, deserved, and rightfully ours. The current state of so-called underdeveloped countries is the result of greed and exploitation from developed countries. The grief, hunger, and horrors that people in the Global South face is directly related to the abundance of food, happiness, and comfort that these volun-tourists have back home.

Poor people have always seen right through this facade of kind-ness, but in times of need we've adapted in order to survive. So, I learned to perform, graciously and adoringly. But even from the tender age of five years old, I understood that they were not here for me. I did not have the words then that I have now for this exploitation. But I knew they were trying to get something out of me: an experience. So I decided to get out of them what I wanted. I remember complimenting a white woman voluntourist's water jug, and she immediately gave it to me. In her guilt, I saw an opportunity. Their guilt won't save us, so we save ourselves. There are many stories of people I grew up with attempting to do some sort of income redistribution, and they have been vilified as the bad ones. As if the voluntourists are not the ones exploiting hardships for their selfish gain.

Their need to come and see our "thankful" and "joyous" faces is fundamentally wrong. Most voluntourists have never seen how the Global South population lives and have not bothered to question why we live as we do. We make them appreciate their lives because seeing what ours actually look like shakes these people to their core. How can it not, when they are accustomed to central air-conditioning and everyone driving a car with four empty seats? And then they come to our countries, where hot water is a luxury and where if one person in your family has a car, then you come from means. Outsiders cannot compare these realities and remain unmoved, but what we need is more than white guilt. We need white people to riot against national trade policies implemented by their career politicians and put a stop to corporate exploitation so that we do not have to live like this.

They bastardize their "acts of kindness" by needing to see tattered clothing. They bastardize their "genuine concern" by paying money to fly into countries that are starving due to white settlers' theft, instead of sending money to support the protestors on the ground working to undo that damage. They bastardize their "good intentions" when their deeds are documented to get a pat on the back, a like on social media, a scholarship for college. They bastardize their "giving back" by expecting something in return, as if our dead ancestors are not enough.

So, I repeat, their need to come and see people suffering is voyeuristic. And I discourage it. Stop this unethical performance of kindness, because most voluntourists have left and told their life-changing stories but dismantled nothing.

—Signed, a poor Brown kid whose picture
was taken without my consent

Generational trauma is really at the core of my anger toward voluntourism, colonialism, and American interventions. American interventions are accepted facts that are historically supported, the United States has interfered and actively participated in the demise of what Donald Trump referred to as "shithole countries."

Voluntourism is a relatively new word that has unknown origins, but it combines both "volunteer" and "tourism" to define a particular kind of unskilled volunteer that seeks to visit the Global South under a guise of benevolence. Yet at the end of the day, in regard to the labor provided by voluntourists, we now know that their impact is minimal.

I am from Central America, so my stories will reflect that. However, each and every country in the Global South has similarly horrendous stories, and as a reader it is important to understand that these are not isolated incidents. To understand voluntourism you have to understand the legacy of outside interference on generations of Indigenous and Black folks. Let's start with catastrophic genocide and forced Christianization in Latin America by visitors who called themselves pioneers, explorers, conquerors, priests, and Christians.

For colonizers in the 1400s, conquest also meant the Christianization of the Indigenous people living in those lands. Conversion and land meant power. The church was seeking power, and do not let anyone fool you into believing otherwise. And let's be clear about another thing: Christianization was not a peaceful act.

Conquest of land and people were intrinsically intertwined for the colonizers then, and quite frankly that narrative goes unchanged today. Today, it is known that these arrivals to the New

World tortured, raped, exploited, and killed anyone who stood in their way and even those who did not. And always, conversion was framed as an effort to "save" the Indigenous occupants of these lands. It's the same language that missionaries use today. The assumption that some people do not have the wherewithal to save themselves implies their assumed inferiority.

Back then, men of the church wrote letters that largely reflected on Indigenous people as nonhuman. These Christian leaders often encouraged forceful conversion. The colonizers were European, but more specifically they were Dutch, English, French, Spanish, and Portuguese. There was no one agenda; each country had its own plans for expanding its territories. But one thing they all seemed to agree on was that the original habitants of the New World were subhuman and therefore could only be elevated through conversion and breeding with the members of the superior groups.

Assimilation was and is a key component of colonialism, and it was required for survival for many Indigenous people. Many were forcefully indoctrinated into the accepted religion. This was a time when nations and religions were intertwined, and spreading a world religion meant having more people to claim as subjects. This whole enterprise was never about saving anyone, though that was the language that was used. Rather, it was all about power and which colonizing nation could get the most of it. Forceful conversion was seen as a necessary act for good, because to be Christian was to be human.

The idea that you must elevate someone's existence means that you do not view them as capable of knowing what is best for themselves. This is a dehumanizing act veiled as a benevolent one, and whether intentional or not this is the history and foundation of missionary work today.

Colonizers "discovered" new lands, but colonizers also stole lands, robbed generations of their religious beliefs, and overall took from people they considered inferior. The Indigenous civilizations they destroyed were marvelous; the few that survived might never return to their former glory.

At the same time that Christianization was occurring, the Europeans were also having children with Indigenous people, Indigenous women. Sometimes pairings happened with consent; sometimes they occurred by force. Some of these early missionaries would even boast that this was their "service to God," to create mixed children between European and Indigenous people. This traumatic act of devaluing entire groups of people based on racist definitions of civilized and uncivilized is still felt today. A lot of Latin America is comprised of mestizos, meaning people who are part European and part Indigenous. To this day, Latin American mestizo people are largely anti-Indigenous, and this is a result of being told that Indigenous people are inferior and mixing means elevation. We did not create anti-Indigenous sentiment; we were taught it, we were forced to accept it, and then we internalized and perpetuated it on our own. That is the insidious nature of colonization. Many people have survived by assimilating toward the dominant group's values, and this internalized racism continues to traumatize entire nations.

This type of horizontal violence is painful to experience, and this violence that we enact on one another is horrific. My trauma and my family's trauma was and continues to be inflicted by rebranded colonizers, known as voluntourists. Seeing voluntourism celebrated reminds me that I am not the first to experience this type of terrorism, nor the last, so it is my duty to speak up against it.

I have Indigenous and Black ancestors. I am a person with deep roots in my country, and therefore I see these visitors who call themselves saviors as the ongoing legacy of past colonization.

My mami's side of the family comes from a poor rural Nicaraguan town known as Jinotega. Jinotega was mostly Indigenous until the late 1800s and early 1900s. Additionally, that side of the family has a history of looking down on Indigenous people. The erasing of one's Indigenous connections is common for a lot of people in Latin America. But recently, mi tio started to study the genealogy of our family in Jinotega. This tio discovered that my maternal bisabuelo was Indigenous and that he spoke his Indigenous dialect, until he did not.

I grew up visiting that great-grandfather: Papa Tingo, as we affectionately called him. He lived to be over one hundred years old. I never knew him to speak much, but I met him. We saw him once a year, and each time mi mami would say that you never knew if esta es la última vez that we would see him, a Latina mom proverb. I grew up not thinking too much of him, but knowing this vital piece of information about him now makes me long for some stories.

My family tells stories to keep people alive even after they have passed. We tell stories to honor them. The women in my family have been the primary storytellers. Papa Tingo did not share his stories with me, nor my mom, nor anyone else who can and will pass his stories on to us. But his experiences and his trauma are in our genes, and our genes remember. Trauma is inherited.

Voluntourism is a multimillion-dollar industry, and it is run and sponsored by white Christian folks who seek to forget the sins of their forefathers. They want that good feeling that comes from helping underprivileged people in underprivileged countries. Not enough thought is spent on why some countries have more than others, and in this chapter I am not letting them forget it.

Coming to the United States of America was never the goal; my family was not in high anticipation for our migration, ever. In fact, mi mami cried often because we had left her family and friends. We left her roots. A tree cannot live without roots, and neither can many people. My maternal grandmother died before mi mami could see her, before she could say goodbye. She just could not get there quick enough. My bones feel that anguish, that displacement.

Uprooting people is painful, and some do not survive this violent removal. Our migration was a hard transition and a hard reality to accept, despite the fact that we all understood that things here would be easier than they had ever been in our home country. Nicaragua is the second poorest country in the Western Hemisphere, second only to Haiti. By the time we migrated in 1992, my country had been in shambles for years. Corruption and poverty were the norm, and class mobility was nearly nonexistent—though much of the same can be said of the United States. Yet the earning potential is different here, and one American dollar equals a lot of Nicaraguan córdobas. The pillaging by Western nations is really what devalues our córdoba. Still, the income my dad could provide for us and our family back home was just too big of a temptation to pass up.

And while the members of my immediate family have all made lives in the United States, that does not erase the fact that my migration is a consequence of American interventions, and many immigrants often pay the highest price for this type of American meddling. If you have ever visited a country that is not as wealthy as the United States, know that these countries do not end up being this poor without some help. Mi Nicaraguita was where she was in 1992 because of years of interventions.

The United States would be responsible for taking down one of our more progressive presidents, José Santos Zelaya. Then in the 1920s, the United States first appointed a Somoza, Anastasio Somoza García, to control our lands and our people. The United States was fixated on Latin American lands and resources, and the US government invested millions of dollars into my home country to exploit those lands and resources. The Americans often install heads of state in the countries they are exploiting, because that is how an empire continues its reign. To the United States, this is a basic business transaction. But those business transactions forever changed my country and numerous countries across the globe. Due to these obvious interventions, several revolutions were attempted in my country, one famously by Augusto César Sandino. Eventually, Sandino was assassinated. This is what happens when you attempt to fight against the United States.

After the United States put the first Somoza in place to rule over my country, Nicaraguans lived through two more Somoza men as our dictators. These men from this family were corrupt and were able to amass one of the biggest fortunes in Latin America due to their pillaging of our natural resources.

The Somozas sold rights to cattle and land to anyone with a robust pocketbook. The Somozas never cared about Nicaragüenses because they were too busy getting rich. When Tachito—the last of the Somoza dictators, also known as Anastasio Somoza Debayle—came into power, he continued the horrible Somoza reign, which overall lasted forty years. Tachito attended West Point, and he was the only graduate of that school with his own personal army. That army was a graduation gift. Tachito was never loyal to us pinolerxs because he barely was one. As the heir to the Nicaraguan "throne," he was raised very differently than many Nicaraguans. He had no allegiance to us, only to our money.

Tachito was raised in the United States and spoke better English than Spanish. He grew up wealthy. The locals referred to him as the "last marine," precisely because he was understood to be an outsider, and because it was common knowledge that the Somoza men and the United States were in bed together. The United Nations cited Tachito in the seventies with numerous violations, and his national guard did monstrosities to our citizens. By that time, much of the Nicaraguan population could not deny the terrors occurring, and a powerful revolution was afoot. Somoza attempted to fight back with the help and training of US soldiers who equipped the national guard with everything they needed to stop the revolution from taking place.

Still our revolution succeeded. Sandinistas overthrew Tachito, but before the dictator fled to the United States he was able to get his hands on all our money. My country's government was left with only $3 million, total. The Somozas had left us in ruins, and we had to rebuild a country from scraps. After the revolution, guerrilla fighters and leaders were vetted for loyalty. They tried to bring us back to the days before dictators had robbed us of our rights.

Mi papi's older brother, my uncle, served in the national guard under one of these tyrannous presidents. My tio served under a dictator, Tachito, because he was promised a scholarship for college. Tio José served as one of the president's personal bodyguards and henchmen. The national guards, at that time, were known to be ruthless killers and would all eventually be charged for their crimes. Against my family's adamant protests, my uncle went ahead and joined the Guardia Nacional toward the end of Tachito's reign. When the Sandinistas won, all of Tachito's soldiers were thrown in jail.

Mi tio only served the dictator for a few months, but when Tachito fled the country, my uncle was sentenced to serve twenty-three years in jail. Mi papi risked his life to save him. Mi papi had a sit-down with the new Sandinista president, Daniel Ortega. Mi papi and his band were invited to play at a presidential party, and that night he made his way toward Ortega to request that he intervene and free my tio. Because of this plea by mi papi, my tio was then freed. I should note that my family does not come from a long line of soldiers; our heritage is in generations upon generations of musicians. But American interventions make soldiers out of everyone.

What I remember of mi tio was that he was an alcoholic. Mi tio would drink until he passed out, and that could occur anywhere.

If he passed out on the front porch of his mami's home, then at least we knew he was safe. God forbid he pass out on the street somewhere, which occurred often, and then we would hear of it through children who played in the streets. The kids would come up to mi abuela's portón and tell her where my uncle was seen last.

Whenever we visited my paternal abuelita, which was often enough, Tio José came. The children, my cousins and I, were usually escorted as far away as the adults could take us from him. It was not because they thought he was dangerous, but maybe because he was a remnant of a past everyone wanted to forget. We were no longer at war, but the echoes of war were felt and they were with us even when we were all actively trying to forget.

And while they wanted to forget, it seems he could not. I will never know what that tio saw and what that tio lived through while helping to keep the dictator Tachito alive. As a kid I did not understand his alcoholism, but as an adult I always wonder what he was trying to escape. I wonder what demons he wrestled with. I wonder what he was trying to silence within himself.

That tio died a few years ago. The story goes that he got so drunk he passed out on a road and a car ran over his body and kept driving. Alas, he passed out somewhere nobody could protect him.

I have only seen mi papi cry a handful of times, and when he heard about his big brother's death, I saw him sob. I will never know what mi papi knew, what mi papi shielded me from, but I will never forget those tears. Trauma is inherited.

He had another brother who had joined the army, but he was on the other side. Mi tio was a teenager and a singer at our church when he was forced into the Sandinista army to fight the US-backed Tachito dictatorship. This uncle was a pacifist. He did not believe in violence, and because of this his commander shot him in the head in front of his entire platoon. These were tense times, and compassion was not what it would take to keep the United States at bay.

Mi tío's death is dark stain on the Sandinista revolution for my entire family. But for me his death signifies a dark stain on the United States. My tío was killed because the United States insisted on keeping its grip on our country; the Americans wanted to keep control of our lands and they wanted to secure their investments.

After the devastation of burying one of her youngest sons, my abuelita stood in front of the gates of her home in her neighborhood of Las Brisas and refused to let the Sandinistas take another son. She said they would have to kill her before she would let another son go. No other son was taken from her home. Trauma is inherited.

The Sandinistas overthrew the Somoza regime, but the removal of a puppet does not remove the puppeteers. Our revolution threatened the reach of US power. The embargo in 1985 was just another American strategy to get the country back in line.

I have seen my country struggle since the day I was born. I was born in 1985, after the revolution and just a few months after the United States placed its embargo. This was a time when even diapers were hard to come by, formula also. I grew up hearing about our revolution and the tension that it created for everyone. I grew up understanding that my parents had lived through a war, and they survived despite the very many people who did not. Mi mami gave birth to my brother and I while also surviving the distress of giving birth in a war-torn country. Trauma is inherited.

I cannot fully blame them for how their trauma has impacted them and thus impacted me. But what I can do is hold the United States and its voluntourists accountable for upholding a narrative where they think of themselves as "helping" people in countries that Americans actually helped destroy. But it took me learning my history and understanding white supremacy to find the words for the generational trauma that has always impacted me. For a long time, I had aspirations to become American—until I learned what America has meant for me directly, and how it has changed the course of my entire family line. Knowledge gave me the power to lift the veil that covered my eyes; knowledge allowed me to see it all clearly.

And still, we have been tasked with welcoming these colonizers to our lands with our arms wide open, as though their country had no role in causing our distress. So, the real question is: What have these voluntourists done, and what can they do instead in their own communities?

Nicaragua is not a special case; Nicaragua has not been ransacked more than any other country in the Global South. Nicaragua is just one in a long list of countries that have lived through similar terrorist acts by the United States and European powers. It takes one simple Google search to find out what has happened in Iraq, Honduras, Puerto Rico, Thailand, the entire continent of Africa—literally every country with Black and Brown citizens. None of what I have shared in this chapter is news, but still there exists an outright dismissal of this information, which remains striking to me.

I am angry that my picture was taken without my consent when these missionaries came to plant some trees at our church orphanage. But in a deeper sense, I am angry that missionaries visit our countries at all. What I require is for missionaries to stop visiting our countries. What I require is that they do something to significantly change the grave situation in our countries by advocating that their government stop pillaging them.

True generosity lies in striving so that these hands—whether individual or entire peoples—need be extended less and less in supplication.

—Paulo Freire

In my twenties, I attended one of the few elite theological institutions in America that lauds itself in churning out progressive movers and shakers: Vanderbilt Divinity School in Nashville, Tennessee. VDS is a wonderfully utopian place where I was challenged and pushed to learn more than I ever thought I could handle, and quite frankly it changed me for the better. However, such progressive liberal havens like these also breed a particular type of white student.

The white people I met there were well-meaning, well-read liberal folks who happened to know all the ins and outs of racism and colonialism, but somehow positioned those problems outside of themselves rather than taking ownership of them. They did not understand themselves to be part of the problem, and they did not see themselves as benefitting from these systems of oppression. Many saw themselves as strictly allies.

It was in this program that I first encountered the term voluntourism. I had finally obtained the word to validate my unsettling experiences and feelings of dissonance. And in dealing with that dissonance as I had experienced it growing up, a new type of dissonance was rearing its head. I found myself surrounded by people who knew the terminology and still found ways to justify their actions as different or better.

I was a typical graduate student, meaning I read all day and drank all night. One day, while drinking and chatting with one of my white peers, we stumbled into his dorm room. We lived in the same building, and he had to get something before we headed out to the bars for the evening. I had never been to his room before, so I started looking around. He had typical pictures and trinkets strewn about, and then something caught my eye.

I was stunned. On his IKEA bookshelf he had a framed picture of himself, a very white man, hugging a group of Brown kids.

You see, VDS talks openly about the problems with white saviorism and the ways that it manifests through consumption of Black and Brown trauma. I guess I had assumed we had all been paying attention in class, or maybe I assumed people knew better.

I remember this moment vividly, because it taught me a lot about myself in relationship to the program I was attending.

I squinted and leaned in, and he saw me looking and said something along the lines of, "That picture is from when I went to Guatemala." He mentioned that he had been traveling with either a church group or a college Christian group. I remember him trying to do a justification dance—this dance of, *I am not like those white people who do not respect other cultures. I am different.* Back then, I didn't know how to push back against a friend. I didn't know how to challenge him for doing what he thought was a good deed.

We headed out, but I could not shake that photograph from my mind. Those children in that picture, those smiling Brown kids, looked just like I had. I kept wondering how many of the missionaries had framed the pictures they had taken with me, of me. I wondered if, when they spoke of their trips, they talked about me or if they centered themselves. I wondered in what context it would be appropriate and in what context would it be inappropriate to have pictures of anonymous kids in your room.

I remember white people taking pictures of me in Nicaragua, but I do not remember ever being asked for my permission. I do not remember ever thinking that those pictures would become trophies of good deeds in dorm rooms across the country.

On that day in Nashville, I felt violated, and that feeling was hard to accept. I felt protective of the kids in that framed picture in that white man's dorm. I felt angry. I kept thinking about consent, and if those kids had been asked for consent for him to take their picture, frame it, and display it in his dorm room. I wanted to ask my friend to name each and every one of those kids. *Who are these kids to you?* I wanted to ask. *Who do you think you are, to visit a significantly poorer country and claim your visit as an act of benevolence?*

Things changed between that friend and me after I saw that picture, and things changed between me and a lot of my white peers in the program. I stayed defensive; I suddenly saw myself as I feared others saw me. To them, perhaps I wasn't just another graduate student trying to survive midterms, papers, readings, and finals. I began to see myself as someone whose humanity was not valued. Those Brown kids looked more like me than anyone else in my graduate program. It occurred to me that my white peers might not truly see me as one of them.

Most people in my program probably did not know I had been a recipient of missionary aid. Most people in my program probably did not know that I was like those nameless kids displayed on fridges and mantels, on IKEA dressers and bookshelves. I realized we had little in common because they saw themselves as saviors while I was seen as someone who needed to be saved. I realized in that instant that we were not friends, and that I would forever be their token Brown friend. I was just there to fill a role in legitimizing their allyship.

Voluntourism is not a conservative person's problem. It's still voluntourism if it's a liberal person doing it. Voluntourism is a product of white supremacy and is a form of virtue signaling that still centers the assumed goodness of whiteness.

If white people are truly looking to permanently free people, to permanently help people, then only real and tangible actions toward liberation can be effective. The path forward requires society to stop rewarding these voluntourists with scholarships, likes on social media, and admiration for their supposed life-changing experiences. To begin healing the generations of trauma white people have inflicted on Brown and Black people, white people first have to hold themselves accountable.

Demanding open borders is how we begin to repair those relationships with people whose countries have become almost unlivable. Demanding and ensuring health care for everyone in this country, including mental health care, is how we can begin to cut away the trauma. Many immigrants have not even begun to heal from war and displacement but still have to live in a capitalist society that demands financial contribution as a justification for their migration. Making the visa process less impossible is a great start. We need to stop teaching one-sided history in our schools. Let people have all the information needed to do better and be better global citizens. We need to ensure that the United States changes how it treats foreign countries, especially those poorer, "shithole" countries. Because these countries are still feeling the effects of globalization, and we have to do better by them.

Most of my family still lives in Nicaragua; it was only my immediate family who got to leave. Visas are hard to come by, and while some of my family has migrated, our hearts are back home.

Through them, I am constantly reminded that I am not free, and I owe it to them to speak up. In 2018, after a few uprisings and protests in Nicaragua, my cousin was kidnapped by the Nicaraguan government under suspicions that he was part of the uprising. I will say this is all alleged, since the government still denies that most of this occurred despite the local press it received and the videos I saw of mothers waiting to hear news of their kidnapped children. Sometimes out of fear of regressing into a previous dictatorship, revolutionary leaders become assassins. Conclusions were made about any young man's involvement in the uprisings, based on age. The protesters were young college students, and being within that age range meant you could be picked up and questioned an unknown amount of times. Many young men have not been returned home. My cousin went missing for almost an entire year. My aunt would hear about unmarked graves, and she would drive there and would try to identify his body. At one point, we heard that he was at El Chipote, an old, abandoned jail that was used to torture people back in my parents' time. They were using it to torture a new flock of young boys who were suspected to have information. Eventually that jail was closed off as investigations were being made by the United Nations about the human rights violations that were occurring. Almost one year after my cousin went missing, we got word that he was somewhere unknown and to get him back his parents had to pay a ransom. After paying off the ransom, they got him back and my family had to smuggle him to another country for his safety. Last time I saw pictures of him was days after he was released. I could tell something inside him had changed.

All this makes me angry, and sometimes I get so angry I cannot even see solutions. But I know that I can begin to heal by naming that anger and finding the true culprit. I live with my eyes wide open, no veil covering them and no admiration for America despite the nationalist propaganda that is prevalent always but especially during election time. I have fallen in love with my people now that I know what we have survived to be alive today. I have healed through knowing, and by knowing I can move toward possible solutions. I am no longer stuck in the trauma and the confusion that trauma creates. Rather, I have learned to exist and resist. I work hard, on a daily basis, to find joy despite everything that was made to take that joy away.

CHAPTER 2

COLORISM

Colorism is not unique to black Americans; people of color around the world—from Africa, Latin America, Asia, and the Caribbean, etc.—are impacted by global colorism, or the widespread elevation of light skin tones over darker skin across all communities of color.

—JeffriAnne Wilder

Mi mami tells me to get out of the sun. Mi mami tells me to put on sunblock. Mi mami tells me to not go to the beach so much. But she is not protecting me from skin cancer; that is not really on our immigrant radar nor our primary worry, unfortunately. She is not telling me to stay out of the sun out of a deep concern for my health. Mi mami does not want me to be too brown.

You see, mi mami is from the mountains of Jinotega, Nicaragua. The mountains, where the temperature stays at a cool sixty degrees Fahrenheit. It is foggy, and people often wear sweaters. Mi mami, like many of her townspeople, is light skinned. She does not tan in the sun; she burns. Mi mami turns bright red, gets sunburned in ways I have never experienced. But she is not as light skinned as my tias and her youngest brother, Tio Ivan. Mi mami has dark black hair and mi tias all have light-brown and ash-blonde hair. Since mi mami is one of the oldest among her siblings and cousins, and since each child born after her was fairer than the last, my family would joke, "la raza mejoró" with every child. And it should be noted that mi mami's skin tone at her darkest is my skin tone at its lightest.

Mi mami was born of a green-eyed, light-brown-haired, light-skinned man: mi abuelito Nicolas. Everyone hopes that my grandfather's light-eyes genes will be passed down and resurface someday, though it seems to've skipped two entire generations at this point. His mother was an Afro-Nicaragüense, but we do not talk about that. I learned about mi Black bisabuela in my late twenties, through a casual, happenstance conversation that left me surprised. Everyone else seemed content with this erasure.

I, however, have my papi's genes. My papi's side of the family is darker. They have Brown skin and very prominent traditional Indigenous features, like flat faces, wider noses, and straight black or brown hair. My papi is not ashamed of his Brownness. On the contrary, mi papi does not worry about his skin tone. He enjoys sitting in the sun unfettered, while mi mami wears a hat, sunglasses, and a long-sleeve shirt if she is able. But my papi is a man, and standards of admiration for men stem from their ability to perform some arbitrary definition of manhood. That is not to say that mi papi has not experienced discrimination due to his Brownness. I have vivid memories of the hyper policing mi papi experienced after 9/11 along with many other Black and Brown men in this country. These random body checks by the Transportation Security Administration were quite difficult to disregard as just coincidences. However, when I was growing up, how much money a man could provide for his household held more intracommunal value than his skin tone. On the other hand, women were valued for our fragility, our purity, and our proximity to white standards of beauty.

I understood this growing up. The "prettiest" girls in my classes were always the ones who had light skin, light eyes, and light hair.

Mi mami tells me to get out of the sun. Mi mami tells me to put on sunblock. Mi mami tells me to not go to the beach so much. Because I have my papi's Brownness but mi mami's gender, a curse—I was born female and Brown, in a cultura that hates females and especially hates the darker ones.

But avoiding the sun feels unnatural and distasteful, when I know full well that the politics of pigmentation have been telling my people that being Black and Brown is bad and that getting darker is your own damn fault. Despite having grown up with meager means, we do not want to appear like we have worked in fields. It is shameful to own your poverty, and more shameful if your skin begins to tell the tale of your misfortunes. Our communities act like Brownness is optional, like we can dim our skin tone by avoiding the sun and hope that the yellow undertones eventually turn pink.

Mi mami tells me to get out of the sun. Mi mami tells me to put on sunblock. Mi mami tells me to not go to the beach so much. Mi mami tells me that I am becoming negra, with rechazo in her tone.

But I cannot undo the fact that my skin glows from all this sunlight. Like magic, my skin turns sunrays into nutrients, into vitamin D. You ask me what color my skin tone is, and I will tell you: It is a morning cafecito con leche with your abuelita. It is a caramelo tint that looks unreal, painted beautifully on my flesh. I do not burn with the sun; I evolve right before my very eyes. My Brown skin is beautiful. In the winter it becomes a lighter shade, the color of walnuts, and in the summer it darkens. I have to change my makeup with the seasons to match my beautiful, evolving skin tone, because my skin is supernatural.

I love my Brown skin, but it has taken me years to realize that and to undo the years of the sun-avoidance dance that many of us Brown girls are told to perform.

Mi mami tells me to get out of the sun. Mi mami tells me to put on sunblock. Mi mami tells me to not go to the beach so much. And I understand what she is doing, I understand what her life has taught her about Brownness, but I insist on living differently. I decline, because I refuse to let the color of my skin and my gender make me hide under ridiculous gorros. I refuse to incomodarme for a cultura that breeds colorism. Instead, I wear my tiniest bikini and I go to the beach, put on sunblock to protect this beautiful Brown skin I have been blessed with, and watch magic happen.

Colorism a byproduct of racism and shares many of the same qualities and characteristics. For example, colorism, like racism, is deeply embedded within societal structures (e.g., education, politics, the media) and can be institutionalized.

—JeffriAnne Wilder

My experiences with colorism are as a non-Black woman of color, and will not claim fluency in colorism within Black communities. I am an expert of my lived experiences. My experiences with colorism at home are hard to pinpoint and relate, because they never felt like discrete incidents; colorism was just always there.

After completing graduate school, I returned home. I was experiencing a lot of the trauma that comes with existing as a nonwhite person in predominantly white spaces. I had lived the majority of my life in Latinx neighborhoods, which meant that I had no real coping skills for the ways white people protected and abused their privilege. But my body took all that in, and when I graduated it felt tired and I needed rest. Fortunately, mi mami is traditional in the way that she assumes her children are her responsibility until her last dying breath, so she invited me to move back home. She insisted.

Mindfully returning home meant acknowledging the ways I had changed. I finally knew how to speak up for myself. I had learned the language to name my experiences, which allowed me to heal from my childhood. Coming back home was terrifying, but I also had no real job prospects at that point. Nobody tells working-class students of color that our reality will not change much even after getting multiple fancy degrees. No one mentions in the "stay in school" propaganda that even when we have our education, the assumption of our inferiority persists. No one told me I had been fooled into believing in a system that was fundamentally designed to destroy me.

When I moved back home, I found myself crying a lot. I took many odd jobs, working at the private agency that handled Section 8 housing in Miami-Dade County, working on the floor at a Neiman Marcus outlet store. I even attempted to apprentice as a piercer at a tattoo parlor. I was mourning the loss of my first marriage, I was mourning my disillusionment with the American Dream, and I was mourning my loss of innocence. Adulthood as a woman of color required that I harden myself and keep my heart shielded. When I mourn, I seek solace in nature; I applied for jobs while sitting on a towel on Miami Beach, and it was there that I wrote often.

After a few months of being home, I remember one day coming back from the beach and mi mami saying that specific comment: "Te estás poniendo negra." When mi mami said that, she was saying that I will darken to an unacceptable Brown, thus insinuating that darkness is inferior. She was expressing both anti-Indigeneity and also anti-Blackness. For non-Black POC, this is our colorism, seen and felt in the constant policing of our Brownness in its many tints and hues.

And while my experiences with colorism growing up had been hard to name and process, hearing this kind of "everyday colorism" at age thirty was different. I was now an adult with better tools to think critically about the things we casually say. That comment by mi mami hit me, hard. I also knew that her comment did not stand alone; it was part of a sea of normalized colorism that our communities enact toward one another. Somehow, among BIPOC, colorism is often disguised as genuine concern.

I did not know the term colorism until I got to graduate school. By learning in adulthood what colorism is, and what it does within my community, I grew to understand how those comments had shaped me growing up as a little Brown girl. I also have to accept how those comments still shape me today as a Brown woman. I refer to that comment mi mami made on that day when I came home from the beach as horizontal violence. This seemingly harmless gesture of concern is in fact an act of violence. We inflict this within our own communities; it is violence enacted by us and to us. We somehow have allowed ourselves not only to internalize racism, but to become Brown white supremacists. This is not an individual critique on mi mami; this is a larger conversation about the normalization of the supremacy of whiteness through colorism.

I grew up in a Latinx city, but more specifically in a non-Black Latinx neighborhood. The majority of the population of Miami-Dade County is Latinx and/or Caribbean. But like most major cities, Miami has neighborhoods that are siloed by race, nationality, or both. For example, back in the early nineties, Sweetwater was a primarily non-Black Nicaraguan neighborhood. So, my exposure to colorism came through a non-Black Latinx lens. The type of horizontal violence that is done in non-Black Latinx neighborhoods mirrors the type of violence that we enact toward one another back in our home countries, where proximity to whiteness is prized. Non-Black Latinx colorism is regularly carried out by our families, friends, media, and sometimes even by ourselves as a survival tactic.

In Nicaragua, I was bought up to believe I was mestiza. I remember when my baby sister was getting her first bath at home, I saw her Mongolian spot and I asked my mom about it. She told me that it was a spot all mestizos have, and it fades as they get older. The Mongolian spot signified our Indigenous ancestors, and she told me that we had all had our own Mongolian spot. Yet, I have a Black great-grandmother on my maternal side and a Black uncle on my paternal side, and their Blackness is not part of the constructed mestiza racial identity I was taught to claim. To be mestiza is to be mixed specifically with Spanish and non-Black Indigenous ancestry—the Mongolian spot reference. However, technically I cannot be mestiza when I know I have Spanish, Indigenous, and Black ancestors. To identify as mestiza is to erase all my Black ancestors. My family, like many mestizos, has absorbed Blackness into our gene makeup, music, and customs but erased said Blackness entirely when identifying racially as mestizo. That is precisely why I do not identify as mestiza. Because in this way, we gatekeep mestizaje and erase the richness of our Black ancestry.

Black people can be Indigenous. There are also other racial categories that have been erased with time. An example in Nicaragua is that we have a history of multiple race categories dating back to the 1800s. The racial categories that existed were casta, ladino, zambo, mulato, mestizo, blanco, and negro. These racial categories include the mixing of Indigenous and Black, which is zambo. The categories also unveil the fact that white people have existed in Latin America. Furthermore, there were entire communities that did not mix and stayed racially Black. But today, mestizo and mulato are the two primary identifications that are commonly used, precisely to erase Indigeneity and Blackness except when in service to whiteness. Mestizo means someone who is European, Spanish specifically, and Indigenous, while mulato means someone who is Spanish and Black. We have erased all other racial categories when we should not have.

For me, to identify as mestiza is to perpetuate the same colonial structures and eugenic thinking. I often self-identify as a non-Black Latina to highlight the issue of anti-Blackness—which shapes our identities vastly in Latin America and the Caribbean—by centering Blackness and my relationship to it. Additionally, this is not to say that there are not exclusively mestizo people, because there are; similarly, there are exclusively European folks living in Latin America and the Caribbean, like in Argentina, which has a substantial German and Italian population. However, since I write in first person, these are my lived experiences, with a very beautiful but complex family history that includes Indigenous, Spanish, and Black ancestry.

Colorism is often thought of as an issue exclusively affecting Black communities, where those who are lighter skinned obtain certain privileges due to their proximity to whiteness. Across the board, colorism means the privileging and prioritizing of lighter-skinned people of a specific racial or ethnic group. So, much to a lot of people's surprise, colorism is global. Other communities of color experience colorism because anti-Blackness and anti-Indigeneity is as expansive as colonialism.

Colorism in my particular non-Black Latina experience is anti-Indigenous. Back when the European conquests began in the Americas, rape, fornication, and marriages occurred between Indigenous women and Spanish men. The children that resulted from such unions meant the need for a new categorization, due to the revulsion that Spanish people had toward Indigenous people. Since these children were partially Spanish, the desire to acknowledge their elevated Spanish blood created the need for a new description. Yet, the children were still considered to be Indigenous, and they were not allowed to be fully acknowledged as Spanish. This new racial category was meant to highlight proximity to whiteness, centering whiteness as superior. That is where mestizaje comes from, a desire to not be fully associated with an inferior race while acknowledging their elevated Spanish ancestry. Mestizaje is steeped in a history of hate and trauma, and through that hate and trauma comes the repulsive scale of colorism that I grew up intimately knowing. The children of this mixing have built nation-states whose entire identities revolve around the maintenance of anti-Indigeneity and anti-Blackness, which is why colorism needs to be undone.

Also, colorism is rooted in anti-Blackness. It is a system that places value on lightness and devalues darkness. Darkness, Blackness, is placed at the bottom rung of this fucked scale. So, while on the surface my non-Black Latina experiences with colorism were in a very directly anti-Indigenous context, this system is also automatically anti-Black in its agenda because the goal is whiteness and not the other way around. Colorism is a child of racism, and both are strategic constructions meant to give whiteness superiority over all other racial identities.

Colorism is about skin pigmentation, but it is also about facial features and hair types. Because the goal of colorism is to position whiteness as superior, white skin is placed at the top of these reprehensible hierarchies. Getting into the weeds, two people with similar skin tones can be differentiated and ranked based on facial features and hair color and texture. So, in addition to skin color, wider noses, bigger lips, and tighter curls are stereotypically associated with Blackness, and the goal is white skin, a small nose, small lips, and straight hair. Proximity to whiteness gives a person of color privilege over other BIPOC, and this inner hierarchy was created to delegitimize BIPOC experiences as a whole. All this is to say, it is self-destructive but prevalent.

Colorism took another form in school and socially. I learned that how I looked was a problem among mestizos. I am racialized as Brown, my nose is wider, my hair is straight and dark brown, and I have a flat face with higher cheekbones. My features fit the stereotype of what Indigenous people are "supposed" to look like. So, I am acutely aware of how white I do not look. Even when I avoid the sun, I still have nonwhite facial features and straight, dark hair. But I learned the extent of my nonwhiteness through some very harsh life lessons.

In fifth grade, I attempted to grow out my hair for the first time. Mi mami, like many Latinas, had been forced to keep her hair long, and her way of emancipating herself was by cutting it into a pixie cut when she first got married. And mi mami never wanted me to feel that pressure, and so she kept my hair short for most of my life.

I never thought much about it; it was a decision made for me. So, in fifth grade, my desire to grow out my hair was not something I had invested a lot of time into. I just stopped getting haircuts. And as my hair began to grow longer, I began to get teased by my classmates. I attended a non-Black Latinx elementary school, so there were a few of us who were Brown; whiteness was understood as superior through the idolization of the popular girls, who were all white-passing. The microaggressions I experienced changed when I began to grow out my hair.

They started to call me what is often still used as an insult or a slur when referring to Indigenous people in Latin America and the Caribbean: "India," they said. What they were teaching me was that I was ugly because I looked Indigenous.

I was only in fifth grade, and the lesson I learned on that day was that it was my job to manage how people would accept me. It was my job to manage my appearance. I have really straight, dark brown hair, and how I styled it and cut it meant a lot to me in terms of negotiating my identity. After that experience I kept my hair short, because growing my hair out still triggered some strong gut reaction that reminded me that I am not supposed to love myself.

Decades later, the act of growing out my hair took a lot of self-awareness and healing. Having long hair meant embracing those roots that are a part of me and embracing my ancestors. Everybody covets long, straight hair, but still the preference is with light-colored hair on white skin. White women can have long, dark, straight hair and still be considered desirable. If it is on the face and body of an undesirable other, a BIPOC—in those cases long, dark, straight hair becomes undesirable. Colorism dictates that some things are not inherently bad unless they are attached to darker bodies. Whiteness is queen, king, and army.

When you are prepubescent and suddenly become aware of the ways your own people think you are inferior because of the features on your face and the color of your skin, you will start to run away from yourself. You'll want to look like someone else. You'll want to hide your Indigenous ancestors.

In middle school, I started receiving the attention of a cute boy in my grade. His name was Juan, and to me he was so dreamy. He was Colombian and had this beautiful caramel skin color. His eyes were hazel, and this was one of the things everyone seemed to love about him, including myself—his claim to fame, his foothold in whiteness.

At first, I thought he was dating me as a joke. When you are made to feel like you are not beautiful, and society teaches you that the worth of girls and women lies in their beauty, then you start to feel unlovable. In tenth grade, a boy would date me as a dare, which further cemented this mentality for me. But much to my surprise, seventh-grade Prisca genuinely captured the attention of this boy, and after a few weeks I was ready for my first kiss. It was everything you could imagine: awkward. Thankfully, both our expectations were low so this did not seem to deter anything. Then he asked me to join him in the mornings before school started to hang with his friends, the cool kids. Cool by virtue of their light skin or ability to pass as white.

I remember walking up to his group of friends while holding his hand, and the girls started to laugh, loudly. They yelled, "She looks like an india," and continued to laugh. I remember him defending me, and I remember wanting to disappear. I did not speak up for myself because I believed what they said about me, that there was something wrong with me. He broke up with me a few days later, without any explanation.

These experiences taught me to hate myself. I learned that I deserved to be mocked for looking like my ancestors. I had my ancestral Brownness scripted on my face and on my body, and I was taught to hate it. I was taught to hide my features. I was taught how to begin to erase parts of myself. I was taught that I could erase myself entirely.

Mi mami tells me to get out of the sun. Mi mami tells me to put on sunblock. Mi mami tells me to not go to the beach so much.

I realize now those were the seeds of my own anti-Indigeneity. For a long time, I felt like I had to express the same disdain for Indigenous people in order to fit in with my fellow mestizos, because that is what mestizaje is built on. I was supposed to have more in common with mestizos due to the nation-state identities that were given to us by our colonizers. Embedded in my survival instincts was this desire to distance myself from my roots, from the real and vibrant communities that still exist today despite centuries of attempted genocide. Through ridicule, I became one of them, and I felt a need to cling onto that. It was not until I read Gloria Anzaldúa, who proudly claimed her Indigeneity, that things began to shift for me. Seeing someone call out our colonizers, and take pride in her Indigenous roots, is still vastly unheard of with so many of our gente.

I am visible—see this Indian face—yet I am invisible. I both blind them with my beak nose and am their blind spot. But I exist, we exist. They'd like to think I have melted in the pot. But I haven't, we haven't.

—Gloria Anzaldúa

I needed to read Anzaldúa to discover ways to speak up against anti-Indigeneity. I realize today that while I was directly hurt because of this embedded prejudice, there are thousands of displaced peoples in my country and here in this country who continue to be hurt by these violent acts of erasure, nation-state policies, and occupation. I was participating in the continued subjugation of Indigenous communities by not owning that side of my ancestral line with the same respect and admiration the whiter parts of my ancestry received. I was also a person, socialized within a racist structural machine that specifically sought to devalue me and people like me. While in some regards my agency was taken from me through socialization, once I became aware of this, I could finally begin the work to actively undo those teachings and counter them.

Media does its fair share of harm by reinforcing negative stereotypes of people who are darker through colorism. Growing up, Telemundo and Univision had actresses, entertainers, and news anchors who all spoke my native tongue of Spanish—but they never looked like me. I grew up on Xuxa, Sofía Vergara, Lucero, Thalía, and Gloria Trevi, and they were all light-skinned, white-passing Latinas who were portrayed as the beauty queens of our countries. These were the women we were projected as our representation, but I did not look like them. Instead, I looked like the nameless maids who were occasionally cast in a telenovela or, worse, like la India María.

India María was an exaggerated and ridiculously racist stereotype of Indigenous people, and she was the only person I saw on our channels who looked anything like I did. She was kind, but was presented as inferior. She stood in stark contrast to a Thalía and was always called fea and dumb by the other characters in whatever movie or show she was in. I became aware that I looked like pop culture's idea of a joke. As a young, Brown, third-world little girl, I understood too well the message behind la India María.

Colorism privileges white-passing and white-adjacent BIPOC. This deserves our attention, because when we eradicate colorism, when we divest from whiteness, we can hopefully find our way back to one another. Colorism divides all communities; not calling attention to it is a disservice to us all. Our darker members will resent those who do not share in such painful experiences. We are resentful of those with proximity to whiteness because we are all socialized to want that too. And Black people are justified in their anger toward non-Black POC for the violence we have been complicit in, knowingly or unknowingly, all in service of whiteness. That desire and longing for whiteness is a shared issue across communities of color; it is enforced through colorism, and our energies need to be focused on divesting from that hierarchy entirely.

Colorism can trick you into believing that you need to change yourself. I am embarrassed and still in disbelief at how much money I spent attempting to erase myself. I am embarrassed and still in disbelief at how much money so many Black and Brown folks spend to distance ourselves from our darker features. At the lengths that many of us will go to avoid the sun, to get that skin-bleaching cream, to contour with makeup to narrow our noses. So many of us became experts in how to erase ourselves, instead of healing from it all and eradicating colorism.

I was in high school the first time I attempted to really change my appearance to look white. In ninth grade, one of my friends, Jessica Otero, would bring to school a large plastic bag full of bootleg colored contacts. She was Cuban and white, and to me that meant she was gorgeous. She would often wear hazel-colored contacts, and I thought she looked stunning. I realize now that I had been told to think that whiteness and lightness was stunning. But at that time, I wanted to look just as stunning, just as white.

I wanted to be like her, so I asked how much the colored contacts were, and she told me she was selling them for $20. I didn't have an allowance, but I was able to save up money, little by little. In about a month and a half, I was victorious! There is very little that can stand in the way of someone who has been taught to hate herself, and so-called improvements become our fixation. I remember when I walked up to Jessica and asked her to show me her stash of colored contacts. She showed me every color and I picked the most natural-looking one I could see: turquoise. I realize now that was a terrible mistake, but in ninth grade you could not tell me a thing.

Of course, I looked like I was sick, with enlarged, ill-fitted, turquoise-colored eyes. The bootleg colored contacts lasted about two weeks before they started to deteriorate. They were probably not meant to be given without an eye exam. But because whiteness is a drug that BIPOC are told we want to be addicted to, I kept saving up more money to keep buying them throughout the school year.

Learning to love myself today meant learning to confess and denounce the alterations I had performed in the pursuit of whiteness. These alterations included wearing colored contacts, bleaching my hair, learning to contour my nose into a thinner shape—all in an attempt to pass as white despite the futility of it. My attempt at transformation was always rooted in colorism, which was basically a learned form of self-hatred. And as an adult, I needed to eradicate all of that from my life.

While colorism is a way for POC to enforce racism, it's also a way for some POC to survive racism. If you are white-passing or white-adjacent, you can survive and adapt to a racist society. If you benefit from colorism, you are also rewarded for enforcing the codes within it.

Mestizos are seen as superior to Indigenous people, and we continue to be rewarded for our proximity to whiteness. The rewards were tangible back in the day, through treaties between our Indigenous and Spanish ancestors, and through the social embrace by the ruling class, the conquistadores. Though the embrace was conditional, it was a step in the direction of having our fractured humanity recognized.

Generation after generation, colorism results in confused, power-hungry mestizos who work tirelessly to become white at the expense of Black and Indigenous people. Colorism in my family meant that I was told that I was mestiza, when everyone knew that we have Black ancestry. Colorism meant that marriages were strategic to elevate one's racial status, where the aspiration was to marry up the colorism scale, not down it.

In this day and age, it is common to hear a liberal white person speak proudly about traces of diverse racial heritage, as discovered through commercial DNA tests. There is this fixation today with being more than just white. As if waves of European immigrants who were reviled as nonwhite—the Irish, the Italians, the Polish— hadn't yearned over generations to become just white. As if their ancestors did not work tirelessly to contribute to the national identity of whiteness by erasing their cultures and differences.

This stands in stark contrast to the genealogy searches that I am familiar with, where Latinx people attempt to find and claim their whitest European ancestors. In Miami, it was common to hear someone talk about being a mut, being mixed with Colombian, Spanish, and Italian, as if all that mixing had occurred consensually and was just a happy circumstance of their ancestors' lives. Mestizaje routinely seek to erase everyone in the family who is Indigenous or Black, by distancing us from them.

In fact, I had once done this myself, creating distance between myself and my Indigenous ancestors. When I was a teenager, mi abuelito, like many in his generation, became obsessed with genealogy. He retraced our paternal family line back to Spain, following our Spanish last names, selectively weeding out of the family tree any claim to Indigenous roots. He also traced us back to Egypt, looking for links to Egyptian royalty—despite the obvious fact that Egyptians are North African and racially Brown and Black. This did not seem to faze him. When he thought of Egyptian royalty, my abuelito thought of Elizabeth Taylor; somehow, to him, Egypt was a path to Europe.

His anti-Indigenous family search allowed him to proudly claim Spanish and Egyptian heritage, and thus I did too. I was not told about our Indigenous ancestors; they were deliberately erased and forgotten. I never questioned this, and so agreed to keep them erased and forgotten. I had already internalized the benefits of this willful ignorance.

In mestizo communities, proximity to whiteness affords people a possible reward of better jobs, better placements, and therefore better opportunities. Back in the 1800s, Nicaraguans were surveyed, and mestizos who promoted their whiteness got to keep lands; those who identified as Indigenous were removed. Claiming mestizaje is how we become whiter. It is tangibly beneficial to identify as white, even when your skin tells a different story.

Mi mami tells me to get out of the sun. Mi mami tells me to put on sunblock. Mi mami tells me to not go to the beach so much.

We don't just have to call out white people for their racism. We also have to dismantle internalized racism within communities of color. The politics of pigmentation cannot continue to be ignored, because denying our experiences perpetuates generations of harm. The next time your mami, tia, abuelo tells you to get out of the sun so that you do not get darker, tell them what they are actually saying. The next time you try to erase your heritage, consider what it would mean to love your Brown skin. Those who have passed as white, you need to think about your privilege and the harms you may be perpetuating on your own communities of color. We all need to start this slow, sometimes painful process of communally unlearning what we have internalized.

And I implore you to wear your tiniest bikinis and enjoy the sun while watching your magic happen, juntxs!

CHAPTER 3

IMPOSTOR SYNDROME

Many victims of racial discrimination suffer in silence or blame themselves for their predicament. Others pretend that it didn't happen or that they 'just let it roll off my back.' All three groups are more silent than they need be. Stories can give them a voice and reveal that other people have similar experiences. Stories can name a type of discrimination (e.g., microaggressions, unconscious discrimination, or structural racism); once named, it can be combated.

—Richard Delgado

Growing up, I was pretty self-motivated. My family immigrated to Miami, Florida, when I was seven years old, and Miami, being a Latinx city, meant that English was optional. Police officers were often bilingual, teachers in school were bilingual, and Latinx judges and school principals were all bilingual. So, although a lot of the Latinx people in power in Miami were white-passing or lighter skinned, I still saw possibilities around me. I saw possibilities when I heard slang Spanish slip out of the mouths of respected Latinx people in positions that felt unreachable. What this meant for me is that I chose to ignore obvious obstacles like classism and anti-immigrant chatter; dreaming while under attack was most likely a survival skill that I picked up while I was being raised as a girl in a strict, Christian fundamentalist household.

In order to thrive, I had to find ways to pick and choose what was for me, and what was meant to keep me down. I could generally do some sort of mental gymnastics to justify my own motivations for my future, a future that was left unscripted beyond an obedience to a future husband and God. All this is to say, yes, there were instances that hurt my pride and times when I had to change how I carried myself to avoid being teased for being too new to this country, too Nicaraguan, too Brown, too working-class, etc. But for the most part I had this raw belief in myself that went generally unimpacted by the low expectations that had been projected onto me.

I understood in high school that other people did not see potential in me, but somehow I saw potential within me. Even when I was able to do things that were firsts for my family line and ancestors, I had little doubt internally in my own ability to do well. There was a spark within me that was probably naivete, but also some willpower that I was able to harness.

But then in my twenties I moved to the primarily white city of Nashville, Tennessee. And in this white city, I began to see that people had different expectations for what I was capable of, and there was no one around that looked like me to prove to me and my brain that I could defy those odds. It was not until later in life that I would develop the skills to create my own spaces for representation, like Latina Rebels.

Impostor syndrome is something that almost everyone experiences at some point in their lives. Impostor syndrome is the name for that fear that people will one day discover you to be a fraud. It is the lingering doubt that you are not worthy of your successes. This type of thinking can have negative effects on your mental health, which in turn can affect your physical health.

Impostor syndrome is believed to affect all genders, but early on when the phrase was first coined and gaining currency, it was discussed as a common experience among women in the workplace. I will further Pauline Rose Clance's theory that it was specifically a white woman problem, because they were among the first to infiltrate the white male corporate world. Women are socialized to be docile, appeasing, welcoming, humble, not opinionated, and deferential to men. Men are socialized to be aggressive, competitive, bold, and proud; they are groomed for power, dominance, and success.

When women began to be recognized for their professional successes, impostor syndrome led them to believe what they had been socialized to believe—that any accomplishments resulted from luck, teamwork, and outside help.

People of color and specifically BIWOC can suffer impostor syndrome in the same ways, but also differently. Society applauds whiteness for the sake of whiteness, and expects greatness from white people, though still within a two-gender hierarchy. These cultural values are affirmed through media, literature, academia, interpersonal interactions, the entertainment industry, and so on. Performing well professionally for BIPOC requires overcoming low expectations; if you do well, white peers now believe you are an exception to a cultural rule. Racial impostor syndrome comes from fears that you will be discovered as a fraud. But the racial dynamics are complex, because you are made to believe that you don't belong—whether you succeed or fail.

While Black and Latino students are not intellectual frauds, the education system often transmits messages that suggest the opposite.

A belief that intelligence is inherited and "fixed" and using cultur-
ally incongruent measures that continue to illustrate, symbolically,
a hierarchy of intelligence will only continue to reinforce cognitive
misrepresentations.

—Dawn X. Henderson

I started to experience intense impostor syndrome in my graduate program. At my undergraduate university, Florida International University, I had graduated at the top of my class. I made the dean's list almost every semester, and I had a side business of writing papers for people for money. I could ensure an A or B grade to all my clients. I felt pretty invincible in my Hispanic-Serving Institution; I felt seen in my undergraduate experience because I felt validated through grades and accolades. I adapted to college very well, despite being the second person in my family to attend college in the United States and having to learn to maneuver this space without much guidance. Seeing professors who spoke broken English with heavy Spanish accents meant that I saw myself through hearing the familiar.

But still, I had been on my own to figure out the FAFSA, college applications, credits and electives, and what coursework was required for majors and minors. And it was touch and go for a bit, as it was hard to figure out and even harder to explain to people why I did not already know some things.

Still, I had managed to do well. So well that I thought, "Why not try graduate school?" in a flippant way that I can only describe as Elle Woods–like. I felt so reassured and valued, through representation and grades, that I managed to somehow see a place for myself within academia. Even when I did not really know what grad school entailed and who was there guarding the entrance.

I did not score well on my GRE, because standardized tests are racist, classist, ableist, and designed to weed out those who do not belong inside the pristine walls of academia. Still, I was able to find a program that knew those flaws in standardized testing, and I was admitted into an elite graduate institution: Vanderbilt University in Nashville, Tennessee. But the process of being admitted marked the entire academic experience for me.

I had great recommendations, I had a 3.5 GPA from undergrad, I had served in leadership positions in various honor societies, and I had also written a thesis for my honor's college requirement. On paper, I should have been a shoo-in. And then I received this phone call from the admissions director at Vanderbilt Divinity School. On this phone call, I was asked to explain my statement of purpose. As a first-generation student, I did not have much knowledge in terms of what a statement of purpose was supposed to be, and I certainly couldn't get help from my family or friends. I just did what I had always done, and that was ask the internet and hope for the best. I had googled how to write one.

I then wrote about my desire for a theological education. When I explained my statement of purpose to the admissions director, she gave me the acceptance over the telephone. I had been accepted without ever having received an admissions letter. I had been accepted into Vanderbilt Divinity School through a screening process.

I remember being confused about this phone call. I also remember being shocked and elated that I had been accepted to this prestigious program. I was so caught up as a first-generation student that I did not question the process that I had just undergone. Many months later, during our new-student orientation, I remember asking other students how they were accepted—because by that point I had had more time for doubt to seep in. The process that I had undergone felt off, and I didn't know why I was screened. So, I sought out answers, and in asking around I discovered no one else I asked had been called. Also, I was one of only two self-identifying Latinas in my cohort of seventy or so graduate students. The other Latina is mixed, and she had attended Duke

University for her undergraduate program. In my mind, I thought maybe I was screened because I had attended a large state school (FIU enrollment at the time was more than forty-five thousand students) as opposed to a small and elite private university. But these were all speculations.

The more I asked people if they were screened, the more strange looks I got, and the more I was convinced that my peers now knew what I assumed they had already suspected: that I did not belong. Perhaps the university, and my cohort, knew something I had not yet fully discovered within myself. That screening process should have been the red flag for my journey ahead at Vanderbilt University.

I couldn't help but see that message—you do not belong—everywhere. I once mispronounced a word, which I had only ever read but had never heard said out loud, in a question during a lecture, and my professor giggled and corrected me under his breath, in front of the entire class. I remember being asked if I even knew how to write, by a teaching fellow in a discussion group in front of twenty of my peers. I remember my classmates using obscure academic references I had never heard before. That lingering feeling, that seed of doubt that had been planted during that screening call, that seed began to grow roots within me.

When faced with a need to perform, [impostors] experience doubt, worry, anxiety, and fear; they're so afraid they won't be able to do well that they procrastinate and sometimes feel they're unable to move at all toward completing the task. In other cases, they over-work and overprepare and begin much sooner than needed on a project, thus robbing themselves of times and effort that could be better spent.

—Pauline Rose Clance

As a way of managing my growing impostor syndrome, I began to overprepare. I would tell professors about my proposed thesis for our final paper during the first few weeks of school, and it became a running joke among my peers. In my attempt to assert my worth, I was ridiculed. There was a lack of understanding from my peers in what it meant to be the first in my family to achieve this level of academic success, and a lack of understanding of what it meant to enter elite spaces that signal your "otherness" often.

I also began to self-sabotage. During my second semester of my first year, I got a B on my first exam for our New Testament class. Most students had failed this exam, and the professor told everyone that a C grade from her was equivalent to an A grade for any other class. Those words haunted me, and I never got a better grade from that professor. I remember wanting to get a handle on my worth, and wanting and trying to do better, and yet continually getting Bs and Cs. The A grades were elusive, and I blamed myself. I was exerting myself beyond what I knew to be my own capacity, and I still felt like I was grasping at straws. I felt like a fraud.

I was reading books my peers had already read in undergrad, and I was researching theories my peers had already studied years ago. I was playing catch-up, and I blamed myself. I had been taught, and had believed in, things like perfectionism and meritocracy—teachings that made me believe there was only one right way to do things, and that hard work paid off. None of that served me when I was trying my hardest and doing my damnedest and still could not compete in this academic environment.

You see, what was missing was that I was trying to find my worth and validation from an institution designed for white intellectuals. The ivory tower is ivory for a reason; it is not ebony, it is not the color of honey, nor the color of café con leche, and I was never meant to thrive there. Until I understood that my validation was not going to come from my predominantly white institution (PWI), I was going to keep struggling.

But back then, I was not well versed in white supremacy and the various systems that uphold it. I had none of the advantages that my peers had from their white privilege; no tutors, no private education, no SAT or GRE courses, no network of family members who had gone to elite universities. My lack made my professors and peers uncomfortable, and I was constantly made to feel that I didn't belong and that any time I fell short I confirmed their suspicions. My modest grades became a marker of my otherness. And my body began to show the signs of buckling under all these pressures.

I began to experience palpitations, and I would sweat through my clothes from anxiety when talking to any person with power, which usually meant that they were white. I felt misunderstood and weird. I could not sound brilliant enough, and I could not bolster my arguments with enough citations, and I could not seem to make sense to my peers, and I began to shrink right before their eyes. When I had once felt invincible, I began to want to be small, to be invisible. It felt like I was in an abusive relationship with an institution, seeking its validation and only receiving criticism, and none of that made sense to me.

> *Impostors are very perfectionistic in almost every aspect of their performances.*
>
> —Pauline Rose Clance

My impostor syndrome came from internalizing white-supremacist models of meritocracy and perfectionism. White supremacy promotes the idea of individualism, because that keeps us busy and unfocused on what the real problems are. Through individualism we do not analyze the systemic problems, the institutions that keep so many of us down. Because of individualism, I was unable to see that this was not about me, but about us all. Our wins are ours, and our losses are ours, and they belong to our communities who encourage us. When we don't seek white approval in PWIs, we can look to our Black and Brown peers and our chosen family, who show us how to resist and how to be seen by one another.

Because I was not yet aware of how much racial impostor syndrome impacts us all and how much white supremacy can infiltrate your sense of worth, by my second year of graduate school I had developed an eating disorder. I felt like I could not control how others saw me, so I spiraled. I felt that when white people saw me, all they saw were my flaws, and I experienced that to be true. It was not just a feeling, it was happening and it was true. So, I began to shrink my body. I wanted to take up less space. I felt that I couldn't be good enough, and the white gaze felt suffocating. Waiting for validation from white people was sucking my ability to value myself outside of their gaze.

I tried to escape the voices in my head that told me I did not belong. American society dictates that whiteness, and proximity to whiteness, was always going to be the measure of success. I was starting to learn about racism, sexism, and classism, and slowly I began to find the language for the forces around me. But while my brain and my lips could finally name the oppression, my heart still hurt from feeling like an outsider all the time, all while trying to graduate.

Two years later, I would develop a mentorship relationship with the admissions director who I had spoken to in that screening call. And I asked her directly why I had been screened before attending. By this time, I had often been made to feel inferior by my peers and professors. I knew that there was an underlying presumption of my incompetence, and I was in search of real answers.

When I asked her about being screened, she told me it was not because of my grades or competence. The school wanted to know that I was willing to learn and grow in my theological training.

My statement of purpose reflected my charismatic Christian, fundamentalist, conservative upbringing. Some students with my background are resistant to learning progressive theologies, and Vanderbilt Divinity School saw itself as a progressive theological institution. I did see students on campus from conservative backgrounds who seemed like they were fighting the program, and those people felt like outcasts. Then again, I also saw people struggle who had liberal backgrounds, so that screening process was not free of faults. Knowing the reason should have alleviated my initial fears, but by this time it was too late. My self-confidence had been worn away by years of negative messaging within my PWI, and the damage would affect me in ways that I would only discover much later.

We rarely have control of the ways impostor syndrome traps people of color. To assimilate requires erasing your ethnicity; you have to perform in a way that puts white people at ease, to the point where you earn honorary whiteness: "You're not like the others." Students like myself who choose not to erase their ethnicity, or who cannot downplay their differences, are othered and quietly outcast. Succeeding through Americanized, white definitions of success means performing to reinforce, or to spite, the greatness of whiteness. We either reinforce or upset the low expectations built by white supremacy. And many of us develop anxiety and other mental illnesses when we are daily asked to compromise ourselves, all while trying to juggle schoolwork, or do our jobs, or live our lives. We dared to believe that degrees and promotions meant success, but no one ever said that success came at the cost of our well-being.

By the time I graduated, despite knowing that the screening process was not meant to delegitimize me, it had. That one seed that had sprouted roots had become a full ecosystem by the time I got home from graduate school. And while my mind and my lips can consistently articulate the ways that I know impostor syndrome was something that was cast onto me, I still cannot shed it. Some days, impostor syndrome feels all-consuming.

A way for me to heal from it is that I take with me all the sweet prayers and communal laying of hands that women in my family have done as they have blessed me into every phase of my life. I moved back home after graduate school, and when I finally was ready to leave again, mi mami came into my bedroom and laid her hands on my hands. Mi mami looked directly into my eyes, and she said: "Yo sé, que tu siempre estarás bien." This unwavering belief in me, this bendición, is what I carry with me. In the past, I had devalued her prayers, I had devalued her words. Today, her words bring me back to myself whenever whiteness suffocates me. I keep mi mami's loving affirmations with me whenever I begin to doubt my abilities. I am still strengthened by this belief that I will be okay because mi mami believes in me.

Impostor syndrome is a daily presence in my life. In 2017, when my now agent, David Patterson, first messaged me on Twitter telling me how he loved my writing and that he wanted to represent me, I did not believe it. In 2019, when we sent my book proposal to various publishers and six editors from top publishers said they wanted to publish my book, I did not believe it. I even cried one night because I was so certain that everyone was lying to me and that this was all just one long con. And when I finally accepted my book deal and signed the contract, I cried again because I kept thinking that someone would discover that I was a fraud and that I was not good enough.

What I have had to do is learn to live with impostor syndrome, and I have learned to not let it stop me.

I write today for high school Prisca, who was told that college was too big a dream and still applied. I write today for immigrant Prisca, who could not read and write at eight years old, but learned to read and write and then majored in English literature. I write today for graduate school Prisca, who was rejected from both the

English-proficient writing center and the ESL writing center and still managed to get her master's degree.

I write for my inner child—who was bold and confident and her own biggest supporter—because I know what teeny Prisca would have said: "Sabía que podías!" And that younger version of me could and would dream big, because she saw herself represented and heard her language spoken in private and public spaces, and she got to develop sides of herself that allowed her to grow. I was born in a country that had a female president, Violeta Chamorro. I saw a woman from my country reach the highest position of power, and I dared to dream.

I would be nothing without the people who indirectly or directly paved new realities for me, and remembering them is how my boldness is fed. I remember my friend Rev. Alba Onofrio, the now executive director of Soulforce, who is queer and nonmonogamous. I recall how they, just by living their life on their own terms, shattered the ceiling of heteronormativity and the norm of monogamy for me. I recall Rev. Dr. Lis Valle, who left an abusive relationship and a successful law career in her late thirties to throw herself into academia and theological education, all to head toward what she felt called to do. She shattered ageism and norms around living a straight and seemingly safe path.

I started gathering friends—queer, working-class, Black, Brown, and Latinx Vanderbilt graduate students—knowing that together we could be unstoppable. Even creating Latina Rebels in the middle of my program, in 2013, was my attempt to harness the joy of people like me online.

This is how I began to trim that tree of impostor syndrome that continually grows out of me. I am nothing without these people and the spaces we carved out for ourselves, and everything I am is thanks to them.

What does it mean to live with impostor syndrome? For me it is about armament. Living in a city that is dominated by whiteness and white people means that whenever I step outside the safety of my own home, I am wearing armor. Armor can take many forms, and can change depending on where you are and where you are going on any given day.

Have you ever watched old war movies, when they would have that scene of soldiers painting their faces? The music that accompanies these rituals of war still resonates with me. Even with the fictitious Hollywood sheen, I have always been entranced by war paint.

When I moved to Tennessee and started getting othered and racialized by white people, my understanding of oppression became more intimate. The white gaze felt hostile. When white people exert their social status and unearned power to target BIPOC, the stakes quickly escalate. Being seen as different is dangerous and life-threatening for too many Black and Brown people. Moving to Tennessee has meant learning defense mechanisms, including applying my war paint.

Every morning before I go out, I put on lipstick and winged eyeliner: my war paint. I adorn my body with my armor. I walk into white spaces with deliberate bravado, to deter even the passing thought of approaching me with familiarity. I make myself unavailable for small talk and I do this every time I go out. It is exhausting, but it makes me feel safe in all-white spaces.

The subtle and sometimes not-so-subtle racism disguised as well-intentioned curiosity has consistently left me feeling disarmed, vulnerable, and exposed. I remember when I first moved to Nashville and had gone out to a bar in an attempt to enjoy myself. A white man approached and rubbed my exposed shoulders and asked, "Is your skin really this color?" He assumed I had on tanning spray or had gone to a tanning bed, because he had never seen someone with my skin tone before. He had touched me without asking, like he would any object he felt entitled to possess.

This is just one example of what I experienced when I moved to a predominantly white city for the first time. These disarming comments followed me over the years, and I never grew accustomed to them—I do not want to grow accustomed to them. I do not want to accept their perception of me, even as I have internalized it.

My war paint is my defiance, on many levels. I did not grow up wearing lipstick, because I grew up in a conservative church where women's clothing, makeup, hairstyles, and even mannerisms were strictly monitored and controlled. Women were shamed for wearing makeup. Heavy makeup was vanity; it was a distraction from God. Essentially, if you loved God then you did not need outside affirmations, because God was all you needed.

Unlearning this was a process. Realizing how heavily policed I was by my church has made me more determined to reclaim these things that were weaponized against me.

Slowly, when I started wearing lipstick regularly, I discovered the power of makeup as a Brown immigrant Latina living in a white city. Many feminine Black and Brown women have also framed their makeup as war paint. Interestingly, a white person's response to the presence of a Latina wearing red can be rather revealing. The spicy-Latina stereotype depicts us as fiery, and thus associates us all with the color red. I learned to pay attention when I wear red lipstick, so I can see just how much of this stereotype each white person has absorbed. I can use this information as I strategize how to manage each encounter.

Red is my color, and I have a feeling it will always be my color. Red lipstick is an homage to the tired spicy-Latina trope, but it is also my middle finger to those people who sexualize me without my consent simply because I am Latina, simply because they have never been exposed to someone like me.

Racism comes from a place of willful ignorance. I am not one who is willing to tirelessly educate white people on how to approach me.

Wearing my defiant war paint and armor, I dare anyone to call me spicy.

I walk with that challenge on my lips and on my body.

I am ready for war, and I have my armor on.

Me being able to exist in this Brown skin, to exist as an immigrant, and still adorn myself with visible pride—it confuses racist white people. They cannot wrap their minds around people like me loving ourselves.

So instead of feeling unprepared, as I initially felt when I first moved to Nashville, I now stand ready to protect myself. Living with impostor syndrome does not mean that I cower in a corner whenever I am in primarily white spaces. It means living fully even when I know I am not supposed to. It means living fiercely. Living with impostor syndrome means doing what I can to provide positive representation for little Brown girls in white cities. I stand proud and strong, for them.

Because teeny Prisca got to see proud Brown people around her, and she got to dream because of it. Even when the current version of me struggles with keeping my lips from trembling when I speak, I still hold myself up and adorn myself with pride. I will take up space, even when it hurts. I will stand with my head held high, even when I doubt myself. I will prove them wrong, even if I have to prove it all to myself first.

CHAPTER 4

MYTH OF MERITOCRACY

Meritocracy is the belief that hard work will pay off. It is the classic rags-to-riches story, a promise that we are told is reachable for anyone, across all races, genders, sexualities, and backgrounds.

However, despite rare exceptions, meritocracy is a myth. Most people are not able to work so hard that they are no longer poor. Some of the hardest working people I know were born poor and will die poor. It's important to accept that hoping to be the exception is not a solution. Radicalization can only occur after realizing that we are cogs in a large and powerful machine. Gatekeepers use the myth of meritocracy to distract busy working-class and working-poor folks with so much self-blame when they fall short that they will not think to revolt against their oppressors. Gatekeepers are everywhere, regulating who gets to live the American Dream and who gets to work hard for others' dreams.

I believed in a meritocracy, deeply, and then I did not believe in it. When I finally stopped believing in it, I found my way back home.

My first memorable encounter with an adult gatekeeper was a high school guidance counselor. I knew how to spot him because I had already encountered young gatekeepers: my peers growing up.

I was never that kid, the kid who was encouraged to go to college. I know what those kids look like, and they are typically middle-class, white or white-adjacent, well-dressed, well-spoken, and well-behaved by white standards.

Me, on the other hand—I was not expected to go to college. Mi mami does not have a college degree. She was a stay-at-home mom, and I was told that being a homemaker was honorable and an aspiration that I should have too. I got this messaging very directly at home and indirectly at school.

I was not one of those kids whose future looked bright. I was told I talked too much, and I seldom paid attention in class. I distrusted my father's authority at home—but feared him due to regular beatings—and I brought this innate need to question authority to school. At home, I could not do anything about my own powerlessness, but rebelling at school seemed to give me some form of satisfaction. It made me feel like I had some control over my life.

I created a different identity at school. I remember mi mami asking me: If she were to spy on me at school, would she recognize me? I nervously laughed and brushed off her insightful prodding. I had a life that felt like my own at school. I felt free, or at least free of my parents' strict structure. I felt no desire to give up any of that freedom for my teachers and their fickleness toward favoring the most indoctrinated, assimilated kids.

I was not a troublemaker, but I hated being told what to do because that is all that happened at home. I did not get detention but was suspended a few times because I was "distracting." I was sent to "in-school suspension," because my attendance still equaled dollars for the school and in-school suspension kept them financially compensated. I was someone who was policed specifically for my behavior, which was not properly muted in the ways that public education, more often than not, prefers.

I was even suspended for reading in class. I read often, because I found more education from my own books than from my teachers, and I was penalized for it. And when my books were not on my desk, I resorted to talking to my peers, a lot.

My mami still has a progress report from ninth grade, where every teacher gave the same comment: "She talks too much!" Mi mami would laugh about that for years, but she never reprimanded me. My education wasn't a priority for my family. I figured that out in elementary school—when mi mami complained about all my honor-roll stickers becoming a nuisance—and carried that energy into the remainder of my schooling years.

Because I wasn't the quiet and obedient model student, teachers overlooked me at best, or, at worst, busied me with other tasks instead of teaching or even encouraging me. In tenth grade, one teacher was so frustrated with me that she tasked me with memorizing as many digits of pi as I could, as a condition for my getting a passing grade for the class. I hated algebra but I ended up learning five hundred digits of pi, and got a C grade for that school year. And while that should have impressed my teacher, she mostly just expressed relief at not having me as a student anymore. Sometimes your favorite teacher is someone else's worst teacher, because maybe what they liked about you was your ability to do what you were told.

I was not that kid the teachers deemed smart. That kid who shined, that kid who teachers believed in. I was not someone who people thought was bright and destined to go places. I did not learn to read when everyone else did. A few factors came into play for all this, including my migration.

In my country of Nicaragua, I attended a public school. Most immigrants from Latin America and the Caribbean will tell you that not many families opt to enroll their children in public schools, because our public education systems can leave a lot to be desired. Most people, if they are able, enroll their children in private schools in hope of a better education. We also migrated right when I was supposed to go to second grade, and by that point I was already struggling with my reading skills.

Like many people who are illiterate and old enough to be aware of it, I did a lot of memorizing and reciting so as to appear as though I could read. But as soon as something came up that I had not memorized, I was quickly discovered. Learning to read was hard, and being the kid who could not read well was also hard, and it began to chip at my self-confidence at a young age.

When we came to this country, we arrived on a temporary visa. Once here, my parents were told by an immigration lawyer not to enroll us in school until after we obtained our residency. Apparently enrolling us in school signified intent to stay, and that was the last thing we were supposed to do while filing for residency.

I had been out of school for nearly six months by the time I started school in the United States, and by then the academic school year was a month or so from ending. Because of the timing of my enrollment, I was not expected to catch up to my peers and their coursework. We had the summer off, and when school started again that August, I was eight years old. I remember walking into my second-grade class and being asked to find my desk. There were name tags on each desk, but because I could not read, I just sat anywhere. My reading skills, or lack thereof, were quickly discovered and I was immediately sent back to a first-grade class, before the majority of my new peers had even set foot into that portable classroom.

Soon after the teachers realized I could not even recite the alphabet, I was asked to stay after school to learn to read, one-on-one, with a teacher. I have vivid memories of learning to make sense of the alphabet. I remember the joy of learning to spell my first name and my last names. The haze was lifted, I could see clearly, and the letters suddenly meant something. This all came at a time when I was also learning that my parents had names of their own, aside from mami and papi. I felt such pride when I first wrote mi mami's name: B-L-A-N-C-A. Because I was behind and was expected to have already learned this, my victories were not celebrated. My teachers just noted that they were making progress in solving my problem.

Soon after, mi mami got me a library card and a rolling suitcase that I regularly filled to capacity at my local library. I inhaled books like my life depended on it. But I still hated school. There was a difference for me: reading gave me life; school was intended to be punitive.

Back then we were living in a neighborhood that was predominately populated by Nicaraguan immigrants. Sweetwater, in the early nineties, was known as Pequeña Nicaragua. This was before gentrification and before the local university bought out a lot of the properties and essentially displaced Little Nica to another part of town.

Our neighborhood had a huge influx of new immigrants, and teachers understood to speak to the students first in Spanish, and then they slowly introduced English. I was able to somewhat hide my lagging reading skills, as we were all learning the English alphabet together. I was only discovered as a student who was "behind" when I was asked my age at the beginning of every school year.

In third grade, we moved to another part of town about nine miles from Sweetwater. My parents packed everything we owned, again, and we moved out from a neighborhood that had quesillos a block from our apartment, fritangas within walking distance, and a middle school named after one of the most famous

Nicaraguan poets: Rubén Darío. We left all these comforts and remnants of our home country and moved to this new school and neighborhood.

This new neighborhood had residents with a mix of immigration statuses. There were a few recent immigrants, including some undocumented, but most folks were born here and their families had been here for a couple generations. A lot of the kids in this new neighborhood seemed more American, more middle-class, with two working parents, and this neighborhood was less racially diverse. While the majority of my neighbors were Cuban, and thus ethnically Latinx, racially they were mostly white or white-adjacent.

A lot of my Latinx peers did not speak Spanish, and many even spoke English to their parents. In this new neighborhood, everything about our migration, and our poverty, stood out. As a ten-year-old in third grade, I was noticeably older. And as a kid who had recently immigrated, I was noticeably different. I was a working-class kid and an immigrant, and I did not know how to dress like my peers. I remember trying to learn and use slang, only to get smirks or corrections. I did not move in our school with the same ease that the second- and third-generation kids did. So, I started to pay close attention.

A funny memory I have in my quest to become more American and thus assimilated occurred in the summer between sixth and seventh grade, when I listened to Power 96.5 FM late into the nights, writing down song lyrics and practicing them. My middle school would play music in the cafeteria, and everyone sang along but me. I was preparing to not be the odd one out in seventh grade, like I had felt in sixth grade. I was not allowed to listen to secular music or even English-language music at home unless I translated the lyrics for my parents. My parents heavily policed what I consumed to keep me from sinning, and to avoid my eternal damnation. Whenever I was asked to translate, I was quickly told to shut down whatever I was enjoying. So, I made concerted efforts to learn these things in private to try to fit in, to avoid being an outcast.

Starting middle school, I just wanted to fit in. I wanted to be a part of the larger American narrative, a narrative that felt white and middle-class.

Adapting to popular culture meant accepting it as my own. I needed to commit and distance myself from my working-class, immigrant background if I was going to be accepted. To succeed, I knew I had to fit myself into the American definition of who I should be. My assimilation in America required my assimilation into whiteness. When I finally realized what had happened, there was nothing I could do but mourn the loss of so many parts of myself.

Systemic oppression and internalized racism keep many of us down. So, to the ones who somehow make it out: it is our duty to become cheerleaders and advocates for those who are struggling. I was never the kid with a cheering squad of mentors and teachers and family members. I was the other kid, whose cheering squad was me, myself, and I. Growing up, I needed more supportive people in my life, because I would soon discover that the gatekeepers only get meaner and more aggressive.

I was not the chosen kid, the kid who was doted on by the adults in my life. It is easy to praise the kid who always looks polished and gets all the good grades. Racism and classism are why it is easy to accept some children and easy to overlook others. Gatekeeping taught these adults which traits were indicative of success, and they perpetuated them onto us.

Entire school systems have found ways to keep the good white kids away from the rest of the student population. We know today that gifted programs were invented to recreate segregation within desegregated schools. Gifted programs were not about the smart-est kids but about appeasing parents who could take their kids to private schools if the public school did not serve their needs. These parents' singular concern for their children is what created the school systems we have today. I was not dumb; I just did not fit into what school systems and teachers have been told to value.

Racism and classism function in the trickiest of ways. Specifi-cally, for this chapter, class creates a value system: your net worth becomes your actual worth as a person. And it should be noted that Black and Brown people are disproportionately part of the working-poor class bracket. So with that logic, white people are more valuable in society, and all those who come close to it also get value by proximity.

I remember the first time I became aware of class. I was in mid-dle school. Before then, uniforms were pretty strictly enforced in my schools. Ibiley, the official uniform distributor for Miami-Dade during that time, sold expensive official uniforms for each school. My working-class family could not afford to purchase uniforms at those prices, so mi mami sent some swatches to mi abuelita, and she made my uniforms and sent them to me before school started. Or sometimes we thrifted them from our local Goodwill store. But while I knew I was wearing Ibiley "fakes," no one else seemed to notice. In middle school, though, the uniform policies were lax enough that class differences became more obvious.

One day, as I walked into my math class and took my seat, and I overheard people talking about someone in our class wearing fake brand-name shoes. This peer was Black, and a minority in this neighborhood by a lot. The boy had made the mistake of showing his class status while being Black, and it was all our classroom could talk about. Before, this peer of mine was considered funny and, I would even say, nice. But then he had made the mistake of wearing fakes, and nobody would let it go. The jokes centered around him being poor and they were relentless. On that day, I learned that what I wore and how I wore it mattered to everyone, and that it revealed everything about my family, my upbringing, my home, my worth, and my future. I became aware of the ways that I should create distance between myself and my working-class context. I had too much stacked against me, and I needed to get people to not pay attention to all those other things about me.

Fast forward to high school, where I often heard anti-immigrant slurs. This was also a majority Latinx student population, but it was common to hear insults like "reffy" (refugee) thrown around. The designation of reffy befell those who merely had Spanish accents. There was an us-versus-them mentality, "us" being the more assimilated Latinx and "them" being the ones who were not. We became gatekeepers, reflecting the media that was available to us and the adults in our lives. There is tangible value in aligning ourselves to whiteness, and we were simply reflecting the society we lived in.

I had to do everything in my power to become an "us" and not a "them." One year, our school was stripped of our soccer championship because many of our star players were undocumented. The opposing school, also a primarily Latinx school, had found out and reported them. Those players were given conditional passes to be included in the "us" because they had something of value, a skill we were told was important. Still, when they lost their title, nobody protested.

There was no allyship with the undocumented folks. Because I was a green-card holder, I could create that distance, even when I found more in common with those newer immigrant students than with the more assimilated ones.

I remember hearing students talk about college; it was an "us" conversation that I knew I had to infiltrate. I was not really part of the assimilated crowd in my high school. I was not part of the few undocumented-immigrant groups at our school either. I did not have many friends. But for my future, I knew I had to latch myself onto the college-bound crew. Those kids were different; they were who the gates helped protect. The AP students and gifted students were the prized children of the school. They had the help of teachers and faculty who defended them against foreign invaders.

I knew I was a foreign invader in more ways than one, despite the historical irony. So, I learned to utilize the skills I had gained and applied them again; I watched and I listened and I learned to adapt. I remember hearing some of my peers talking about college, and many sounded matter-of-fact about their college prospects. Meanwhile, I had never even imagined such a thing for myself. I watched and I listened and I learned to adapt. I spotted the gatekeepers, and I learned to work around them.

During my junior year of high school, with a laughable grade point average of 2.8, I marched into my school counselor's office and told him that I was going to enroll in five of the college-bound classes known as Advanced Placement classes. I was already enrolled in two that year, and it had been quite a shift for me in terms of teachers and peers. But there seemed to be a difference between dabbling and total immersion in these classes, something I would realize once I got full access. You could tell these students were valued by the school. To solidify my "us" status, I had to emulate the "us" students and enroll in as many AP classes as I could. The "us" students, the college-bound students, did not slack off in their senior year; they fluffed their transcripts. So, I wanted to enroll in five AP classes for my senior year, to reflect my moral goodness and, hopefully, get the keys to open new gates and new opportunities.

This was a big leap for someone like me, someone who did not excel academically and had never before expressed college aspirations. My counselor denied my request and told me to take more electives and give my GPA the boost it needed through easier classes. He implied that I was dumb; he told me that being book smart was not a skill everyone had, and maybe I would excel at sports instead. I remember feeling really embarrassed, but learning to move past shame had already been normalized in other ways for me, so I knew to move past the shame in this instance as well.

Being a working-class, Brown, immigrant Latina, I knew by then that I had to become my own biggest advocate. So, I went to the one person who could convince my public school counselor at one of the biggest high schools in the country to change his mind: my mami. I spotted a gatekeeper, and I knew his weakness: parents. So the next day, I brought my mami to school to force him to put me in those AP classes.

As we were sitting there, I told the school counselor that mi mami wanted him to put me in the AP classes, even though she was not asking for this and did not even fully understand why she was there. I was the interested party, not mi mami.

The counselor then had the audacity to tell me that he felt it was not a good move because he would be setting me up for failure. He said I would need help with these classes, and then he looked at mi mami and said that her lack of English proficiency meant that she would not be able to help me. This gatekeeper upped the requirements for entering this classroom and made them personal.

My high school counselor had all the power in his hands to either make a path for me to attend college or rob me of that opportunity entirely. He was saying I shouldn't have such high aspirations for myself, all because we were immigrants and my parents did not speak English. I had not imitated proper indoctrination into the American school system, which my grades reflected but was not indicative of my potential.

He had devalued my abilities and my resilience, and had overlooked the simple fact that I had already learned to assimilate in the United States without the help of my parents. This gatekeeper decided to reinforce the walls that should have been doors, as gatekeepers do.

My counselor underestimated me and my ability to win. I had been paying attention, I knew that the AP students were college bound, and I had to be around them to get to college. I knew that the AP students were the ones college recruiters courted, while the other students were approached by predatory military recruiters during our lunch hour. The school made concerted efforts to support the AP students, and I knew that I needed that support when it was not provided at home. I knew that the AP students were the ones who got recommendations, networking opportunities, and preferential treatment from teachers and school counselors. I knew that AP students were coveted because they got the school more funding; a teacher had told me to my face that AP students were worth double what regular students were worth. What I learned was that if I was an AP student, the school would place a higher value on my Brown immigrant body, and they would invest in my future. The gatekeeper knew this and saw me as unworthy. The school counselor failed to see that having no support at home meant that the school should provide that support instead of penalizing me. I was a child, and the adults around me were failing me because of their own internalized biases.

As I sat there contemplating how I was going to build my rebuttal against the counselor's xenophobic and classist remarks, I remember mi mami turning to me and attempting to negotiate with me to listen to the counselor. I remember my heart breaking, because I knew mi mami did not understand the gravity of this moment, the gravity of this refusal. Mi mami seemed to believe that this gatekeeper was telling only truths and not reflecting a larger, more fucked-up narrative, which was meant to keep us down simply because we were not white and middle-class. I knew—I had been paying close attention—that if I did not overturn my counselor's opinion, I was going to struggle to get into college. The gatekeepers in society just get more heartless and harder to outsmart; this high school counselor was relatively low-hanging fruit that I knew I could reach.

My brother is two years older than me but four school years ahead of me because I was behind academically. He had graduated from high school before I even started, and he struggled trying to figure out what to do next. I remember he worked in the roofing industry for a year or so and then decided to enroll in the local community college, but he was navigating this school system with blinders on. FAFSA, applications, class selections were all foreign concepts to us, and we had not received any help on how to navigate it all. It was assumed that all families just inherently knew how to jump through those hoops. That assumption cuts opportunities out of the equation. I knew I needed the help, even when I did not know the exact details of what kind of help I would need, and I was going to get what I needed even if I had to fight for it.

Internalized isms taught many of our parents that they could not fly even before they were aware that they had wings. I remember seeing mi mami trying to find common ground, trying to accommodate this man over her daughter, and trying not to cause a scene. I also remember not caring that they did not believe in me; I knew I could do it. What I did in that moment was commit to believing in my unreachable dreams. I purposefully mistranslated what mi mami said and insisted that she believed in me. I used all the conviction I could muster to tell this counselor that I was getting into these AP classes. I insisted that mi mami was not going to back down.

My school counselor sighed and rolled his eyes, and then he quickly typed out a short *contract* on his computer and printed it out. The *contract* stated the risks associated with my taking this many rigorous classes. The *contract* stated that mi mami had been warned and had decided to ignore the counselor's suggestions. The counselor was wiping his hands clean of us; he was ensuring he was safe in case I failed. This gatekeeper used every tool in his tool kit, and winning for me meant knowing all his tools—and finding better ones.

I was never his concern; he was protecting those inside the gates from me. I remember mistranslating the contract to mi mami and having her sign this document that, quite frankly, should never have been made. That senior year, I was put into my AP classes and ended up applying to and attending a four-year university after high school.

All of which would not have happened had I listened to those voices and low expectations that are meant to keep us down. All of this would not have happened had I been intimidated by this gatekeeper or believed what he believed about me. The assumption was that success looks white and middle-class, and I defied that not because I am smarter but because I rejected his perception of me. I did not work harder than my college-bound peers; I did not work harder than the hundreds of students in my grade who were not given the access I had demanded. I know a lot of brilliant Latinas who should have been in those AP classes with me, but were not because they had believed the lie that the school counselor had told me: the classes would be too hard and they would fail. They believed that the gatekeeper had their best interests in mind, when that was a lie. That is how gatekeepers win, and continue winning. As an immigrant, I was constantly taking notes and constantly observing what was meant for me and what was not, and then I decided to defy gatekeeper after gatekeeper and take their power into my own hands. None of that came easily, because it is a broken system and it leaves a lot of brilliant people behind.

In my AP government class, during the first week of school the teacher had us raise our hands to see how many of us worked when we got off school, and no one raised their hand. Then he told us how he had asked that in his regular government class, and over half the students had raised their hands. I remember feeling that in my gut, because I knew I was just a stone's throw from that context, and while I had no after-school job, I also knew that there was a difference between me and my new peers in these AP classes. And that reality was palpable.

Their differences were not that they were smarter than other students; rather, they simply had the financial ability and support at home to be solely students. Resegregating schools between AP students and regular students was a way to separate by class and race. This system benefits white, wealthy parents because their kids are isolated in a bubble of privilege, and it benefits schools because they get more funding. The only people who lose are the "regular" children, whose potential will never be tapped because their parents are poor, immigrant, Brown, or Black. They lose because they cannot outsmart a system meant to reward their docility and punish any resistance.

When I graduated, I still had a 2.8 GPA, because I was the same student. I never did find community in those AP classes; there was a lot of elitism and a lot of open name-calling of those who were considered dumb. Our school prioritized us, and many of these AP students believed that made them better people. We were all creating identities; we were all trying to become the capital "US" of USA. We were all sheep in wolves' clothing, trying to become American, trying to become the standard, white. We were kids learning to be the predators and not the prey. We were being taught to become gatekeepers in our own right. We were being taught that we deserved to be treated better because of our assumed class status. We were being taught that we deserved access, but were given no tools to critically think about why others do not get this same access.

And while it was lonely, I still managed to find the help I needed during the college-application season and was able to get into what the AP students regularly called their "safety" college, Florida International University. This Hispanic-Serving Institution was my top and only choice.

Lying about my class, my family's finances, became important when I sought community with people whose families clearly had more money than we did. There is also a taught shame around poverty that is hard to undo, so lying became easier. We are taught that being poor is a reflection of your own laziness. In my church, we were even taught by the prosperity gospel that poverty was a moral failing, reflecting your lack of devotion and bendición from God. So, I began to lie about my class. I began to lie about what my parents did for a living. I did not want people to know my mami and papi could not afford what my peers' parents seemed to have no problem affording. I did not want to be any more different than I already was. Mi mami knew about this and would call me Julieta, from the *Soñadoras* novela. Julieta was a character who came from the projects and pretended to have more money than she did to fit in.

It was a known fact that I created distance from my background, but it was to survive the cruelty of a society that ranks people based on their financial status. One way I hid my class was through school lunch. I had been on free and reduced lunch for all the years I had been in American schools. I noticed when entering high school that those who relied on free or reduced lunch ate inside and away from everyone else. Those who ate inside were the Black students and the undocumented students. It was an unspoken rule and created a lunchtime segregation based on class, race, and citizenship status. My school had a courtyard, and the pizza was sold outside. The kids who could afford the $1.75 would pass on paying for the cafeteria lunch and opt to eat pizza instead. If you ate the pizza, you could eat outside, in the courtyard. I stopped eating school lunch, and since I couldn't afford the pizza, I basically just stopped eating lunch. All this, just so I could be a part of the outdoor social culture of the school.

This is how I actively attempted to erase my working-class background, and it seemed to mostly work. People just accepted that I did not eat lunch, and lunch hour at our school was functionally a social hour anyway. Being a kid who ate inside the lunchroom meant social isolation.

I continued to pass somewhat as middle-class through certain acts that kept my class identity ambiguous. That ambiguity meant social capital. I was mostly able to manage and hide my class status—that is, until graduate school. At that advanced academic level, at that elite institution, there were distinct class differences. I couldn't disguise my disadvantages, and I almost flunked out of my first semester.

For undergrad I had attended a Hispanic-Serving Institution. It was one of the most affordable colleges in the country. Few students paid for on-campus room and board; most of the students were commuting from their parents' homes. Each credit cost roughly $100, and my financial aid covered all tuition costs, a laptop, and even sorority membership fees. I was brilliant at maneuvering class and finding spaces for myself, for a working-class person.

Graduate school was truly the first time I knew I could no longer hide my class. I was sitting between two peers from my cohort, both absolutely book smart. And they started talking about Michel Foucault, and then about Judith Butler. They were laughing and referencing literature that we had not even read yet—heavy theory we had not been introduced to—but they had already read it. I even recall one of them saying he read Foucault because he found his books in his father's library. I remember the shock and panic that overcame me. I knew none of those theorists; I had no clue then. But my peers did. Their socioeconomic upbringing had given them access to knowledge I could never dream of and I could never even pretend to know.

With the Latinx AP students I had encountered years earlier, there was this performative aspect of their class entitlement. That same entitlement felt different in white spaces; it felt dangerous here. These white students were not trying to perform their advantages to differentiate themselves above other students of color. Instead, they were so clearly from advantageous life circumstances that their blatant privilege viscerally made me feel sick to my stomach.

In my home, a simple traffic citation could set our family finances off course for weeks, if not months. Cavities went untreated until teeth fell out or broke in half, readers were used as regular glasses by both my parents, and the black market was often used for prescription medicine we could not access or afford. I felt so out of place at Vanderbilt, in ways that I did not even know how to describe to anyone else.

And so, I resigned myself to reading faster, taking more notes, and starting papers at the beginning of the semester that weren't due until the end. I resigned myself to believing that hard work would pay off, to believing in meritocracy. Much to my surprise, all of this did not work. This was not a competition for who could work harder to get an A; this was about whose parents had provided their kids with enough access to succeed at this academic level. This was about whose parents even had the ability to know where to supplement their children's education with home libraries, tutors, extracurriculars, after-school enrichment programs, summer school, and so on. This was about competing with students who never even understood the concept of gatekeepers. This was about students who felt entitled to extensions, help, compassion. This was about students whose teachers had invested time and energy in them. This was about students who had mentors before I even knew what that meant. These students were all the chosen ones, and I felt alone.

I remember one small-group discussion, when I was attempting to describe a paper I was planning to write. The teaching assistant asked for a volunteer, and in an effort to outsmart a gatekeeper,

I attempted to outsmart her. Except this gatekeeper was smarter and way more prepared to gatekeep than my high school counselor had been. I wasn't ready, and when I stumbled, she ridiculed me and said I clearly did not know how to write. Maybe to her I was just another entitled student she needed to break, but I was not. I needed encouragement, because I was already drowning. But that did not happen. Instead, the teaching assistant proceeded to tell me that I was welcome to write my paper in Spanish, since clearly English was not my forte. Telling me she had majored in Spanish in undergrad and was comfortable grading my paper in my first language.

I did not have the heart to tell her in front of everyone that, while Spanish is my first language, I speak a slang Spanish and never learned to write in proper Spanish. I was not ready to write a graduate-school-level paper in Spanish. I was not even ready to write a graduate-school-level paper in English, but here I was scrambling, trying to find the door to access and insider knowledge, and it seemed to be fading into the distance.

In that moment, I just wanted the ground to open up and swallow me whole. I wanted to cry, I wanted to run, I wanted to quit. But I knew how much it had taken to get me there, and I could not allow myself to fail. I remember one of my peers writing me a private message after class, saying that what the TA did was not okay and that I should say something to the professor. In his well-intentioned attempt to be an ally, my classmate effectively left me feeling hopeless. There was no way I was going to out myself to our professor as an outsider. And I just kept thinking, did this peer not understand that gatekeepers reflect the institutions? All I have known are gatekeepers, and here the gatekeepers were stricter and more forbidding than any I had before encountered.

Hard work and luck were not going to cut it anymore. What I needed were two college-degreed, upper-middle-class parents who had the advantages of immersing me in a lifetime of leisure visits to museums and art exhibits, home libraries full of advanced books from the Western canon, dinner conversations full of critical and intellectual discussions, and access to parents' friends to give me mentorships and internships and recommendations and advice.

I began to understand that school in general has a certain student in mind, a wealthier and whiter student. Academia is an entire environment that was built for that student. The gatekeeper I met in high school; he was gatekeeping AP classes but also gatekeeping everything else that came from that type of access. I was not supposed to outsmart my high school guidance counselor; I was not supposed to get past those gates. And still, somehow, I did—and I was starting to realize why there was a gatekeeper to begin with.

Just like BIPOC are overrepresented at the poverty line, we are underrepresented in academia—for the same reasons. I finally understood that it did not take ability and hard work to be where I was. No gatekeeper had decided to create a path for success for people like me; in fact, I was expected to fail. Since institutional support would never materialize, that meant I had to innovate my own strategies for succeeding.

What my high school counselor should have said on that fateful day, and should have said with the full weight of the reality before us, was: "You are not white enough to dream, so do not bother."

I did not understand that class had everything to do with my sense of panic; I did not understand that class differences created my impostor syndrome. I did not understand that hard work does not always work. In fact it just leaves you exhausted, to your own detriment.

I was recently told by a white man that he pursued a PhD because it was fun for him. People like me do not get degrees for the fun of it; we do it because we believe it will open new doors for us, new opportunities. I felt like I needed a degree for my life to be different, for things to be better.

I was told a college degree was the ticket to a great job, but when I graduated with my bachelor of arts in English literature from FIU, I had zero options. I was qualified for secretarial entry-level positions, and those were the only jobs available to me. I did not have a family friend who could find me a job in the publishing world. I did not have the means to take unpaid internships and hopefully end up with a great job years later. My parents did not have the means to pay my rent somewhere so I could focus on working my way up to a living wage.

Since a bachelor's degree had zero impact on my marketability for a job, I somehow believed that a master's degree would give me access to better-paying jobs. I had to make it, and I had to find new strategies. These new strategies came from the kindness of some wonderful people.

During my second semester in graduate school, I received my first D, on a paper I thought I had written flawlessly. As I flipped through the pages, smeared in red ink, I found a note at the end written by New Testament scholar Dr. A. J. Levine, who advised me to go to the writing center.

I was devastated but knew that failing out of graduate school was not an option. So, I made an appointment at the writing center, and when I showed up a few days later I was turned away. The writing center said that my writing errors resulted from the fact that English was my second language, and I was told that they were not "proofreaders." I was advised to go to the international student writing center. With a broken heart, and my pride down the drain, I made an appointment at the international student writing center. I had not attended a PWI for undergrad, and therefore I could justify this entire writing-center debacle, keeping off some of the blame and retaining some dignity for myself. When I showed up at the international student writing center, I was told that I wrote English fluently. They also said they were short-staffed, so they could not help me since they had to help the other students who were further behind in their English. I was turned away again. I felt like I was going to break. All this class-passing and cordiality was not working. All the hard work and overpreparation was not working. All the tightness that I held within me began to feel like it was strangling me. I was wrecked.

I walked up to my professor who had given me that D and told her the situation. She looked shocked. She also immediately took my side. She personally committed to correcting the grammar, proofreading all my papers, and helping me improve my writing.

I eventually told a dean at my program, who looked equally shocked. Everyone was shocked. They could not believe that this elite institution was creating even more barriers for the diverse students they were so proud to showcase in their pamphlets. The people who make it to these institutions to teach are often so disconnected from the experiences of working-poor people of color that they simply cannot help, because they cannot even fathom the full extent of systemic inequality in this country. They cannot fix what they cannot understand, and in their ignorance they maintain those gates as strong and unmovable.

This is when things began to shift for me; this is when things began to shift within myself. I could not hold all of it together, I could no longer pass, and I was tired.

But the American Myth also provides a means of laying blame. In the Puritan legacy, hard work is not merely practical but also moral; its absence suggests an ethical lapse. A harsh logic dictates a hard judgment: If a person's diligent work leads to prosperity, if work is a moral virtue, and if anyone in the society can attain prosperity through work, then the failure to do so is a fall from righteousness.

—David Shipler

By my third year, something clicked. I learned that there was a new language, an academic language, that I just did not know. I learned it, to the best of my abilities given the time constraints of our program. And I ended up being okay. I earned occasional As, and learned to accept my Bs and Cs. I learned to use all the anger as fuel to start demanding more from the institution that had so benevolently admitted me while providing so few tools for me to succeed. I eventually became the Student Government Association president of our program, the first Latina to have that peer-elected position in the history of the school. With that position, I got the ball rolling to create a club for Latinx students, and we had access to funds that we got to use to help us succeed.

Over time, I also learned to value my background instead of distancing myself from it. I learned to claim it with pride. I learned that integrating myself into American values and ideals made a difference in my ability to infiltrate academia, which is vastly white and elite. But I also learned that adaptation did not mean that I had to relinquish my love for my roots.

Over time, I learned that my circumstances were not created by me—but also, I learned that I was more powerful than my circumstances. My friends, my community, helped me realize this. I met a handful of BIPOC who were owning where they came from, and who utilized all that experience to fuel their work and writings. I began to see that there was hope. I met a queer, biracial Latina who had been raised in Appalachia, and we valued her keen skills at pickling. This wasn't a hobby; resources were scarce where she grew up and she knew how to gather and preserve for the winter. She carried that knowledge with pride. Out of little, she had survived—and it made her special, it made her stronger. I met an undocumented Latina who had grown up quickly, taking odd jobs at a young age, and after she entered Vanderbilt she spoke out about her struggles to force the institution to look within itself. It's cruel to expect people who have pushed themselves past gatekeepers to then perform gratitude. Those gates never should have existed in the first place. Those of us who make it into these spaces have to serve as mirrors.

We must reflect the realities of their gatekeeping back at them, and remind them that they are not better for allowing us in, but rather that we are remarkable for making it in despite them.

I met people who were rejected by society, and somehow they had used that friction to energize themselves. They did not make themselves small for anyone. They used their accomplishments as armor—not only to break into these institutions but to then to smash the walls and glass ceilings so that more can come through. More of us are needed. Not enough of us have a chance to make it.

I learned how wrong I was to distance myself from those very people who were there to bring me back to life when I felt like nothing was working anymore. I was failing at whiteness, but that didn't make me a failure. I didn't need to assimilate with my white, privileged peers; I had to learn survival skills from my BIPOC peers. I learned to lean into those friendships and fight alongside them.

There are always going to be moments when the gatekeepers will try to clip your wings. So here are some reminders, for those times when things get harder and when you're tempted to see your differences as problems and not solutions.

Some days, you will forget that your mami is brilliant and strong, because she might make herself small around gatekeepers and might not have the same strategies you use for maneuvering in uninviting spaces.

Some days, you will forget that you papi is hardworking and strong, because everyone says that if you work hard enough you will make it, and he works hard every day and has not made it and might never make it.

Some days, you will forget that you are capable, because you are mocked for where you come from and the clothes that you wear.

Some days, you will forget that you are smart and worthy, because you might stutter when you have to speak English in front of a room of native English speakers.

Some days, you will forget that our music is an important contribution to society. Instead, outsiders will call our music spicy and sexy, misunderstanding our people and our resilience in one fell swoop.

Some days, you will forget that your abuelita was sharp and witty, because of her cultural differences.

Some days, you will forget that oppressed communities have been using laughter to deal with our oppression for centuries. Instead, you will be kicked out of restaurants and told you are being too much.

Some days, you are going to be made to feel like you are not good enough to go to their schools. And you have to remember that this has nothing to do with being smart enough or worthy enough. Your feelings of displacement mean that these institutions were not built to include you. They were not built for your betterment or for you to have more opportunities, and they rely on your complicity. Do not play nice. Shine despite them. Use them anyway, because they are actively using you regardless.

Remember that we have been outshining and outliving their low expectations for some time now. And now, we are entering these spaces en masse and showing them what all of this diaspora excellence looks like. It is their strategy to make us forget. It is their strategy to keep us at bay, keep us quiet. They will use every tool in their gatekeeper fanny pack to stop us.

But you are the sum of generational resistance.

You are the sun, the moon, and the motherfucking stars.

You have never stopped being great; your ancestors have always been great and you are here because of them. Do not allow these gatekeepers to make you forget.

We must remember the years of historical evidence and national traumas in our home countries that show us what is really happening. Research the history of Chiquita bananas, the forced sterilizations in California, the children in cages at the border, the Panama Canal, the forced pipelines on Indigenous lands, the Tuskegee experiment, the AIDS epidemic, Henrietta Lacks, the syphilis experiments in Guatemala, and international trade policies like NAFTA and CAFTA.

Remember that there are systems in place that stay in place because we are so busy doubting ourselves. Remember that we need to make demands and take back our humanity.

I have to actively remind myself, on those tougher days, that my Brownness is beautiful and brilliant. I have to actively remind myself that meritocracy is a lie, told by powerful white people, meant to keep people like me busy, docile, and quiet.

Remember that you deserve to be here, and you deserve to take up space, and you deserve to make demands of your schools, workplaces, governments, and institutions. For all of us.

Remember who you are, and the rest will come.

CHAPTER 5

POLITICS OF RESPECTABILITY

I am exhausted.

I learned quickly when I enrolled at my PWI that I had to be extraordinary. I had to be special, to justify occupying my seat at this elite institution. And when I graduated, I could not waste all the effort that I put into that degree; I had to make something of myself and I had to do it well. I had to dot all my i's and cross all my t's if I was going to be worth anyone's time.

I felt pressure to speak and write Spanish fluently, lest I be criticized for not being in touch with my roots.

Not only that, but I have to speak the highly enunciated, "acceptable" Spanish. You cannot just speak Spanish; you have to speak the selected version of Spanish that someone decided was superior to the others. I also had to learn to allow my tongue to relax and let out a "chavala" from time to time, to remind myself of where I came from and how my countrypeople speak Spanish. I had to practice both, like there was a test that I was told I was going to fail but I still spent all my time practicing for anyway. Once you allow yourself to become palatable, you can get lost, so I knew that I had to keep my Nica slang within me, even if just in private.

I have to speak and write English flawlessly. What is minimally accented English good for if you cannot write it well? "Well" as defined by academics, "well" as defined by upper-middle-class white people, "well" as defined by spaces that are meant to exclude you. And then the parameters for "proper" English are also rigorous. I have to be fluent in the big-words-nobody-can-really-understand-except-a-select-few-elites English to be respected in academia. Not only that, but I had to figure out how to pronounce these words before I had ever heard them spoken out loud. I was the kid who devoured books and encountered words I had never heard before—and then practiced saying those words privately first, in hopes of not embarrassing myself publicly. And I had to become comfortable with doing all of that.

I have to also be able to switch back to my Miami-English. In my Miami-English, my accent gets to come out more and my tongue gets to rest a bit. To be relevant in the region I was raised in, I needed to keep that.

I have to be soft and kind and approachable, because for Black and Brown people to succeed, to play the game, to make it, we need to make white people feel "comfortable" around us. White people tend to feel most comfortable around people who look like them, who dress like them, who sound like them—people they can recognize.

I have to be gentle and smart, and all my actions have to overtly signal my respectability. I have to perform a version of myself perfectly to prove my humanity. As a woman, as a smart woman, my duty is to signal to people that I am smart and somehow, accidentally, I happen to be a woman. I have to be just the right amount of angry to be respected and taken seriously. And I have to do this signaling with what I wear, how I adorn my face with makeup, and how I do my hair. Nothing too feminine, nothing too sexy, nothing that could indicate that I might have a body and a brain.

The delicate dance required to make my white peers feel safe sucked the life out of me. And even when I was trying to not "be the issue" or "cause drama," I still got the same responses:

"You're taking things too seriously."

"It's not always about race."

"Not all white people . . . "

"Not my experience . . . "

"I have a Latina friend."

"Are you sure that is what happened?"

This is white peoples' coded language for: "You're being too aggressive," or "You're being too Brown," or "You're making me uncomfortable about my racism." Instead of addressing their own issues, they will vilify you.

White people will go out of their way to claim themselves as victims, as if the entire system is not built for their benefit.

You have to be ready for those moments and not let them disarm you. I want these white people to know that I have agency, even when we all know they wrote the playbook. I have to make them believe in my devotion to success, even though success is measured entirely on their terms.

The pressure to fit into all these boxes was suffocating. I felt pressured to be a lot of things for a lot of people.

When I say I have to be extraordinary, what I mean is that:

- I was the first in my family to go to college, and was fully funded.
- I was the first in my family to present at an academic conference.
- I was the first in my family to graduate with honors from college.

- I was the first in my family to move away from Miami, the only city we lived in other than Managua.
- I was the first in my family to get accepted into a graduate program.
- I was the first in my family to get a graduate degree.

And still, at some point I began to realize that white people did not want me in their elite spaces no matter what. After performing beyond what was expected of me, I began to realize that none of my sense of belonging was real or for my betterment; instead, it was all for their comfort. I was the diversity that would enhance the experience of white students on campus. I would be the Brown friend that white people could use to assure themselves that they were not racist.

Being respectable was killing me. Performing perfectly was not serving me. So I had to go through, and admit, some other firsts: I was the first in my family to attend counseling. I was the first in my family to be vocal about my suicidal ideation. I was the first in my family to leave my husband even when he did not hit me.

Being respectable was killing me, and actively attempting to disembody myself for this illusive notion of respect was getting me nowhere. So, keep your perfect. Keep your accolades.

Keep your trophies. Keep your fellowships. Keep your grant money. Keep your scholarships. Keep your degrees and your awards, if they will only be given to me when I behave well and in accordance with what you think I should do.

I am exhausted.

Oppressed peoples are always being asked to stretch a little more, to bridge the gap between blindness and humanity.

—Audre Lorde

In my experience, the politics of respectability intersect with my race, class, and gender. I will parse out the ways that I experience respectability. And I will tell you how I reject respectability through those intersections, as a reclamation practice through chonga subculture.

"Respectability politics" was coined by a Black woman, Evelyn Higginbotham, and it was intended to describe the experiences of Black women and a strategy they have adopted to subvert stereotypes. My resistance to respectability politics is not a criticism of what has a been a survival skill; rather, it is how I have chosen to move through the world, consequences and all, as a non-Black person of color.

We all adhere to a version of respectability politics—"we" being BIPOC. We all switch our speech, accents, behaviors, appearances into more palatable ones around normative culture, which I will rightfully refer to as white culture. For example, professional spaces, which were created by white cis hetero men, have only really been infiltrated by women, openly LGBTQIA+ folks, and BIPOC in very recent history. So, everyone who is outside the normal parameters learns to code-switch so as to affirm our sense of belonging—to ourselves but mostly to white middle- and upper-middle-class America.

Whenever I have explained respectability and its performance to anyone who is not a BIPOC, they have consistently perceived this act of self-preservation as disingenuous. Specifically, when I have told white men about respectability politics, the word "tease" has come into the conversation. It is an old sexist trope, that a woman who is thoughtful in how she maneuvers spaces is untrustworthy. When, rather, what is happening is our attempt to thrive in the world these men have created. The idea that women are to behave differently in different contexts for the sake of getting jobs, raises, better grades, invitations to events, married—that all seems preposterous to men. Yet so many of us do it on a daily basis.

Some of us switch to survive in white spaces, and some even attempt to thrive in the depths of that switched persona. Respectability politics also dominates the policing of women and how we define someone who is marriage material or not, always under the umbrella of a heteronormative patriarchal society. Since colonization, women have been expected to be modest and not even hint at their sexual desires.

The expectations around respectable womanhood are very much something that women experience. Then if you are a BIPOC who is also a woman, that double consciousness dominates how you move through the world. For me, that particular policing came from school dress codes, which overly policed girls and seldom boys—unless those boys were wearing what white people deemed as gang-affiliated attire, which is usually just code for anti-Blackness. This policing of my appearance also came from church and what was considered God-like modesty. Later in life, my own sorority would police how we would behave and dress when "wearing letters"—which is another shit show all on its own and could be its own book, if I am being honest. Being a girl, being a woman, in this society means contending with respectability at every event, at every institution, and in every space. Women know that, in any space, you will be judged for who you show up as and how you present yourself.

Once I understood that code-switching in white spaces meant presenting myself as civilized by white standards, I could not just continue to move in that direction. I felt the weight of everything. I could recall hearing mi mami talk about my abuelita dying too soon because she cared for everyone but could not stop to care for herself, and I knew I had to stop this generational curse of prioritizing how everyone felt about me, rather than how I felt about myself. I had this wild idea: What if I wanted to thrive, as myself? What would thriving fully as myself mean?

I remember when I intentionally began to embrace my working-class femininity in academia. I was warned against it. I was told to mute myself and I was told that because I am a woman, I am going to be considered incompetent—and that it was my job to be twice as smart and twice as witty. It was my duty to prove myself, but I did not want to live like that anymore.

I did not like being told that I had to be all those things for the comfort of men. So, slowly but surely, I began to step into my femininity. I began to get my nails done, a thing I had rejected doing since middle school because I was told only cheap women wear long acrylic nails. I began to do my hair, something I had been told would lead me to sin because women who were vain were not God-fearing. I began to wear bright colors and heels. I didn't want to have to convince anyone that I deserved to be respected. I wanted to embrace the feminine culture I had been told explicitly to stay away from. I wanted my humanity to be valued, regardless of what I wore and how I spoke.

I knew this was setting myself up for failure, but I wanted to try and figure out where I was actually safe and where I was not. Divesting from whiteness required me to investigate respectability. I wanted to know who I could not trust, and I wanted my body to test my surroundings. I wanted to dress as myself and see how others responded. If white people responded poorly, then I knew I needed to get away from that academic space, or that romantic relationship, or that friendship. Up to that point, I had presented myself in the most palatable, nonthreatening, decent, and modest way; up to that point, I had worked hard to put white people at ease. Now I wanted my body to work for me and not for them.

> *Latina bodies are read as out of control and used against the commu-*
> *nities they "represent."*
>
> —Jillian Hernandez

I wanted first to prove to myself that the standards for being a respectable Brown Latina were ridiculous. I wanted to dress the way I wanted, and I wanted to test my friends and colleagues to see if they would still respect and accept me. In the end, I found that being myself meant losing some friends.

And not just white friends. Even BIPOC and some queer folks kept me at arm's length, revealing that they had bought into respectability politics and so did not want to be associated with me. People in my parents' church began to whisper about me.

I vividly recall one visit in Miami, when my parents asked me to go to church with them. They weren't trying to save my soul; the invitation was part of a family ritual, Sundays being family time. Growing up, we had always attended church together—first to arrive, last to leave. I had no real desire to step back into a place that brought on waves of negative memories, but that question of self-definition kept lingering: What would it mean to show up as myself in that space? So, I picked out a short, tight red dress, and I headed to church with them.

I remember walking in and being greeted by all my old acquaintances. It felt like I was the prodigal daughter coming back. Growing up, I had been the dance leader of the church's dance team and a huge presence in that community for years. And here I was, retuning as an entirely different person, and I was not going to allow them to define how I stepped into this space.

I sat in the pastoral seats, right in the front row—a seating arrangement I had always resented because of the hierarchy it created in this already toxic environment. And then it happened; to protect the senior pastor from my indecency—my short, tight red dress—an usher attempted to lay a white cloth over my lower body, and mi mami was not having it.

She was sitting next to me, and I remember seeing her face react before I noticed what was happening. I recall her reaching over and then past my legs, then I realized she was looking past me and her face was getting redder and redder. I saw her yank that white rag out of the hands of the usher before it even touched my legs. I never even saw who the usher was, I just saw her face: mi leóna.

Like I said, we were in the front row, and everyone could see us. Everyone did see us, and I am sure she heard whispers about her blatant defiance later, after I returned to school. But mi mami knew and knows how I feel about church, and she was not going allow my return to be tainted by the purity culture within it.

Mi mami held me on that day, and I knew mi mami understood me and understood that what I was trying to do was bigger than just that one moment. I wanted to be myself and expect more than the crumbs I would have gotten if I had adhered to respectability. Code-switching is for the benefit of white people, whether they are in the room or not, and in this Spanish-speaking, Latinx church, the demands of respectability became evident. Good Christian women are well-behaved, because God is watching. It is not a coincidence that white people benefit from our good behavior, and that their theologies are what we are taught today.

But church was not the only place where I was pressured to hide parts of myself to render my Brown female body into something more palatable. I remember hearing what other Latinas were saying about me behind my back in grad school. I recall people keeping their distance from me, seeing peers visibly roll their eyes when I entered a room, friendships that never flourished because the Latinxs in those spaces did not want to be associated with me, people in my community refusing to speak with me. And this taught me hard lessons around the fickleness of feminism within elite academic spaces.

I now dress more feminine as a daily practice, in order to embody the dual identity of being smart and feminine. I want working-class feminine Latinas to know that we do not have to shed our identities to be allowed into elite spaces. Seeing someone with tattoos, long nails, and bold clothing who is still successful—that creates a counter-narrative so that more of us can actually thrive.

I hope, through my example as a Latina who rejects the white gaze and still makes a living in elite spaces, I can make it easier for someone else to be respected without first being required to dim themselves. Not only am I a woman of color experiencing misogyny through the demands of respectability, I am also bilingual, which adds another layer. Code-switching, which is often required to gain respectability, has a deep history that includes bilingual people who have had to switch between their two languages.

I become a different person when I speak Spanglish. I slouch my shoulders, my legs part, and my hands and shoulders become a part of my language expression. My overall posturing in Spanglish feels like coming home and taking off my bra.

At my essence and at my happiest, I speak Spanglish fluently. I came to the United States when I was seven years old, and my parents never learned English. I have always spoken Spanish at home. English is the language I use in school, and I am comfortable in both languages for different reasons. While Spanish is my first language, I also speak English. American English has insider and outsider codes, and "good" English demarcates insider knowledge and access to insider privileges. Despite the United States not having an official language, there is value placed on people who speak English; the age-old Freudian slip always rings true when a xenophobe proclaims, "Speak American!"

I speak English well and can even claim some fluency, but all that drops off when I am expected to understand sarcasm and idioms. I do not always catch the minor intonations and will often take something meant ironically literally. That is how insiders can and often have noticed my outsider-looking-in position within the English language. It is my code-switching poker tell.

Code-switching is not a benign form of respectability politics; it is not an extra set of skills that BIPOC happen to have. When you demand that BIPOC speak in a way that is palatable to white audiences, that demand supports white supremacy.

Black folks who may be more comfortable with African American Vernacular English (AAVE) are often required to change how they speak in white spaces, to seem safer and avoid making white people uncomfortable. Immigrants and bilingual folks of color who may be more comfortable in their native language are often required to speak unaccented English in white spaces, to seem safer and avoid making white people uncomfortable. Everyone has to perform for white audiences, making white, middle-class status and privilege the norm, even if that is not the lived experience of most Americans. Even when speaking English, regional accents or accents that come from speaking multiple languages get toned down for the comfort of white ears—a lot of BIPOC call this their "white voice."

The term "white voice" seems to imply that only white people speak well, which is not the case. When I say I am using my "white voice," it doesn't mean that I agree with the assigned hierarchy of acceptable speech. I use my "white voice" because I have to adapt in order to exist and thrive in a white, capitalist society. I gain advantages when I sound white at school, at work, even when I visit my family. I am not saying that my "white voice" is better; in fact, I am not placing value on that skill at all. At least by calling it what it is, I can demand that listeners understand that I'm using speech that is designed to erase me.

To accept something outside of myself as superior would be to accept my inferiority—which is really what is happening when I code-switch. Over the years, I knew I needed to somehow resist those very tools that had helped me succeed in white spaces, because success should never require my own erasure. So, I decided to speak Spanglish.

I was with one of my good friends, Lis Valle. She was driving us somewhere, and her then-teenage son called. He was doing some errand and needed to use her credit card. Lis had to keep her eyes on the road, and so she asked me to take her wallet and her phone and read off the card numbers to her son. As I read them, I switched from Spanish to English without skipping a beat, as I often do with close bilingual friends.

Her son laughed on the other end of the line, and he said: "You can read them to me in one language."

And I shouted back, "No! Spanglish is the language of my people."

I was being somewhat tongue-in-cheek in the moment, but the more I thought about it after, the more I know this to be true. My ancestors were Indigenous, and without much consent involved, Spaniards came and created this new raza: mestizos. The mixing of Spanish and Indigenous people resulted in a large majority of the population in Latin America. The language of mestizos is primarily Spanish.

Spanish is my home language; it reminds me of tajadas con queso. Spanish reminds me of where I come from, but I also speak a slang Spanish that brings me specifically to a certain neighborhood in Managua, Nicaragua, called Chico Pelón. I construct sentences like a Nicaragüense, sentences that do not make sense to Spanish speakers from other countries, like: Te vas a joder si andas fregando con esa chavala. Were I to use a more dominant, palatable Spanish, I would say: Si sigues molestando a esa nina, vas a tener problemas. I make deliberate choices even with simple words like "sandals"; in Nicaragua we call those chinelas, but I realize that the palatable Spanish wants me to say sandalias.

Spanish is the language of mi mami and mi papi, and how they say my name in Spanish makes me feel safe: Priscila, Priscilita, Prisi, Pris.

Spanish is also the language of oppression, and I am aware of that reality constantly. When I hear other Spanish speakers express frustration toward US-born Latinx people who do not speak Spanish, that rings especially true. We forget that we were force-fed Spanish by Spanish people, Europeans. Spanish is the tangible reality of our colonization.

Conversely, Spanish is also a language of liberation, because what our countries have individually done with it is artful. Tell me you do not get goose bumps when you hear the beautiful Spanish spoken by someone in Puerto Plata, or by a Jinotegan kid, or even by a Cundinamarca-born person. We have taken this thing that was imposed on so many of us, and we have transformed it into a beautiful expression of survival.

When you learn to dream and think in both languages, when your migration has scripted two languages into your essence, you learn to feel safest with those who can speak both fluently. Those people get me. They understand what it means to translate complicated documents for their Spanish-speaking parents, abuelxs, and tixs. They understand what it means to grow up too quickly because you were reading court summons, filling out government aid documents, or just hearing an English-speaking doctor talk about your mami like she deserved whatever illness she came in with due to her lack of English comprehension. Learning to take the blows for your parents, and learning not to translate the ugliness that comes with language hierarchies, means you cannot pretend those hierarchies do not exist.

Bilingual people understand that English-only speakers never had to unlearn their native language, never had to have their cultura taken from them.

Spanglish doesn't come with a grammar book, a class or a dictionary.
It is in the air, existing only for those who have developed an ear for it.
—Juliana Delgado Lopera

Those of us who speak Spanglish fluently know that sometimes you will not know the name of something in one language or the other, which means that one side has exposed you to books while the other has exposed you to love. I can make declarations of love in Spanish that will usually make my partners swoon, because I learned to amar apasionadamente in Spanish. And I can fight with my words unlike anyone else fights in English, because I had to learn to fight and protect myself and mi gente in that language.

Spanglish *is* the language of my people: a specific kind of immigrant or kid of immigrants who learned two languages fluently but also opted not to prioritize either one, because we are products of two worlds. Also, we opted to recreate ourselves as displaced people, and that shit is resiliency at work.

From a really young age, I understood that there are only particular instances where your best self feels safe to come out. When we first migrated to this country, my entire family went to Santa's Enchanted Forest in Miami. This seasonal fair is a staple for locals. This was my first time going on fair rides and rollercoasters. This glorious moment, where I was just tall enough to do the big-kid rides, meant that my brother and I got to stand in line together. I remember us speaking excitedly about the ride and about who was going to sit where for optimum enjoyment, and then I heard something behind us. Two English-speaking kids said: "Speak English. You are in America." And my entire mood changed, I felt so embarrassed. I remember nothing else from that day but that feeling of getting the air taken out of you.

From a really young age, I understood that there is a version of me that white people prefer, because it is the version that gets rewarded. This version does not get teased. This version gets to exist, if only on their terms.

Spanglish is generally seen as a nuisance to white people. I have learned that, while I feel most like myself when I speak Spanglish, it feels threatening to white people.

And sure, some people might speculate that it was excusable for monolingual folks to require that I switch to English. But it wasn't just my language. I also had to shift my tone and my expressions. Not only did I have to switch to my "white voice," but I also had to switch to my "white behavior" for the comfort of the white people around me and, sadly, for my own advancement.

When I am my happiest and truest self, I am an embodied experience. When I speak Spanglish, I speak with my entire body. When I laugh, I laugh with every muscle and every part of me. How I talk to people is how I engage myself. I do not have curt little English exchanges; I divulge in Spanglish.

When I embody my Spanglish fully, in public, I get kicked out of restaurants. I have also been silenced in common university spaces for being disruptive. I have been scolded and told to simmer down, when all I was doing was showing up fully as myself.

White people's comfort levels seem to be the priority for everyone, especially for themselves. And their discomfort means that we must, in turn, alter ourselves in order to enter their spaces—and they have claimed a lot of spaces. They run the government, armed forces, corporate America, academia, the legal system, you name it. They not only created those spaces but ensured that only the approved version of you is allowed to enter. You will no longer feel like yourself.

This is today's racial segregation. The ability to exist in their spaces is restricted at best, forbidden at worst.

Respectability politics has robbed so many of us of the joy of being ourselves, and so many of us have decided to accept the version of ourselves that white people prefer. When I accepted their preferred version of me, I felt like I was in a constant state of bodily displacement. It was always a show, a performance for them. I felt like a clown.

> *[Evelyn] Higginbotham (1993) describes [respectability politics] as a way to counter racist stereotypes and structures, respectability requires condemning behaviors deemed unworthy of respect within one in-group.*
> —Mikaela Pitcan, Alice E. Marwick, and danah boyd

A collective revolt against all these systemic tools of social control is necessary for our liberation.

I remember the first time I realized that I was being misread as aggressive. I was at a party with my white peers, and someone said something to me and I casually responded. The exchange was so minimal that the exact details escape my memory. But later, in the kitchen, some of my white friends said they were frightened by my response, and they said they were afraid to upset me. I was bewildered. I wasn't angry in the exchange; I had felt neutral, and the conversation was instantly forgettable.

You see, where I am from, I am seen as the pastor's daughter and a "good" girl. For better or for worse, I had bought into that identity and had behaved in ways that enforced that image, but somehow in white spaces that did not translate. I lacked the ability to adjust my presentation to accommodate the white gaze, because I was not raised around white people. So, after immigrating here,

I had to learn to not scare white people. Being a woman of color, a Brown Latina, means that when I am around white people, they tend to just default to seeing me as a stereotype: the fiery Latina.

At that point in my life, I did not understand nor could I wrap my mind around this seemingly innocent misunderstanding—but the thing about misunderstandings with white people is that they can be dangerous for Black and Brown people. Being seen as a stereotype can result in our incarceration and even our death at the hands of police officers. Survival often depends on understanding how we are seen by white people and then adjusting the parts that they misunderstand as scary and aggressive. To that, I call bullshit.

We know now that cops view Black children as dangerous adults. We know now that white people view Black children as deviant and white children as angelic. We know now that racial biases have informed the entire carceral system in the United States. White people correct deviation from respectability through punishment and incarceration. But "misbehavior" is just code for not acting white.

White people can behave however they want and are still viewed as having their humanity intact. BIPOC have to act respectably toward the white gaze while in white institutions, otherwise they are silenced, strongly reprimanded, jailed, or even killed. And even when we act as we should, as soon as a campus-wide alert is sent about someone who is dangerous, the color of your skin will determine if you are protected or approached with suspicion. Respectability politics is only required for BIPOC, and the darker you are the more policed your behavior will be, which is why our framework for understanding respectability politics was created by Evelyn Higginbotham, a Black woman.

Respectability politics function as social control. It is dangerous to go outside those parameters. While white people defined those parameters, too often even BIPOC enforce them within their own communities. White supremacy is designed so treacherously that we can stand in our own way.

Coded, racialized words used against our communities are often used by BIPOC to distance themselves from stereotypes: *reffy*, *illegal*, *ratchet*, *ghetto*. Too often, some BIPOC will accept these definitions as real, internalize these racist ideas, and turn them against other BIPOC. By accepting those words as negative adjectives and distancing themselves from them, misguided BIPOC are supporting the stereotypes. By uplifting the white-approved versions of themselves, by distinguishing themselves as *professional*, *classy*, *well-spoken*, *elevated*, misguided BIPOC are supporting white supremacy. In trying to gain safety for themselves by saying they are one of the "good" BIPOC, and thus claiming proximity to whiteness, misguided BIPOC just reinforce white supremacists' beliefs that most BIPOC are "bad."

Respectability politics is a circular trap.

To panic about being identified within perversity can too easily lead us to strive toward self-restricting normalcy.
                                        —Celine Parreñas Shimizu

Growing up as a working-class Brown Latina impacted how I moved through respectability politics. Whatever I choose to wear, however I choose to act, the white gaze redefined my choices as those that either confirmed or refuted prescribed stereotypes.

So, let me introduce you to chongas. In some ways, chongas are similar to cholas. These are regional terms, so your familiarity may depend on where you live. Cholas are a West Coast Mexican American Latina subculture. Chongas are a primarily Florida Cuban Latina subculture. Aesthetically there are similarities, but overall I would argue there are notable differences. One big difference is that chola scholars have reclaimed that subculture from the clutches of respectability politics in ways that chongas have not. I can name several chola scholars, but I can only name one chonga scholar: Dr. Jillian Hernandez.

I grew up aspiring to be as beautiful as the chongas I saw around me, but the media turned it into a taboo identity that no one wanted to claim, even those who were still emulating it.

Being a chonga was the goal, for me, until it was not. Personally, I blame the Chonga Girls—a comedy duo of millennial, white-passing Latinas who assumed the roles of chongas as a costume to mock them—but I also know that this turn against the culture was bigger than their act. Back when I was in school, the Chonga Girls made a parody music video mocking chongas for their cheap aesthetics, accented English, and assumed sluttiness. In truth, these two women were rejecting chongas by further stereotyping them as other—in contrast to the performers, who aligned themselves as different and therefore respectable by ridiculing this particular subculture. Through their ridiculing of chongas, they normalized the communal rejection of immigrant, loud, and poor Latinas. And Miami Latinxs ate it up, and doubled down. The Chonga Girls used their bodies to signal to all of us that we should stop trying to emulate this Latina subculture. At the time, I was an impressionable young Latina only beginning my journey of simmering down for whiteness.

> *The hyperbolic, stereotypical representations of Latinas often found in visual culture are measured against an imagined (white/middle class) construct of U.S. citizenship.*
>
> —Jillian Hernandez

Today, according to most Latinxs in Miami, chongas:

- are nasty
- have bad attitudes

- are cheap
- are too sexy
- speak with accented English
- speak "improper" Spanish
- wear too much makeup
- or, as my US-born Latina sister-in-law once said, are just "too Hispanic."

Chongas proudly claim their migration in a way that is contrary to white culture, which demands that immigrants feel shame for their differences and immediately assimilate into the dominant white American culture.

What does a chonga look like? A chonga is a Latina, usually an immigrant herself, from a working-class or working-poor context, who has adapted a tough exterior with an aesthetic to match. It is important to note that many chongas don't regularly refer to themselves as such, because the term has become an insult.

I have a decolonized perspective on chongas, which means that I reclaim this racialized and classist slur into what it really is when we take the layers of self-hatred and oppression away from the subculture.

Chongas are beautiful, strong, assertive badasses who will love as passionately as they will hate anyone who tries to harm them or their loved ones. Chongas are bold, resilient. They use their bodies and assert themselves to resist assimilation and whitewashing.

Chongas have the agility to maneuver around violent situations. They are raised in working-class neighborhoods and barrios, and they have learned that the police are quick to show up to their neighborhoods to arrest people but slow to come and protect them. They learn that their families and close communities are the only people who have their best interests in mind.

It is because they have seen corruption in their motherlands, and erasure in the land of the free, that they have come to know that everyone around them is trying to take advantage of their poverty.

When they get the torn-up or nonexistent textbooks in schools, when they live in food deserts and dangerously unregulated housing, they learn that the system is not meant to protect them, so they protect themselves.

Chongas have sharp tongues. When the Teach for America teachers and the counselors tell them to stop dreaming because someone like them could never get into college, they learn to stick up for themselves.

I identified as a chonga for years, and after facing ridicule I decided to go for a more muted aesthetic. In my midtwenties, I sought to reclaim my identity. But it took me years to get to that place.

Chongas inherently reject white culture and the white gaze. Chongas learn to not let people tell them who they are. Chongas demand that they are seen as they are.

And if anyone doubts us, if anyone thinks they can make us feel inferior for having accents, we will show them otherwise. We know how to tear them up, piece by piece, with our quick words and sharp responses. We had to learn to have sharp edges; we have been chiseled into a weapon of self-defense.

As a chonga, I realized quickly that I was seen as deviant and dangerous. I remember being asked by a cashier in a casual exchange at Whole Foods (a mecca of whiteness) if I had ever shot anyone. I understood that my Brownness was scripted as dangerous.

Chongas adorn themselves in their chosen armor. We dress like goddesses. We see our femininity as a tool for our survival, as femininity was used by our mothers, grandmothers, and great-grandmothers. And in this land of the free, we intend on using those tools to maneuver spaces that seem uninviting to us.

When I wing my eyeliner, outline my lips, put on my miniskirt and crop top, I am adorning myself with my war paint and armor.

Because to you, I am not human. But it's okay, because to me and to those who understand: I am a goddess.

Chongas oscillate between Spanish and English with an ease that can only be described as brilliant. We are primarily immigrants, and success here usually means assimilating into a white upper-middle-class embodiment and comportment, and accents in those spaces are viewed as a nuisance. When we ignore the insistent requests to get rid of any signs of our migration, we are pushed aside. But you see, this entire side of the world belonged to our ancestors before yours even arrived, so although we can speak your forced languages, we will speak them however we please. You're on stolen land anyway.

We may accent it, spit it out, speak it quickly, and speak it loudly—it is our resistance to your uninvited presence and your extended stay.

Chongas are everywhere. When a chonga is around, you know it; we will make ourselves known. We are hyper-visible so you will remember our names, what we wore, what we said, and how we said it. And in a land that tries to ignore our existence and push us into living as the least of these, our visibility is power. Because you cannot erase what you have no control over, and you cannot control those who have never bowed down to your notions of a hegemonic America.

We are loud, we are proud, and we do not back down.

Ask anyone who has gone up against a chonga about their experience, and they will teach you to see us as we are: divinas. And to any chongas who may be in a highly inaccessible space: you matter, and you do not have to shed your toughness to exist in any space. Spaces are only elevated by your existence.

Re-embracing a subculture I knew to be deviant within normative society meant that I put myself at risk. I am always looking out for myself. I park near lights when I go shopping, I park close to entrances at all costs, I look behind me often to ensure I am not being followed, I never have headphones on in public so I can stay aware, I always have my keys in my hand when returning to my car, I smile at service workers to create allies as often as possible, I wear Vanderbilt gear or dress up when seeing doctors, dentists, and anybody who can harm me because they do not like my Brown body in their white space.

I do not smile at white people. I do not let them think I am welcoming to anything, well-intentioned or otherwise. Too often, my humanity is a matter they believe is up to their judgment, and I have learned to not get affirmed by them. I affirm myself.

I do not try to make new friends with white people; I have all the white people I need. Instead, I am constantly on the lookout for people who are like me, people who know what it is like to live a life of moderation for our own safety. Also, a group of us together is stronger than one of us alone, so those are the people I rely on to disrupt white spaces.

And if you have never thought about those things when you're in public, then you feel safe in your context and that is a wonderful gift that I envy. We are not the same. I have learned to survive whiteness, and living without all the weight of seeking their approval.

CHAPTER 6

TOXIC MASCULINITY

Before jumping into this chapter, I want to acknowledge that toxic masculinity affects women's lives every single day. Yes, I understand that men also are affected by the toxicity of their masculinity, but this chapter is not about centering how men feel and how men heal from it. This chapter is specifically about father and sibling abuse, but it also goes beyond that. Because, at the end of the day, we are all affected by toxic masculinity, even when the behavior you are seeing does not seem explicitly toxic.

This chapter intends to give you language for what you have already seen to be true. I have chosen to heal from male toxicity, and my methods may be helpful to you. But my healing isn't tidy; it's not neatly wrapped up with a cute bow.

I start this chapter addressing the monster under my bed: toxic masculinity.

You take up space. You take up so much space that people are left without room to breathe. You, mi papi.

Mi mami lost herself in this energy, and as a kid I saw her struggling to find herself. I saw her struggling to figure out how this happened to her, struggling to blame herself because you always blame her. I saw her struggling to protect you when your daughters began to see through the charade.

You hurt others around you. You care about your looks entirely too much. You wear all the right clothes, all the right jewelry, hair always done, shoes always polished. You make people feel lucky to be around you, to be associated with you. But it is all an illusion; inside you hold darkness and anger, covered up by pristine, ironed clothing and nice watches. You create the illusion to distract people from what is within you. You are a master of disguise.

You drive like you have something to prove. Your vehicles have become extensions of your manhood, and you drive like someone is always watching, always judging. Like every vehicular decision is going to reflect on your masculinity. No matter what is happening, your car needs to represent you. You drive like the world owes you something, like you are always late, like you do not understand how traffic works, like the rules were not meant for you.

Appearances are a total package for you, and status is of utmost importance. You speak confidently about everything that you know and things you do not know. When someone proves to have more knowledge than you, you lose interest. If someone you know attempts to take up more space than you, that is grounds for terminating that relationship and ridiculing them publicly. If that person happens to be your daughter, then so be it.

You are proud. Your reputation is more important to you than your actions. You will present a face in public that is different from who you are in private. You will blame everyone else around you for things you did, to save face, even if that means blaming mi mami for things she never did, for thoughts she never had.

How you look, to the few men you admire, is currency to you. You hate yourself so much that you pretend to love yourself, and eventually you sabotage yourself.

And still, my heart has always wanted to embrace you, even if you did not embrace me.

Not only did I not understand men, I feared them.

—bell hooks

I had an aversion to anyone who embodied toxic masculinity, or who could potentially embody toxic masculinity, for a long time. In fact, up until my first marriage, I would say I created barriers that I thought would protect me when dating or making friends. Because the monster under my bed resembled the monster sleeping next to mi mami. I had to learn to preserve myself outside of mi papi and brother's reach, because for entirely too long I left myself vulnerable to these men. The harm they inflicted in me is still felt.

I was a daddy's girl. I look identical to my papi, and my nickname growing up was "cara de papa," because I had a cute little round face much like a potato, and because I looked like mi papá.

It took me years to mourn the loss of my daddy's girl status. As a society we revere daddy's girls. Daddy's girls are the cherished girls of society, in the opposite way that mama's boys are ridiculed. Those extreme reactions are both products of toxic masculinity. Within heteronormativity, to align yourself with your male parental figure as a girl is a gift, and to align yourself with the female parental figure as a boy is a weakness. I knew that the status of daddy's girl was something to boast about.

Being a daddy's girl was my reward for being the best kind of girl. I defended him—I felt like I needed to, even against mi mami. Mi papi casually gave me that burden. Mi papi would confide in me, and he would talk about mi mami negatively, constantly. I began to believe that mi mami was a bitch, growing up. Mi papi would tell me about all the things that mi mami would not let him do, which sounded like a lot of the things that I was not allowed to do, like hang out with my friends and stay out late.

Mi papi got to align himself with his children because he was not home often, and mi mami was the parent to all of us, it seemed.

Mi papi was El Proveedor, and mi mami did *everything else*.

It was easy to pick her as the enemy. It was easy to see her as the focal "problem" for all of us. But it was also easy to isolate her and turn her children against her. And for years she and I rarely spoke, because he had painted her as a dictator. I resented her for doing that to him.

I bought into what he said about her, and I wanted his approval more than anything else. In fact, mi mami and I did not become close until I myself got married. I started to imagine having my own kids and how I would react if my husband talked badly about me to them. Suddenly it became so clear how unfair he was to her. Things started to fall into place in terms of how their relationship worked, and how isolation was the tool that was used against both of us, because he not only isolated her but managed to isolate me from her. When I needed her, much later, I had to find my way back. And when I did, I began to ask mi mami some tough questions.

I remember telling mi mami about how mi papi talked about her to me, and I asked her why she never talked negatively about him to at least counter what he said to us. She said something that sticks with me, even to this day: "El es tu papi y el es un buen papi," defending him still. Mi mami protected him, like I protected him.

Yet still, I held a special place in my heart just for mi papi. Mi papi is funny, and I am not just saying that in the way that everyone is sort of funny. I mean he is hilarious. If you hang out with him long enough, you will find yourself cackling on the floor with laughter. I have seen mis tias pee on themselves from laughing so hard with him, and I have gone to bed to the sound of laughter many nights because mi papi had friends over. As a kid, I thought laughter just followed him around.

For mi papi's birthday this past year, mi mami sent me a video of him. In the video you can only see mi papi, my niece, and my brother. There are cupcakes in front of him with candles on them. They let my three-year-old niece blow out one of the candles, and she is filled with joy about this. And then it is his turn. In this video, I could see mi papi dramatically preparing to blow the candles out, opening his mouth wide and loudly filling his lungs with air. Then, as he exhales, he pretends to forget where the cake is and "accidentally" turns away from the cake and blows in the wrong direction. Then he pretends to be shocked that he missed, which my baby niece loves. I could hear her squealing and laughing. This is peak mi papi.

He did this head fake four or five times, sending my niece into fits of giggles. Her laughter filled that entire video. Watching it, I cried, because that is the papi I knew as a kid. He was funny and favored me above anyone else. I felt immense love for this funny and warm man in my life; I still do when I reflect on some of my childhood memories with him. For that reason, it took me years to accept what happened, to accept that something had changed. I could never really reconcile that change until I finally understood it through reading bell hooks's retelling of her own stories with her family and her dad.

Mi papi was a phenomenal father to me during my girlhood, but he got lost when I became a teenage girl and then a woman. As I got older, he tapped out entirely. I was no longer his chosen one.

I write about mi papi from a place of pain and with a deep longing to heal myself. The last time I let mi papi treat me like I was subhuman was in February 2016. When he lashed out at me, I almost cried. I almost showed him weakness. I almost acted like a girl, like mi mami. I was almost right back to where I started, despite all the work I had done to undo what he had done to me my entire life.

On that day, that fateful February, I know that my papi attacked me with explosive remarks because he had felt that his status had been threatened, that he had been insulted and excluded. He had felt inadequate, and his pride was hurt.

I know that my papi attacked me because he felt disrespected. He thought I was stealing attention and respect that were rightfully and exclusively his. He thought I was taking up too much space, which was any space—more space than women are allowed to take. My confidence made him feel less than, and he could not allow himself to feel less than a woman, when he knew not to place any significant value in women.

February 2016, we were in Guatemala. I had insisted on going with him on a trip he was taking to both Nicaragua and Guatemala because I missed my motherland. I missed my cousins, the food, the climate, the scenery—and I needed to just get away. Traveling back home to heal is a luxury that many of us aspire toward. But some of us have to make concessions to take this type of healing journey. My concession was to travel with this man I no longer had a relationship with, and I tricked myself into thinking that the trip could heal that relationship.

I also ensured that I took care of myself in the ways I knew how at that time, so I escaped often with cousins and friends, and I drank. I connected with old friends, and when I was with mi papi I made myself as small and as invisible as I could be. I did not want to be the reason we got into a verbal altercation. I wanted to be easy, uncomplicated, just like mi papi liked.

I had moved in with my parents after graduating with my master's degree, because mi mami had insisted and I had no other choice financially. I had been accepted into another master's program with a wonderful fellowship that covered the majority of my expenses, yet I felt like I needed to get away from academia for my health. My graduate program had been hard for me, I had gotten divorced halfway through it, and I recognized within myself an exhaustion I had never experienced before. So I was living with them, because I had no other choice and I convinced myself that I had the skills I needed to survive living under the same roof as my papi again.

Yet, on this trip, I ran out of money and made myself vulnerable to him. Mi papi has used money as a means to control others my entire life. Money is how his grip on mi mami remains as strong today as it was years ago when they first were married. Allowing him to take care of me meant allowing him to have dominion over me. I knew this to be true, but after a week of being away from home I had run out of my own money and turned to him.

A thing to note about my dad is that his favorite pastime is being the center of attention. He thrives off of being the funniest person in a room. Growing up with a dad like that was fun, until it was not. One of the worst things that both my parents did was hit me and make me believe that they hit me because they loved me. I was hit because they said that they wanted the best for me. They framed spanking as their God-ordained right, and they explained it as a loving act to keep us "good." As a result, as an adult I struggled to separate physical pain from love. And while the beatings hurt, mi papi's words are what I hear over and over in my head whenever I do something outside a very narrow definition of "good."

So, here we were in the last leg of our trip, and something happened that I will never forget. While in Guatemala, Andrés, my dad's good church buddy, kept talking excitedly the entire trip about theological gatherings he would host in his home. He talked about his guests and said that they would talk theology and philosophy. Women were invited, which was surprising for me to hear, considering how this church did not ordain women or allow women to do much in terms of leadership roles. On one occasion, I got to meet some of those intellectuals, who were all men. These men had gotten wind of the fact that I had just graduated from divinity school, and so they were intrigued by me. A girl, born in Nicaragua, now living in the United States and obtaining a graduate degree from an American university, and a theological institution nonetheless. That was what Andrés dreamed for his daughters: an American college education. And I was sitting there, in front of him, living his dream for his own children.

At church they had learned that God created man to rule the world and everything in it and that it was the work of women to help men perform these tasks, to obey, and to always assume a subordinate role in relation to a powerful man.

—bell hooks

One morning, Andrés gathered a few of his buddies to join us for breakfast. I remember him bragging about me based on what he knew from social media, and the other men proceeded to ask me questions. I tiptoed around responding to them, giving short answers, because I know my place in these spaces and I had no reason to believe that these interactions would be safe. We got into the topic of the election in the United States, because Trump was just running. One businessman in the group talked favorably about Trump, and I pushed back in the most demure and muted way I knew how. Having studied theology and ethics, I feel generally comfortable marrying those topics, but I did not feel comfortable with these men. Every time they asked questions, I responded, but I did not invite follow-up questions and generally avoided diving into the conversations. Instead, I listened to them talk about a slew of issues. In some ways, they seemed to be pushing against the very gendered theologies I knew my dad still believed. Again, no other woman was present at this discussion but myself. The men were respectfully engaging me; therefore, they seemed to feel entitled to have those conversations with me. They had no awareness of how traumatic the years of misogynistic church teachings might have been for me. They didn't perceive that my clipped responses and wary stances came from a place of distrust and pain. They were just *intellectuals* doing what *intellectuals* do, and that is ignore context, emotions, and pain and continue talking just to hear themselves talk. Talking in circles about everything and nothing, all at once—that is masculine *intellectualism*. I am afraid to say I disappointed them, but I will not put myself into situations that trigger my own trauma for anyone's entertainment, and so I did not engage and did not cooperate.

During all this, mi papi was exceptionally quiet. Generally, mi papi is far from quiet, and that also kept me tense. I know this man; I grew up understanding him and I know when he is displeased. He went about minding his business while we were there, and then on the final day Andrés drove us to the airport. Andrés pried further into my studies. I have known him my entire life, so while I was curt with his intellectual buddies, I felt like I could talk to him. He has two daughters, and he treats his wife like an equal. So, I started to speak and was candid about my theological views and where I stood. I mentioned that our church had done a lot of harm by not equipping the pastors (all male) with better theology around women, and then my dad cut me off.

My dad began to scream at me with this reserve of pent-up anger that I knew was not entirely meant for me. He said he did not need an education to understand God's will. He said the theology he knew was the only theology that is God-ordained. He said that anything else is a lie from feminists—spitting out the word "feminismo" like it was a curse. And he said that I was wrong to question our church theology because that was not my role.

I clammed up.

All the trauma around that man, my father, came rushing back. I thought I owed him the respect that would be due anyone who had paid for my meals while we were traveling. Andrés, his friend, looked at me and then looked at him and just stayed quiet. This man who I had thought respected women as equals, he stayed silent.

But then I remembered: my childhood church in Miami had a sexist and vile pastor. Edgar is in a very high senior position in our church governing board; he is in charge of all the church plants on a national level. Both Andrés and Edgar had attended the same church in Guatemala until Edgar immigrated to the United States. And every churchgoer, at one point or another, has seen Edgar belittle his wife and call her things I would never call another person. All the congregants talked about it; nobody ever did anything to stop it. How these church men treated women told me everything I needed to know. To them, the way men treated their wives was unimportant and a private matter. If a pastor had been chosen by God, no one, especially not any woman, could question him. These men were respected and admired, even when they terrorized the women in their family. I remember hearing my parents talk about how Edgar treated his wife, both expressing disdain for this man. My dad and Edgar had a personal feud, rooted in power and proximity to it, but I always had the feeling that mi papi was willing to work toward a resolution, despite how horrendous this man was to his wife.

That is where people often fall flat: they would rather stay silent and look the other way than dare correct a husband's treatment of his wife or a father's treatment of his daughter. It is a club. And a club rule is protecting one another and maintaining men's power over women.

After he screamed at me, my father and I stopped talking. The rest of the car ride to the airport was a silent one. We hugged

Andrés and said our goodbyes, but we did not speak to one another. We checked in, boarded the plane, sat next to each other, and did not speak. We did not speak when we landed. We did not speak when getting our luggage. And then, while waiting at the airport in Miami, mi papi made a joke about my having gotten a stomach bug and losing so much weight while traveling. And I laughed while avoiding his eyes. I made myself as small and as invisible as I could. I did not want to be the reason we got into a verbal altercation. I wanted to be easy, uncomplicated, just like mi papi liked.

That is what mi papi does. He explodes at the women in his life for falling out of line. After whatever explosion, which he thinks was deserved, he pretends he has done nothing wrong and puts the responsibility on me to release whatever resentment or hurt I may be harboring. And if I do not let it go, then I am the problem and the hateful one. That is the game, the only game he knows how to play. The rules are clear, and I should have known better.

But I did not want to know better, so I stopped trying to mend my relationship with my dad. I seldom tell him that I love him, because I fear him. When I am with him, I shrink away and long to make myself invisible. So in order to deal with my fears, I do not engage him. I have created the strictest boundaries, where I do not even pick up his phone calls. I do not allow myself to visit my parents without being fully prepared: I make sure I have a car and money for a hotel in case I need to escape, and I bring a friend or partner to protect me when things get heated. I cannot depend on my parents to take care of me, so I take care of myself.

I have learned that trauma is intergenerational and complex. Mi papi was raised under high pressure due to his gender. He had to grow up fast. Mi abuelito died by suicide when mi papi was sixteen years old. Mi papi was one of seven siblings. Right before mi abuelito died, he spoke to mi papi's two eldest brothers and told them that he was going away and that it was going to be their responsibility to take care of the family. Mi abuelo attempted to pass the torch to these adolescent boys, and was found dead the following day. Soon after his funeral, both those brothers left town. They ran away from the immense pressures they had been left with because of their gender.

Mi papi, as the third eldest boy, was left alone to take care of his siblings and mother. The torch was not passed down to him, but he took it before it hit the ground. He not only took the torch but ran as fast as he could, and has not stopped running. He took care of his family better than his own dad ever did. My abuelita Candida never worked. My papi was a musician, as my abuelito had been, so mi papi got my grandfather's band together and began to run everything. He played at clubs before he could even drink, and he even got to play for the president of our country. My dad's band was successful, and he was able to pay off mi abuelita's home and for the private education of his older sister and all his younger siblings. Mi papi at sixteen had to become the breadwinner for his siblings and his mami. Mi papi at sixteen became el hombre de la casa. Mi papi did not get to be a teenager for more than three years before his childhood was taken from him.

Mi papi is a proud man who cares for the well-being of others and would die trying to take care of everyone he loves. He has felt that responsibility longer than I have even been alive. That type of pressure, along with living in a country that was going through its most devastating civil war, meant that mi papi adjusted to his context. A war that was prolonged due to US interventions impacted mi papi, and whether he knows it or not, that trauma has stayed present in our lives.

Men in many communities appear to assign ideological weight on the outward attire and sexual purity of women in the community because they see women as 1) the community's—or the nation's—most valuable possession, 2) the principle vehicles for transmitting the whole nation's values from one generation to the next, 3) bearers of the community future generations—or, crudely, nationalist wombs, 4) the members of the community most vulnerable to defilement and exploitation by oppressive alien rulers, and 5) those most susceptible to assimilation and cooption by insidious outsiders.

—Cynthia Enloe

Dr. Cynthia Enloe was the first person I read who indirectly humanized my experience with mi papi. My parents lived through war and interventions by the United States, and they did not go unscathed. Enloe specifically talks about militarism and gender and the ways that it impacts men. Gender binaries become reinforced in times of war; for survival, women get restricted to the home and men get to protect them from "outsiders." Learning this shaped how I view mi papi. I learned that the dangers I was being protected from came from the real dangers he protected his mami and sister from during Nicaragua's civil unrest. I learned that the monster under mi papi's bed was not just toxic masculinity. He had to contend with more than any child should have to, and he managed to do it well—and he is joyful despite it all.

Mi papi lived through traumatic experiences and he stepped up and did what was asked of him. He is a survivor. This does not excuse anything that occurred to me due to his unresolved trauma, but it gave me the ability and the skills to better comprehend it all. And there are so many things about mi papi that I love, things I will never forget, even as I try to heal from his abuses. I know now: hurt people hurt people.

Finding Enloe's work gave me my life back. Finding the words allowed me to begin to self-soothe and then heal. I finally understood that it was not entirely mi papi's fault, and I knew better where to direct my anger.

Women tend to do a lot of work to justify the actions of the men in our lives, while our men do little to nothing to acknowledge our pain, much less try to alleviate it. I thought of enrolling at the institution where Enloe teaches to earn my second master's degree. Her work helped me understand mi papi. But while I was accepted into the program, I decided not to go in the end. I'm glad I did not go. I had almost made an academic career out of justifying mi papi's behavior and treatment of me, my sister, and mi mami. I had almost allowed the monster under my bed to take over my life by becoming an expert on it.

[Women] learn to make an identity out of their suffering, their complaint, their bitterness.

—bell hooks

Dealing with mi papi has been hard. I have felt unfaithful and ungrateful for creating boundaries, even though they have kept me safe from him. I still experience the negative effects of fearing the most important male figure from my childhood. I struggle with doing anything that is not perfect, because the fear of being hit still lingers; my last beating was when I was twenty-three years old. But more so, I have a fear of authority figures. When I first encounter any authority figure, I'm still visibly insecure. I tend to assume that I bring nothing to the table. I get flooded with childhood memories, and I have to work hard to stay focused and present.

I do not trust easily, because I fear that trust will be exploited. I do not show vulnerability to romantic partners without calculation. I'm always on guard and anticipating that my vulnerability could be used against me. I go to a lot of therapy and I try to make sense of the lovelessness I felt in a home that lauded itself as being full of love.

But generally, I have the tools I need to frame mi papi's experiences and my experiences with him. Yet I have not quite found a way to deal with sibling abuse, other than understanding that these behaviors are generationally passed down. I have not read much that talks about sibling abuse, and I have not talked to many people who have experienced it. But having an emotionally abusive older brother in a household that placed more value on men's abilities meant that his abuse was routinely excused and tacitly supported. He was constantly emboldened to do and say whatever he pleased to me and my younger sister. Our church and thus our household revered patriarchy, which meant men in general were considered superior. Our brother was not treated like our sibling; he was treated like our prince.

My brother is cruel; when he is angry, he is vicious. He has this ability to make you feel interesting and funny, until his mood shifts. And his moods are never predictable. You never know if you are getting Jekyll or if you are about to interact with Hyde.

He can be calm and relaxed and engaging, or he can suddenly turn and start screaming insults for no reason. Then he'll tell me that I deserve it and I am to blame. And then he'll apologize. In this, he is very different from mi papi. My brother is a master of apologies.

After he has blown off some steam, said every cruel thing he could imagine, gotten close enough to my face that I can actually see his pupils dilated from rage, then he apologizes.

I will dare to say that my older brother is the best at begging for forgiveness for his rage-fueled tantrums. He will have tears streaming down his face after having called me names and insulted my appearance and my intelligence. He will make big promises of never saying what he said again. He love bombs, maybe to secure his place in our hearts despite his behavior. But these grand apologies are empty, always. He has always broken his promises to me of being better and curbing his temper. It is like he has no control over his anger, and I just have to accept it and know that he will come to his senses eventually.

Keeping a relationship with someone with an unpredictable and uncontrollable temper means that I have to make myself as small and as invisible as I can. I did not want to be the reason we got into a verbal altercation. I wanted to be easy, uncomplicated, just like my brother liked.

His rage is literally bursting at the seams, and you can almost see him building up for a temper tantrum. My brother scares me in ways mi papi never did. Without mi papi, my brother would not be who he is. His behavior was tolerated and his anger was seldom corrected. He freely became who he is today because of how we were raised.

I rarely write about my brother. I rarely mention him. I have made his existence minimal in my everyday life, as a way to erase the worst parts of my childhood. But he is crucial to understanding my childhood; I just choose to not give him that power. Unlike mi papi, who traveled for work often, we were stuck with the proxy "man of the house" twenty-four hours a day, seven days a week.

My brother understood that our household monitored the girls. Everyone was trusted to follow the church doctrines except my sister and me. My brother understood that his role was to police us, to "protect" us from ourselves, so he took it upon himself to weaponize this power he was given. The girls were to be controlled.

If he caught us breaking the guidelines for pure, Christian girls—even just watching a television show that seemed too secular—he would tell mi mami. I would then be reprimanded. On the surface this feels normal, this feels like "proper parenting," but just underneath it was clear that it was a game that was built for his benefit. He knew this, and he enjoy playing this game of making me feel powerless. He needed to remind me that he was ranked higher and he was untouchable. I resented how often he did this, because it was not just sibling rivalry—it was a wielding of church-sanctioned, gendered power.

Our home was strict but conveniently stricter whenever my brother wanted it to be. I did what I could to subvert these rules, if only in secret. In my logic, if rules did not apply to my brother (who was only two years older than me), then they should not apply to me. But I rarely got away with much. And getting the truth beat out of me meant that I eventually gave in and just made myself as small and as invisible as I could be. I wanted to be easy, uncomplicated, just like everyone liked. And I waited for the day when I could leave.

If my brother got wind of me dating someone, he would drive to where he knew I would be, trying to gather "proof" for my parents of my impurity. My brother became the patrolman for my purity and the purity of my sister. It was he who revealed to my parents that my sister was no longer a virgin, which she was reamed out for. It was he who took it upon himself to find evidence of my sinning. It was he who eventually turned himself into our parents when he fornicated. He felt so ashamed, he suffered, too, at the hands of all this. He thought he had done a horrible thing, when all he had done was have sex with his girlfriend. I get it, it was not all him, it was bigger than us, but he took it upon himself to be judge and jury over my body and the body of my younger sister. Our church and home told him that was his rightful role: above us, acting as a constable.

After seventeen years of rage followed by exaggerated apologies and declarations of sibling love, I stopped talking to my brother. I had grown numb and I had grown tired of being told all the things I was doing wrong. I was tired of being small and making myself invisible. I understood that our church placed him on a pedestal, a place I could never reach. I grew cold, and I learned this very unreal skill of going from seeing someone every day for an entire childhood to shutting him entirely out of my life. I learned to not engage, to shut down my emotions around him. I learned to keep him away from me and everything I valued.

When I decided to bring home a boyfriend for the first time, I sought to protect him from my brother. I also wanted this boy to protect me from my brother. It was funny to discover that my brother did not challenge men. It was only little girls he liked to ridicule. I was safe whenever my boyfriend was in the room; my brother would be on his best behavior. I resented that only another man could rein him in. I resented that being born of the same parents meant nothing to him. I resented that he felt so cold toward me and so warm toward the men I dated. I resented that my boyfriends would meet my brother and then question my childhood stories of his abuse. I resented that these young men longed to like one another. I resented that my stories of abuse seemed "not that bad," until one boyfriend actually witnessed my brother slip into cruelty. I resented that he had to see it to believe it.

I learned to tell my brother nothing. I knew anything I said would become ammunition against me. I trusted nothing about him. His intentions were always suspect at best. This way, I could be ready for whatever came at me. I was protected from being charmed by him.

The less he knew about me, the better. The less he heard about me, the more I knew I would be okay. My logic was: he cannot hurt me if I am always prepared.

I rarely write about my brother, because it requires me to ask hard questions of my parents. Why did they allow him to rule over me, to mistreat me, to belittle and dehumanize me? Mi mami would often say that her older brother was worse, as if that was supposed to answer my and my baby sister's pleas to have his behavior corrected. I would never understand why this was allowed to happen to us.

My sister and I still bond over his behavior. She will call me and tell me about his new antics and his new insults and his new manipulation tactics. We find solace in knowing that we were not alone growing up and that we had one another to rely on and protect from him, even when our parents did not protect us. In fact, I was the one who threatened to call the cops when he hurt my sister badly enough that he made her sob from pain one evening. This all occurred in front of mi papi and mami, and mi mami left the room while mi papi told my sister that it was her fault.

I rarely write about my brother, because it requires that I turn the lens on myself. I rarely write about my brother, because I fear that I have not done enough to make him better, to stop his misogyny. But then I remember that voice that keeps telling me: I am socialized to rationalize the behavior of my abusers in order to survive a patriarchal culture. I have been socialized to do the emotional work to understand and heal relationships with men who believe themselves to be superior. This same culture socializes men to do little to no emotional work to heal my pain. So, I have chosen to walk away. And yet my brother will never be okay with my existing outside his control.

He has spent years telling me he loves me anyway. Mi papi plays that trick also; they passively stand back and give me room to apologize to them. They patiently wait. They position themselves as the victims of my shunning. I am the resentful person who cannot let anything go, and they are the victims of my self-preservation. They believe all this to their core. They do not see that surviving being around them means that I have to make myself as small and as invisible as I can.

They do not see that I do not want to be the reason we got into a verbal altercation. They do not see that all I want is to be easy, uncomplicated.

All they see is that I am a woman, and therefore histérica whenever emotional, and that their role is to dominate me at all costs. That is the thing about emotionally manipulative, toxic men: they will always frame themselves as innocent, and we will be led to believe that it is true. We will become their defenders and tell our own daughters to focus on the good. We are taught to be swallowed whole by someone's foundational belief that he is better than us.

I have always suspected that our migration hit my brother harder than it hit me. I was younger and was able to pick up more of the culture. I learned English more easily, without much of an accent, while his accent remains. He was nine years old when we moved here and was bullied for his accent, a lot. His personality seemed to transform here.

In Nicaragua, he had a lot of friends and played outdoors often. He had his independence. We would bike to and from our school. But when we moved here, he became quiet and shy. His first experience with a bully in the United States was a girl, a fact he would be teased about by my dad for many years. He could not keep the few friends he managed to make, and so he rarely had friends. He is a loner and severely misunderstood. I have always believed that our migration was traumatic for him, and nobody really helped him. Toxic masculinity tells boys to bury their feelings, and I wonder how much that has impacted him. But I won't excuse his behavior when he will not work to heal his own trauma.

Today I do not make myself small and invisible, for anyone. I have learned that if men do not like me or my work—and especially if they encourage their girlfriends, wives, or femme partners to stay away from me—then I must be doing something right. I am attempting to create a reality where women like me get to live boldly as ourselves—not like men, but as we are, in all of our fullness.

My friends, all who have been intentionally mutually selected, have helped me build this reality. I am part of a group of three recovering pastor's daughters. We're all from the same church, but from different church plants. I attended the Managua church plant and eventually the Miami church plant, and they attended the Guatemala church plant and eventually the Chicago church plant—same church, doctrine, and leadership, but in different cities. We call ourselves Las Brujas, as an attempt to reclaim a word that Christians have long used against female outsiders. All three of us migrated to this country at around the same time. All three of us have been rejected by our home churches. All three of us have been the child that shamed our Christian pastoral families at some point or another. Together we process our pain, celebrate our victories, and honor our humanity.

Through them, I am attempting to create arenas where we do not have to make ourselves small for the comfort of the men in the room. I am attempting to find joy in my visibility, rather than safety in my invisibility. We do not all live in the same city, but when we gather, we revel in our vastness and take up all the space.

Both of them live in Chicago, and when I visit we go to a steak house that is owned by a Colombian husband and wife. The husband uses his wife as a punch line for his jokes often, and we have all made the decision to take her side and openly do so. These moments of not being silent and not rolling over, that is how we recover from the complicity we saw around us growing up. When the owners see us enter the restaurant, even if it has been months, they recognize us. In this restaurant, a space we lovingly refer to as "our restaurant," we have created a home. Home is with us, with each other, and in the places where we can be ourselves. With these friends, I am attempting to find comfort within myself and radically accept all parts of myself. We hold one another accountable, and we challenge one another to grow. With them, I am the version of myself I could not be at home. My friends are my chosen family. We all have experienced rejection in our home and home church, and we have chosen to radically accept one another. We have accepted the tragedies within us.

I have found my identity not because of my experiences with intimate-family toxic masculinity but despite them. In my own tragedy, I had to find ways to honor my strengths and my ability to take care of myself, despite the monster under my bed.

In my country, like many countries in Latin America and the Caribbean, there is a series of stories we pass down orally. One famous story is that of La Llorona. In the La Llorona story I knew growing up, a mother, when she discovers her husband is having an affair, kills her children. She comes to her senses only after the act is done, and today her ghost roams the streets looking for her children. In the story, all children are in danger of being taken and claimed as her own.

The story lacks details like time and place, and serves as a warning to keep children indoors after the sun goes down. Like many stories, there is a lesson to be learned, a warning. This ghost story is a very common tale growing up in a Latin American household. Telling and retelling this tragedy is a cultural norm.

In graduate school, I discovered a series of these stories shared by many Latin American descendants. La Malinche is one of those stories. As I have heard this story, La Malinche was an Indigenous woman who served as a translator for conquistadores and helped in the colonization of the Aztec empire. I have also heard that she was bought and sold throughout most of her life, and that is how she was able to know multiple languages and serve as a translator. La Malinche is generally seen as a traitor.

Her story also goes on to say that she eventually becomes the mistress of Hernán Cortés, a Spanish conquistador. La Malinche has children with Cortés and she, too, kills the children, after the conquistadores depart to return to Spain.

Like La Llorona, La Malinche's story is a tragedy. Many scholars believe that both of these stories are the same, and many have reclaimed La Malinche. They believe that she had no agency. As a slave and mistress, she was not willingly abandoning her people but was a tool for a larger and more powerful empire. La Malinche is a victim of colonization and male domination, and today she roams the streets crying, mourning the tragedy that was her life.

In a patriarchal society, the focus of the story is on the evils and emotions of the crying women, rather than on the male aggressors and the injustices that brought about these tragedies. And that is why I tell my own stories, because I am not my anger, my fear, and my sadness. My emotional responses to trauma are just a small window into the larger experiences I have lived through.

> *Women's main activities are reduced to two: suffering the male presence and mourning male absence.*
>
> —Elizabeth E. Brusco

In my household, tears are a display of weakness that is scorned. Growing up, mi mami had a parrot that could speak. This parrot called me "llorona" whenever I entered a room. She called me that because everyone in my home called me llorona. For most of my life, I believed that I was a crybaby, but in hindsight I can see things more clearly: I was crying out for help after years of mistreatment, but our culture had desensitized us to female mourning, female tears. We have been taught through La Llorona that those tears are a trick at best.

As I got older, I realized that this was neither healthy nor normal. When I learned to reclaim these particularly female tragedies, I learned to stop being ashamed of my own tears. So today, I allow myself to cry often. I know now that crying is not exclusively a female trait and not a weakness. Rather, crying is a way to name the tragedies in our lives, and it is a way to release them. I've learned that I did not cry because I was a llorona, just as La Llorona did not only cry because she killed her children. La Llorona was mourning her life, a life that was robbed from her. And I cried because I did not know how to explain emotional abuse or how to deal with it as a little girl. Yet I was dismissively called llorona, while no one ever corrected the behavior that caused my tears.

We do that. We call mujeres locas, lloronas, putas, and a slew of other terms that are specifically meant to shame women for not following the rules and for speaking up for themselves.

I was called a loca when I left my ex-husband. A puta when I decided to enjoy sex and have lots of it. And a llorona for trying to thwart abusive behavior. I now know that this coded language was used to stop my protests and stop me from living life on my terms.

I hope that we can move away from being a society that blames women instead of protecting them. I hope that people continue to reclaim the pantheon of Indigenous deities who were discarded or vilified for the preferred Christian God. I hope that we can dare to look female tragedies in the face and try to heal from them instead of running away, like I was taught to do.

I identify with La Llorona because I wanted to be loved. Instead, I was abused by this monster under my bed, who also slept next to mi mami and in the room next to mine. And for years, nobody listened. And until we learn to listen, I will remember my childhood self as La Llorona. A little girl, desperately crying for help, who had to figure out how to survive in a household that placed so little value on her that they managed to mock her instead of coming to her aid.

Yet, still, my heart has always wanted to embrace you, even if you did not embrace me, and that is the real tragedy.

CHAPTER 7

INTERSECTIONALITY

Intersectionality [is] a way of framing the various interactions of race and gender in the context of violence against women of color.
—Kimberlé Crenshaw

This one is for the hairy girls. This is for the girls who were not allowed to shave their legs until they were at least twelve years old, and then when you were finally allowed to, it was strongly advised that you shave below the knee and not above it. Because only putas wear clothes short enough to show the upper part of your legs.

This is for the girls who pleaded, begged, cried to be allowed to shave sooner and were met with unsympathetic glares from your mami and papi. This is for the girls who secretly shaved the hair on their toe knuckles just to wear sandalias, since pants were all they felt they could wear once someone pointed out their hairy legs.

This is for the hairy girls. This is for the girls whose arm hair was the butt of jokes in elementary school. This is for the girls who found the bleaching creams for body hair at Eckerd's one day. For the girls who then bleached their arm hair blonde, only to realize that it did not erase the thickness of their mane. The bleach only seemed to highlight their hairiness against their darker skin.

This one is for the girls with hairy knuckles, for the girls who shaved those knuckles once someone else pointed out their hairiness.

This one is for the hairy girls. This is for the girls who never noticed that women also grow mustaches, to differing degrees. This is for the ones who were happy and enjoying their lives, until their older brother made fun of the hair above their upper lip in front of a guy they thought they were going to marry.

This is for the girls with happy trails. For the girls with that thick patch of hair on their lower back. This is for the girls who were told that "only boys" have hair on those parts of their bodies.

This is for the girls who were made to feel less like a girl, less like a woman, because not only were they hairy but their hair was dark and it was thick.

This one is for all the girls whose eyebrows have a life of their own. I started wearing prescription glasses my senior year of high school, and when I first tried them on, my eyebrows touched my lenses. I remember mi mami laughing at me, saying I had mi papi's eyebrows. I began to trim my eyebrow hairs on that day.

This is for the girls who tried everything to eliminate their eyebrows once they discovered tweezers. This one is for the girls who obsessed over trimming and maintaining their eyebrows, only to find out that thick eyebrows were the new trend for white girls.

This is for the girls who wondered where all this hair had come from and wished to be free of it. For the girls who cried because they just wanted to look like those girls in their magazines: the hairless, cute ones, the ones who did not have to worry about when they would have to shave next.

This is for the all the girls who have had to love themselves despite everyone telling them otherwise. Being a hairy girl means that this world has taught us how to erase ourselves with lasers, waxing, bleaching, shaving, tweezers, and the like.

Being a hairy girl means learning to love yourself in this new hairless version that you've created or learning to love the hairiness as it is—but it means learning to love yourself either way. It means that for a long time you were discouraged from looking like you did, and that you had to take that information and either reject it or run with it.

This is for all those tears you've shed and all that work you've put into loving yourself.

I see you. I am you, and I am still learning and unlearning all the Eurocentric ideals of beauty that fueled my own self-hatred. But we will overcome and raise a proudly hairy generation who will be forces of nature.

Body hair readily denoted this evolving regard for self-ownership and self-determination.

—Rebecca M. Herzig

I started this chapter with this particular hairy girl experience because, despite what feminism has insisted, our experiences as women—whether assigned female at birth (AFAB) or otherwise—are vast and varied. This vastness, including the vastness of impacted oppressions, is addressed within intersectionality. Black, Indigenous, and women of color do not have the option to separate their oppression due to racism from oppression due to sexism; they experience both, from all communities. As a facet of that violence, white beauty ideals are both patriarchal and racist, and they suffocate Black, Indigenous, and women of color.

When I wrote this particular story, I was not thinking about all the cute, white hairless girls I had grown up being taught were normal through television, magazines, and the Limited Too. When I wrote this story, I was thinking about all the hairy Black and Brown girls who were socialized to believe that something was wrong with them because they did not reflect European standards of beauty.

Seeing things through an intersectional lens allows me to decenter the norms of whiteness and maleness. The white male experience has been taught as the universal, representative human experience. It is not. I remember learning about intersectionality in graduate school and feeling struck, because up to that point I had assumed that the "universal" included me. Even when I had experiences that told me otherwise, that universal assumption seemed to overwrite those experiences. I had to accept that the default human experience had never included me. It hurt that my differences were not recognized, much less honored. Instead, I was expected to absorb the dominant white worldview, even when whiteness did not want me to exist. This displacement was painful.

Sometimes I think I just assumed that displacement was always going to be my reality due to my migration. I had to learn to carve spaces for myself by reading the work of Black, Indigenous, and women of color. I first had to learn about intersectionality before I could even begin to do that work.

The word "intersectionality" gave me the language I needed to name the experiences I had been dealing with my entire life. It gave me the tools to turn that displacement into something generative and healing, for myself and for others.

The act of writing this opening letter to hairy girls, for me, is layered. I first published a version of it online, on the *Huffington Post*, to carve out one small place where my hairiness was not shamed and my experiences as a hairy girl were not erased.

My assertion of pride in my hairy female body was never meant to include any white women. The pressure to shave is present for all women, but hairy Black and Brown women experience it in a different, violent way. This letter allowed me to speak to people who would intimately understand this as a distinct experience for Brown and Black women. I have read this story to a room of more than fifty BIWOC who all had tears in their eyes, and I have read this story to a room of mixed races and genders, where I saw a white man get up from his seat and leave mid-story. This story is not meant for a mixed audience; this story is meant just for us.

Because the hairy Brown girl story is not meant for a general audience, it does not center a white experience. White people are used to having their experiences constantly centered as the norm; so much so that they cannot read any other experience as a legitimate human experience. By utilizing an intersectional framework, I am decentralizing this normative culture. This story is for people whose intersections mean that they are women with darker genetic traits and a predisposition for hairiness.

I wrote this for the BIWOC who had grown up tormented for something that they could not change about themselves. I wrote this from a place of wanting to improve our regard toward hairy folks. Starting this chapter on intersectionality with a specific marginalized perspective was intentional. I wanted those folks who are not familiar with this experience to be confronted with and feel the discomfort of being excluded, perhaps for the first time in their lives. I also want those folks who are intimately familiar with this experience to sit in the magic of having our specific reality named. I want my readers to enjoy the magic of an intersectional story that does not prioritize whiteness.

A failure of mainstream feminism is that it is white and elite. The concept of intersectionality arose, in part, as a critique of gender-only feminism. A feminism that sees the white cis female experience as the universal female experience simply cannot address the issues faced by most women on the planet—because most women on the planet are Black and Brown. And mainstream feminism lacks awareness that, while women can share some experiences (such as the pressure to shave), how we experience them is based on our intersections of race, ability, class, and sexuality, which can make that similar pressure feel very different.

It is in the details of your experiences where you will find uniqueness, and it is in the uniqueness where you will find the intersections of your layered identities. If your movement refuses to honor our differences, then your movement only serves to reinforce the status quo. A "universal" feminism only serves the default narrative, which is always white above anything else.

> *Recent studies indicate that more than 99 percent of American women voluntarily remove hair, and more than 85 percent do so regularly, even daily. The usual targets, for the moment, are legs, underarms, eyebrows, upper lips, and bikini lines. Those habits, furthermore, appear to transcend ethnic, racial, and regional boundaries.*
>
> —Rebecca M. Herzig

Hair seems to be a unifier for BIWOC, to differing degrees. And while not all BIWOC will identify with this narrative, there are things within it that still feel true and uniquely ours in ways that white women can never understand.

Women are socialized to depend on male approval. This means that, as BIWOC, to be considered feminine, we are pressured to be beautiful in a world where only white women are upheld as the standard of beauty. If you are not white, there is already something considered inferior about your body. When you are both Brown and hairy, you are also coded as somehow masculine, and therefore your body is a betrayal to femininity. White women have been complicit in cementing these standards.

White women have routinely stepped into their liberation from the injustices they have faced due to their gender by growing out their body hair. Yet, our fights are not the same. Even when white women face social backlash for their unfeminine body hair, they are still white. Being of the "desirable" race means that their resistance will land differently than when an "undesirable" Brown woman grows out her body hair as an act of resistance.

This piece is not for a dark-haired white woman; this piece does not center nor validate those experiences. Black and Brown women are forced to shave our hair to become desirable in a society that has taught us that our bodies are already undesirable because of the color of our skin. This chapter is about self-love and standing firm in however you have decided to thrive.

> *A woman of color's self-love is political and radical, and it is unsettling for the status quo because she is choosing bravely to dismantle the narratives of racist aesthetics against her. So when people bully a girl of color for being content and satisfied with her appearance—a reality that is subjected to racist, sexist slurs in cosmetic industries—and when they tell her to be "humble," which is normative code for "Nah, you're not special, you're not light and delicate in a Eurocentric way," then she has every right to chew their hearts and spit them out. A non-white girl's self-love is revolutionary and anyone trying to water it down needs to back right off.*
>
> —Mehreen Kasana

Mehreen Kasana's quote is precisely why this piece is for BIWOC with dark hair. If you have never had to walk through CVS scanning the aisles for that body hair bleaching cream that your other BIWOC dark-haired friend told you about, that means we are not the same. And differences are beautiful; intersections are full of richness and variance. I should also note that the body-hair bleaching cream fails us terribly, and it fails due to the exact fact that your Black or Brown skin is meant to have dark hair. This story can only be experienced by other BIWOC with dark hair.

Because feminism has not actually figured out that women can also have other layered identities, feminism will continue to fail to see all women.

I am a woman and I am Brown. I am a woman and I grew up working-class. I am a woman and I am an immigrant. But also, I am a woman and I was AFAB, meaning I am cisgender. I am a woman and I am in a heterosexual relationship. I am a woman and I have multiple degrees. All that means that when I go into a job interview, those intersections will either advantage or disadvantage me. Those intersections also inform how I approach everything, and that is what intersectionality means. It means various realities can simultaneously inform who we are, why we think the way we think, why we care about what we care about, and why we cannot be expected to join movements that do not consider all those realities. It is also the first thing that people want to reject when creating movements. The women's movement erased women of color. The civil rights movement marginalized women of color. Both movements sidelined queer and disabled women of color. Whenever a movement wishes to focus on a "unified" experience by erasing specific experiences, that means that these movements erase too many of us.

Embracing all my intersecting identities has meant everything to me. I was finally able to talk openly about things I had been told to keep silent about, like my Nicaraguan roots. Discovering and embracing the complexities within myself meant that I no longer had to hide. That is why intersectionality matters.

Now, realizing the ways that my intersections affected romantic relationships was a slow process for me, but it was a necessary one. For me, dating someone outside my gender, race, and economic background meant addressing those very things that made us different instead of pretending those intersections did not exist.

When I began dating the man who would become my second husband, I knew that stepping up to that relationship meant transparency about our differences. He is a white man. I am a Brown woman. We had to be able to openly address the power dynamics between a person our society overvalues and a person our society does not value at all. And naming my powerlessness was powerful. Naming the ways his intersecting identities are privileged above mine is my way of attempting to address the differences in order to create a symbiotic relationship.

To do this, I wrote him a letter. It was initially intended to be kept between him and me. But now you are all welcome to dive into our relationship and the foundation that had to be laid:

Gringuito,

I am going to need to be frank about what it means to date a Brown girl from Chico Pelón in Managua, Nicaragua. Because since I arrived to the United States, you white boys have been attempting to recolonize my already colonized body, and I have generally avoided falling in love with someone who cannot fathom how to accept all this brown sugar. I generally avoided dating white boys, for one obvious reason: I am a white boy's nightmare. I know my history, and I know how much white privilege and white supremacy has impacted my life, directly. So I do not submit to any man, and I do not submit to white men.

I will not teach you Spanish. People get paid for that type of labor, lots of money. People get degrees and have taken out student loans to become translators. This is undervalued work. And I want you to understand, though you will never really understand, what it feels like to be an outsider. I want you to see and feel, even if just for a minute, what my Spanish-speaking mami and papi experience in this country. I want you to have to watch shows like Plaza Sésamo to begin to gain entrance into these spaces that will be foreign to you. I want you to need to ask me what people really mean.

I will not tell my friends to take it easy on you. Because, you see, my family will embrace you with open arms and "like" you almost too immediately. There are reasons for that—deep, colonized-folk reasons—so it will be my friends who will vet you. My friends will not be interested in you as a ticket to proximity to whiteness. I want them to ask you the real questions. I want them to ask you if you have a "thing" for Latinas, and no matter what you say they will give you a nondescript "Hmm."

I want them to ask you how much of your attraction is a fetish for my cultura, and what you think about capitalism as a white man. I want to watch you squirm and see your true colors seep out through your pores. I want to know where you stand on solid issues. I want to know how much heat you can take, because I am going to need your support when I meet your friends and family.

Your friends will call me "caliente" and ask me if I love spicy food, as if all cuisine from Latin America is spicy. And they will even venture to request that I speak some Spanish to them. All this will be a product of yours and their whiteness and privilege, but I will not sink. But I expect you to swim just as furiously when my friends come for your head (figuratively), because your friends and family, intentionally or not, will come for my heart and I will handle it.

I will expect you to say my name, in my accent. I was born Priscila Dorcas Mojica Rodríguez. One L because two makes a Y sound in Spanish. Your very American name will be said properly in all your spaces, and even my own spaces, and my name will be consistently butchered. So, I expect you to at least hold my name, my entire name, with the same protection and care that has always been given to you due to the color of your skin.

People in my community are going to love the color of your eyes, your baby-blue eyes. It might even inflate your ego; it probably already has. Please remember what it has cost people to value light features and lightness in general; there are skin-lightening industries and even a whole industry of colored contacts that thrives off the self-hatred of BIPOC. My communities have been told our entire lives that white features are superior to our own darker ones, with wider noses, flatter faces, etc. Your whiteness is going to be coveted, but that comes from my subjugation and the subjugation of my people.

I may jokingly call you an "honorary" Nicaraguan; it is a joke. It is my simplified way of acknowledging that you, as a white man dating a pinolera-born goddess, will have access to things within my culture that you cannot get while visiting on a mission trip or vacationing. Please do not repeat this light-hearted sentiment to your friends, nor to any other Latinxs you encounter. You do not get to speak for me, because the struggle of being Nica is unique and is a lived experience. Being Nicaragüense is my birthright, much like having the ability to never fear being killed by a cop on a simple traffic citation is yours.

My Brownness is special, and I will talk about my Brownness and my food and my culture with pride. I have learned to do that despite the socializing I received in this country. The United States required the total erasure of my background in order for me to gain access to anything in this country. My self-love is countercultural in a society that wants me to assimilate. My pride is political.

Above anything else, learn to sit in the discomfort of being on the highest rung of a pigmentocracy, a privilege you did not earn but were born with. And then learn to protect me and the way I have chosen to reject this mentality every day, though I need no protecting.

These are just a few things that you will encounter if you in-sist on dating a Brown girl from Chico Pelón in Managua, Nicaragua.

Sincerely Mine and Never Yours

Before learning about intersectionality, I had never had a conversa-tion like this with a romantic partner. For much of the time when I was dating, I had never thought of bringing up the intersections of race, gender, and class. When I dated other Latinos with the same economic background as myself, gender was really the only issue that had to be addressed. But once the dating pool became increasingly white in Tennessee and I started dating white men, whose entire existence benefitted from the subjugation of people like me, I soon had to learn to have that conversation exhaustively, with intersectionality in mind. White people taught me about my otherness, and then I challenged them with it—because white people will still claim colorblindness to avoid admitting their own privileges.

So, if I was going to step into a relationship with someone whose intersections were so vastly different from my own, I un-derstood there was some work to be done on his end to ensure that I was actually safe. My letter to my now-husband was a valuable moment for us.

My intersections come with me wherever I go, whether I am ready for them or not. And in white spaces those intersections feel heavy and they feel burdensome. It takes work to understand that whiteness is not universal, and it takes work to center yourself by decentering the status quo. Intersectionality legitimized the layers of oppression I had felt: racism, classism, sexism.

Without intersectionality, I would have few tools to combat the dominant narratives and norms. I would have been left to make sense of my dehumanization all on my own. If you accept that whiteness is the norm, then being a BIPOC means that, no matter where you go, there is already something wrong with you. If you cannot articulate all the ways society has erased you, you begin to think your voice is being ignored because you did something wrong. BIPOC often find ourselves invalidating our own experiences and memories. Even social interactions feel fraught with our discomfort. A great and simple example of this is my lack of pop-culture knowledge, due to my conservative, Christian, immigrant, working-class upbringing. People often will be aghast that I do not know any actors by their names, with the exception of Nicolas Cage. I do not know most cult classics and only recently watched the *Star Wars* movies, at which point I felt like I finally understood decades of references. The same can be said about music, specifically classic rock. And my response to my lack of knowledge in the past has been one of shame and self-blame. Yet with intersectionality, I have been able to reframe those experiences. Instead of feeling that displacement internally and silently, I now can name it and become an active participant. Something as simple as knowing what people are even talking about can make you feel connected or not, present or othered.

Due to my intersections, I experienced a particular kind of dehumanization in my graduate program every Halloween.

Every single year of my four-year graduate program, a student would ask me if they could dress up as me for Halloween. After the first year, you would think that I would have become accustomed to the question or been better prepared. But somehow, I was always caught off guard when asked this ridiculously dehumanizing question: "Can I wear you as a costume?"

In my self-estimation, I thought I read as fashionable and glamorous in my phenomenally curated closet of homemade clothes, secondhand items, and some fast-fashion, affordable, trendy pieces. I valued my ability to look like a million bucks while wearing secondhand clothing, but I soon realized that this is not a skill that is celebrated outside my community. How I was read in my mostly Latinx community was not how I was read in white spaces. Because I am racialized as Brown and Brown is coded as inferior and less than, and because whiteness functions to regulate anything that is outside itself, I had a harsh reality to contend with when I began attending my PWI.

The first year, the girl who asked me if she could dress like me for Halloween was a "friend." That is what I call white people who disguise themselves as friendly, but really they are just disarming you and waiting for the moment when they can ask what they have been wanting to ask since they first met you. Her name was Julie, and we were at a party sometime right before Halloween. Our department had an infamous annual Halloween party that was hosted by our program's Student Government Association. Most people dressed up for this event.

I remember that she came up to me and said, "Can I be you for Halloween?" I think she saw the confusion and slight anger in my eyes. She began to clarify and say that she just thought that she could never wear what I wore, and some other remarks that were meant to sound like compliments but were not. She then pulled out her phone and said that one year she had dressed up as a reality TV star, and that was the "look" she was going for this year. She insisted on digging herself into a nice little hole the size of her entire body.

She said she wanted to wear a cheetah-print dress and a fur jacket. That was her perception of me, and when I saw the blurry picture of her wearing her previous DIY Halloween outfit, I only read one thing: cheap. I was immediately ashamed. But she never brought it up again, and I dropped that entire conversation and tried to pretend it never happened. I ended up not attending said Halloween party, to avoid the weirdness of attempting to have fun around white people who seemed to enjoy making me feel shame.

When I was in the moment, I did not know what was happening, and took the blow in stride. I tried to pretend my pride was not robbed from me, and I tried to pretend that the things that were said were not said. Realizing I read as cheap was never something I could take in in one sitting. It would take me a while to peel back all the layers of this racism onion.

Still, I attempted to become close to Julie, possibly to prove to her that I wasn't what she had initially perceived me to be, which was a mistake. You cannot force someone to see your humanity after they have already decided you are inferior. I realize now that when she had asked me if she could dress like me for Halloween, she was making a coded statement about my otherness. She, a white woman from an upper-middle-class background, embodied intersections that were prioritized over mine. My intersecting identities must have been fascinating to her at best, a costume at worst.

The following year, a man asked me that same question. My memory is a little blurry, but I do remember we were standing outside our graduate school building and he mentioned his desire to dress like me for Halloween. He said it as if it was the funniest joke he could have made, but I was not in on the joke. Today he is a doctoral candidate at an elite institution.

Those first two times, I was caught by surprise and I did not know how to react. The following year, I attempted to get ahead of these racist interactions, and I held a panel about Halloween in our campus building. The panel was about how to avoid being insensitive, and twenty or so people came (out of a more than two-hundred-student graduate program). The event mostly seemed to piss off the white students. They couldn't believe that a panel of their peers of color would dare tell them how to behave humanely during our Halloween party. But then I remembered that intersectionality was taught to me in an elective class and barely mentioned in the mandatory classes. And of course, the elective classes that prioritized nonwhite people were over-attended by BIPOC and under-attended by the white people in our program.

For me, though, when I think about intersectionality, I also need to think about my privileged identities. I am a cis person and grew up with a Judeo-Christian understanding of the world that made my ethnic and racial differences feel less threatening to white people at times. My Christianity made me palatable to white people in ways that, if I was not Christian, I would not have been. Furthermore, I think that to some of my peers my Brownness felt less threatening than Blackness might have. Dr. Myra Mendible talks about Brownness being scripted as an in-between identity, a "mediating color" between Black and white.

As I was experiencing anti-immigrant rhetoric and blatant stereotyping in Nashville, it felt strange to think about where I had advantages. But there was one particular incident that made me realize that my intersections with race had placed me at a more advantageous position than my Black peers and even professors.

In academia, there is this rhetoric around not engaging in what they call "oppression Olympics." With this language, the experiences of all BIPOC are flattened and put on an even playing field. I did not interrogate this thinking much then, but have since learned to push back on this desire to avoid the topic of global anti-Blackness.

I remember when I took my first class with a Black female faculty member at Vanderbilt. This class was titled Feminist, Womanist, and Mujerista Theo-Ethics. This professor is a leading womanist scholar and one of the best lecturers I have ever had the privilege of calling my instructor. Her courses were crucial in my own radicalization, and I enrolled in as many of them as I could until I graduated. I remember clearly how she paved a way for me to find the words I needed to survive academia. I remember that, when we hit the mujerista track of this course, the professor opened the class for discussion on where we stood in terms of Latinidad.

I will never forget the questions the professor posed to the entire class; they were designed to confront the students with their ignorance of the experiences of Latinx people. Dr. Stacey M. Floyd-Thomas asked my peers to raise their hands if they had ever been friends with someone who was Latinx, if they knew Latinx people, if they had friends who were friends with Latinx people, and other questions to interrogate the students' lack of proximity and familiarity with Latinxs. No hands were raised during this entire line of questions, except for my own.

In seeing this, I finally understood why I had felt so misunderstood this entire time, and I was finally able to figure out that how I moved within this white space was going to be seen and analyzed and assumed to be representative. My example could possibly be used by ignorant white people against other Latinx people, due to my white peers' lack of exposure to people like me.

Understanding just how completely we live in a segregated society meant that I finally had the information I needed to take some weight off myself for constantly feeling misunderstood. I had always been an outsider in jokes, social gatherings, and academic spaces, but I finally understood that this was not because something was wrong with me. It was them, my white peers, who had zero clue about how to deal with me. All they had were stereotypes; that was the only reference they had to figure me out.

I remember when I received an email from a white woman in this class; it was sent to mostly white students, but I was included. This email talked about wanting to discuss ways to deal with what this student and others in this email perceived as aggression from our professor. I remember being taken aback, because I had never picked up on any aggression. Quite the contrary, in that class I had felt embraced and welcomed. It was the first class where my experiences were not a secondary thought. Rather, they were constantly being centered in the texts we were reading and the papers we were writing. That email was sent by someone who had attempted to align herself with me through her familiarity with the Spanish language. She was, for all intents and purposes, a well-meaning white woman. But good intentions mean nothing if your actions are not good.

What I did next was a decision that I stand by: I told our professor about this email. Because I understood the intersections that she embodied, as taught to me by her. For me this was a significant moment, because up until this point I was no snitch. Because of my experiences with men and my very dogmatic church context, I thought of most authority figures as unsafe. This moment made me realize that while there are power dynamics between student and teacher, pastor and congregant, parents and children—race, gender, sexuality, class, and a slew of isms add complications to this entire framework and made me investigate my previous allegiances. I also had been noticing that, while I was treated in certain ways due to racist stereotypes of Latinx and Brown people, my Black peers and professors faced something else. I knew that there was a racism problem at my institution, and all institutions, and that white students were driving the ship while the white faculty and staff mostly kept their heads down.

I realize that there are ways that my intersections function to oppress me, and that simultaneously these intersections function to privilege me—depending on whatever circle I am in. This white woman, for some reason, had picked me as someone she wanted to align herself with, and she had also picked our Black professor as someone she wanted to vilify. I could not stand aside while she asked me to choose between the white students in my program and this cherished Black female professor.

I had finally understood that anti-Black racism meant that this professor's ability to be where she was in her career was and is a feat, and there was no way in hell I was going to participate in her demise in any way, shape, or form. So, I told our professor everything, and this moment was important for me because it was the first time I had chosen to defy whiteness. Before this moment, I was a passive and therefore a complicit participant in the oppression of Black, undocumented, and LGBTQIA+ people as a way of self-preserving—or so I thought. This moment was the beginning of me becoming who I am today, and while this small act of telling my professor about the email may seem unimportant, for me it carried a lifetime of aligning myself with whiteness and finally saying, No more and never again!

After I told this professor about the email, she brought it up in front of the entire class and explained the racism implied in the note, and she made a lesson out of this incident. I learned a lot about what it meant to be Black in academia in that class, and what it could mean for me if I decided to stay in academia. I learned that there would be ways in which my Brownness would be weaponized against me, and there would be ways in which my Brownness would be weaponized by white people against other BIPOC, and I needed to decide where I was going to align myself and who I was going to stand alongside. This was my moment of reckoning with whiteness, and it changed everything for me. Anti-Blackness is a worldwide phenomenon. And no matter what my intersections are, the fact that I am not Black means that I am an outsider who can choose to stand alongside Black people and fight for their liberation. Or, like many non-Black Latinas, I can allow my voice to be used against Black communities. Non-Black Latinxs may align themselves with whiteness for any number of reasons; to feel less oppressed, to be liked by white people, or to hope for safety within white supremacy. Because I am not Black, my "mediating color" can be used for good, or it can be used for the advancement of whiteness.

I call this my moment of reckoning with whiteness because I have idly stood by and not done enough for our gente in the past;

I have also not done enough even for my own family. I was finally beginning to accept the nuances of race and ethnicity, and I could see the various ways that I benefited from my intersections, depending on the context.

I had idly stood by when mi papi had begged me to translate things growing up. I resented my parents' lack of English proficiency because I thought our moral goodness was measured by our ability to assimilate. I had idly stood by when the undocumented immigrants in my school were teased for their accents. Up to this point, I had done nothing but try to focus on my own education and emancipation. But now, while still fighting for all those things I wanted for myself, I knew that I also had to fight for others.

I had become so fixated on getting a seat at their metaphorical table of insiders that I never stopped to think that maybe what I needed, and what other BIPOC needed, was to create a whole other table. We needed a space where we did not have to change parts of ourselves to become insiders. Put another way: fuck their table, we are going to make our own.

As a non-Black women of color, it is up to me to reject anti-Blackness even when I can stand to benefit from it. I remind myself constantly that no matter how enticing whiteness can seem, and how much safety can be promised through proximity to whiteness, those allures are all an illusion, and history has shown that time and time again.

To protect myself from whiteness, I decided to change the name that white people could use when referring to me.

In graduate school, I began to go by another name, a name other than my birth name. In many Latinx households, there is this inclination to find white/American names more attractive, so a lot of people in our communities will be named Zoe, America, Cindy, and my legal name, Priscila. Often, these American-sounding names will be spelled differently, for a few reasons including lack of English proficiency.

So, while mi papi is named Ricardo Enrique Mojica Fonseca and mi mami is named Blanca Azucena Rodríguez Jarquin, my siblings and I all have these more white/American names. I am named Priscila, my brother is named Richard, and my little sister's name is Linda. In our communities, none of that is seen as odd; it is a common practice of what I call a fascination with whiteness. I come from a family of Rosa, Candida, Ilse, Carolina, Lesbia, Álvaro, Jesarela, Arelis, Alcira, Nicolás, Dara, Jemima—I come from names that do not sit well in an English vernacular. These names demand attention. They perk up muscles in your tongue that otherwise go unused and require more effort to pronounce.

My name was something of a challenge for me growing up, because while I can say my name in Spanish perfectly, I struggle with pronouncing the Americanized version of it. And so, when I moved to Nashville, all the white students could say my name "better" than I could in its English, Americanized version, and it felt like my name was taken from me. So much was taken from me in white spaces—like my pride and my ability to believe that I was valuable—that I decided to take my name back from white people and only allow people I love to call me by my legal name.

In the middle of my master's degree, I requested that everyone call me by my chosen name of Prisca. Because I felt like the white gaze had consumed me, I decided to take the parts of me that felt more sacred and protect them from it.

I told white people to say my name. My full name. I told them to let my name weigh heavily in their mouths and let it tangle their tongues. I told them to say: **PRISCA DORCAS MOJICA RODRÍGUEZ**.

No, I tell these white people, do not call me P, or anything other than **PRISCA DORCAS MOJICA RODRÍGUEZ**.

My birth name is Priscila Dorcas Mojica Rodríguez. Priscila with one L, because in Spanish—my native tongue, my first language, the language of mi mami and her mami—I am Priscila, con una L.

In the United States, people like to think that because you are on their conquered land, they can take your name and make it fit into their language. This is covert colonization—to take my Spanish-spelled name and claim it without any regard by turning it into Pur-si-lah instead of Piri-si-la. There is a difference. Mi mami says my name how it is meant to be said; mi papi says my name how it was always intended. I do not know who the fuck Priscilla pronounced PUR-SI-LAH is.

In 2013, I changed my name to a name that you could not colonize as quickly, a name you had to ask twice to fully hear: PRISCA.

And I also started to add my middle name into the mix. Not just the middle initial. And my mother's maiden name. Because Latinxs are pressured to shed those long names in the United States, because that is what Americanos do. Americanos do not know that in Spanish, in the list of last names, the last name after the middle name is the official last name. We rank our names by order of importance. Here in the United States, if white people see a long name like ours, they will pick the very last name and decide to use that as our primarily last name.

So I have been called "Priscila Rodríguez" often. I have been called this by employers, by journalists who have written about me and my work, by doctors, by therapists, and by my professors. And this is a common mistake that occurs, but the real injury is in the lack of inquisition that goes into the white colonial tendency of overriding people's cultures with white people's own. So, in 2013 I started go by Prisca, and then I added the already legally listed surname of mi mami's family, because I wanted to be seen and not absorbed by my colonizers.

I want you to struggle with my entire name. This is political and strategic and filled with resistance, because you have butchered my name long enough and you accepted me as a nice Latina for too long.

So, you will say my name—my full name.

And I will watch you struggle and not let you call me anything else, because it is the least I can do when other white people attempt to recolonize my body and my name on a daily basis.

My name is **PRISCA DORCAS MOJICA RODRÍGUEZ**. I would rather hear them struggle through pronouncing that name than hear them butchering the name mi madre gave me.

So, when I introduce myself as **Prisca** and white people struggle, I breathe with more ease, because they can butcher Prisca all they want but they will never have the privilege of saying my beautiful Spanish-spelled name with their tongues.

I am

PRISCA DORCAS MOJICA RODRÍGUEZ.

I have chosen to not allow whiteness to erase
any parts of me, especially my name.

Give your daughters difficult names. Names that command the full use of the tongue. My name makes you want to tell me the truth. My name doesn't allow me to trust anyone who cannot pronounce it right.

—Warsan Shire

Allowing myself to step into my intersections with pride is something that has had positive effects in my life, despite the constant bombardment of racism that I still experience. I feel protected by my chosen name, as I still live in Tennessee. I feel shielded from the pain that used to come whenever my name had been taken from my native tongue and shoved into the spin cycle of American English.

Intersectionality sits in this very uncomfortable place for white people because intersectionality asserts the validity of identities, of several identities, other than whiteness. It tells white people that we are different, and that difference is good for us. Intersectionality matters because white culture is most comfortable when erasing us with colorblindness. If we don't assert the validity of our differences, we slip into our consumption and erasure.

Intersectional methodology seeks to create visibility where there often has not been any. Names, for BIPOC and LGBTQIA+ folks, can be life-giving. So when a BIPOC and/or LGBTQIA+ person tells a white person their chosen name, the white person must comply. What we are asking for is very basic. What we are asking for is for them to acknowledge our agency to decide how they will approach us. This is a human right that we have to demand, since they have decided to ignore it for this long.

CHAPTER 8

THE MALE GAZE

I remember the day I stopped depending on the male gaze. For me, it is very specific. I clearly remember the day my friends and I performed a ritual, a celebration, a healing circle to help me transition from being a subject of the male gaze to relinquishing it.

It occurred in 2014, after I had left my ex-husband. I was struggling, living without the security of male companionship. I felt betrayed by my fundamentalist Christian upbringing, which had instilled in me patriarchal values about marriage. I felt alone. I was devastated. Although if you saw me around campus—since I was still in school when my marriage dissolved—you would think I was handling it well, and possibly even happy about the change. But my good friends, mis hermanxs, knew.

My friends would kidnap me in the middle of the night and insist that I eat, because they knew I had stopped eating. They held me while I cried. They slept over the first few days, because they knew that I couldn't cope with sleeping alone. They helped me move into my new place and made demands of my roommates, telling them to paint my room another color. My friends weren't successful, but it was still beautiful to see them advocate for me.

When I divested from the male gaze, I felt horrified, even when I knew that it was for the best. When I divested from the male gaze, I felt alone, even when I was not. When I divested from the male gaze, I spiraled, and it took a strong community to gather around me and bring me back.

So we did a ritual. In my queer Black and Brown friend group are healers, pastors, justice seekers, and activists, and they understand symbolism. Some even studied rituals for their doctorates. Our ritual was a gathering to perform an act of defiance, as a symbol of dismantling my commitment to the male gaze.

It was early spring 2014. The weather was still a bit chilly in the evenings. All my close friends gathered; I had summoned my greatest loves to transition with me. My friend DJ hosted us, because their home had a firepit. We needed fire for our ritual. With my friends around me—Alba, Andrea, Lis, Tatiana, Carlin, Anna, and DJ—we played drums and tambourines and burned my wedding dress.

I brought all of my grief to that fire and asked the fire to take that from me. I wrote my grief onto a piece of paper and threw it in the fire. I did not want to grieve the thing that had controlled me my entire life up until that point. My total devotion to the male gaze had to be burned with flames.

When I understood that, at a wedding, everyone stands up when the bride walks in because this is considered the most important day of her life, I knew that I needed another ritual to cancel out that initial wedding ritual. A transition had to be made.

My wonderful friends danced around the fire and celebrated me. I knew that was what I needed and wanted, but I still could not completely silence what I had always been taught about needing a man in my life. My wonderful community celebrated me, held me—even when I was not sure if I could in fact be safe out-side the male gaze.

After many tears, we all walked into DJ's home and drank hot tea to warm us up. We gathered and allowed the moment to linger. Staring at nothing, thinking about everything, I found myself experiencing immense pain, but I also felt profoundly loved.

This ritual was a way for my friends to walk me back to earth, back to myself, and it was the most loving act I had ever experienced. My platonic friendships accompanied me through one of the scariest moments of my life. And that night, my friends helped me unload the burden of the male gaze onto that fire.

My ex-husband was not the problem. The problem was that I believed what I had been taught: that successful womanhood meant having a successful hetero marriage. I got married precisely because of that belief. So the ritual had allowed me to release all of that.

I had watched all my expectations of successful womanhood burn, right alongside my intricately beaded white wedding dress. I stared at the dress to confirm that it had completely disintegrated. I needed to see all those dreams destroyed, physically, to begin to heal from them.

Functionally, oppression is domesticating.

—Paulo Freire

That wedding ritual, that acknowledgment of marriage being a fulfillment for the women in hetero relationships, is still felt today. Existing "successfully" as women means adhering to patriarchal structures. We risk losing a lot in our rebellion.

I grew up attending a *very* conservative, nondenominational, Spanish-speaking charismatic church. If that does not already indicate the layers of misogyny that shaped me, let me elaborate the ways. The church we attended was a patriarchal fundamental-ist church, which is the type of church that believes that men are the head of the household and guide the lives of everyone in their home. Men are responsible for guaranteeing that the household follows everything in the Bible, which is the word of God, in order to ensure entrance into heaven upon our deaths.

Men decided how to interpret the Bible, and their word was the word of God and therefore indisputable. For example, according to my father, tattoos were banned because "la Biblia dice," although sometimes this was not true at all. The same text that references tattoos also talks about kosher foods, but my father ignored the latter part. There are selective readings behind what verses were to be followed strictly and which were left open to interpretation, and men got to decide all that freely. Theological interpretations were only invited through a pastoral presence. Pastors are believed to be chosen by God, and God only chooses men.

Congregants were kept in line in their devotion entirely through fear. I grew up constantly hearing about demonios and Satanás. I have no real memories of Walter Mercado, because that channel was quickly changed on our televisions at home. Mi mami called him endemoniado, and I believed it. I feared being exposed to de-mons. In childhood, magic feels possible and imaginations run wild, so I ate it up and believed it all with conviction.

If you were not aligned with God and what God wanted for your life, then you were aligned with Satanás. And I feared Sa-tanás. The psychological warfare was intense, and I often had nightmares about being in hell and meeting Satanás. I experienced sleep paralysis a lot, and when I would cry to my parents about this, I was told that it was a demon trying to enter my body. I was taught how to rebuke the demons, and I did just that whenever I experienced sleep paralysis. They linked my sleep paralysis, a natu-ral phenomenon, to my possible demonic possession, and well into adulthood I believed this to be true.

We also grew up understanding the concept of the capital R: Rapture, or the end of times. It was common knowledge that one day soon, God was going to come and take the true believers to heaven while the pagan non-Christians were left behind and tortured by demons as punishment for their sins. Now as an adult all that sounds silly, but as a child and a teenager everything in my life was about not getting "left behind" or appearing like you would be—because that would raise some flags within this Christian community of people who took it upon themselves to police one another constantly out of "concern" for everyone's soul. Women were policed more than men, and young women were considered to be the most susceptible to sin.

My parents had both been raised Catholic but converted to a more charismatic Evangelical Christianity before my siblings and I were born. And we basically lived at our church. My papi was a pastor, my brother played drums in the worship band, and my sister and I were on the worship dance team. We defined ourselves by our Christianity. We defined our morals through the church. We were only allowed to befriend other God-fearing Christians. Everyone outside was aligned with Satanás.

I recall one day when my parents picked me up from school, and I was talking about my day. I made the mistake of referring to my friends as just that—mis amigas—and my papi stopped me dead in my tracks and said: "Ellas no son tus amigas. Tus amigas solamente son las de la iglesia." I was constantly bombarded with counter messaging to keep me faithful to our Lord and Savior.

Women were not leaders and did not have a voice in this church. My patriarchal fundamentalist church does not ordain women. Feminism is talked about negatively. I have been told to stay away from the deceit of feminism and the traitorous claim that women and men are equals. When I was in middle school, the church leaders from across our various church plants, which expanded across the world, all got together to discuss whether women would be allowed to lead the prayer for the offerings and tithes on Sundays. It was a whole discussion, and they voted on this simple handover as if we were electing a new leader for our cult. The men in my church took seriously their God-ordained role as leaders and cabezas de casas.

Like I said before, mi papi is a pastor. Therefore, he was not only chosen by God to lead an entire congregation, but he also was the head of our household. We had this double understanding of where mi papi stood in relationship to everything, and consequently where mi mami stood. As a little girl, I understood what the reality of my future life in a household and in our church would be. Our patriarchal fundamentalist church was shaping me. Slowly but surely, they were indoctrinating me.

> *Patriarchy is a political-social system that insists that males are inherently dominating, superior to everything and everyone deemed weak, especially females, and endowed with the right to dominate and rule over the weak and to maintain that dominance through various forms of psychological terrorism and violence.*
>
> —bell hooks

Girls in this type of church received only one form of parenting, and it was punitive. My sister and I were guarded like we were porcelain dolls who could be easily swayed away from God. We also were guarded because our purity was a form of male currency. In a church that values female virginity, fathers were valued for their ability to guard our purity.

I was not allowed to have friends who were not Christian, because they would tempt me away from God. I was not allowed to have boyfriends because we would be lustful and have sex, and as mi mami would say: "Para qué calentarse." I was only ever allowed to have amigos, meaning I was not allowed to date. When I was at a marrying age, I was expected to have a friendship with a man with supervision for a short amount of time, always staying at a respectful distance, and then get married. My close community believed that for a woman, a good Christian husband is the prize. The only prize.

And I believed all these things because my parents raised me by these messages. These lessons were taught, they told me, out of love for me. And they'd hit and spank me for any wrongdoing. I had a very real fear of being hit whenever I went against my parents' wishes.

In fourth grade, I was allowed to go to a birthday party. I had begged for days, and my mami finally obliged and gave me a two-hour window to attend this party. We had just barely moved from our neighborhood in Sweetwater to a more assimilated Latinx neighborhood. I lacked the assimilation skills that my peers seemed to have, and social gatherings were where I got the most tangible evidence for how I was different and how to adapt.

I ended up having such a good time. I remember the secular music was cranked up, and everyone started dancing. I also started dancing. My mami and brother came to pick me up earlier than expected, and they caught me. As I was doing the Crybaby, I turned my head to check my surroundings and saw my brother peering at me from the backyard gate of my friends' home. They were spying on me, and I had been caught.

I was hit for going to a party and dancing. And I was laughed at, because it was ridiculous to engage in this type of dancing. This dancing was not done in worship of God, and I was told it was not approved by God, and so was discouraged through the rod, porque la Biblia dice.

According to our church, good girls like me were not supposed to dance or otherwise sexually tempt anyone. To the church, dancing resembled sexual availability. All this was strange to me. I did not think dancing was inherently bad, and it was what defined my role in church; I led the worship dance team. But I also knew how to survive, and so I accepted this contradiction as my reality.

Anything I did other than reflect a good Christian upbringing would lessen my value and therefore diminish my odds of finding a good husband, the prize. I understood that and I had to accept it. Otherwise, I'd be accused of being possessed by demons or spanked until I agreed with them.

I was constantly bombarded with these messages about my place in the world as a woman. I remember talking about my future husband at eight years old. Any interest in marriage and childbearing was encouraged and coded as honorable. When playing with my dolls, my perceived maternal instincts were praiseworthy.

I remember the first list I made of my future husband's qualities. It was the first of many. I was twelve or thirteen years old at the time, and we were attending a Christian event tailored for Christian youth in downtown Miami. At one point, the speaker separated the boys from the girls, because those were the only genders that could exist in that type of church. The girls were given blank sheets of paper, and the female speaker went on to say that she had made a list, which she put under her pillow, with all the attributes that she wanted in a husband. She said the most important thing was that her husband be a God-fearing man. Then she instructed all these young girls to make our own lists about our future husbands, and I remember not knowing what to put. Don't get me wrong; I was a boy-crazy, hormonal preteen, but I was also just a kid who was not thinking that far ahead. Yet, no one around me seemed to skip a beat. We were pitched this future of marriage and happiness as the ultimate goal, and when everyone around me seemed to believe in it, I knew I had to believe in it too.

Anyway, as instructed, at the top of my list was "pastor's son." I remember going home and my mami coming into my room and asking me about the conference. I told her about the list, and she was so proud. She encouraged me to pray, and I went ahead and kept that list under my pillow for about a week before I lost it.

My parents talked about my future husband so often that I knew how dating would look before I was even interested in boys. I was told that if an honorable, God-fearing boy wanted to marry me, he would first approach my parents and then we would be allowed to be friends for a short period of time. Then we were to quickly get married so as to avoid the sin of fornication. Long relationships were discouraged because the sin of sex was considered unavoidable.

I knew that the God I had grown up learning about did not want me to have a boyfriend, so I began to hide things. God cannot compete with hormones; my church taught me this, and then I experienced it. I felt reckless for wanting to kiss people without first figuring out if they feared God. As I got older, I got better at hiding my "lust," and I would do cartwheels to just satiate those hormonal impulses.

Finally, I was nineteen and thought it was time to bring someone home. I thought I was old enough to be on the marriage track and therefore did not need to hide my boyfriends anymore. When I brought José to meet my parents, I was deeply disappointed to learn that, no matter what I had on my list, they had their own list. My parents had their own expectations of who they thought I should be with, and it was all informed by what they were taught in our church. My boyfriend was a self-proclaimed Christian and had attended a Christian school, so I thought I was in the clear— only to discover that his divorced mom was a deal breaker for my parents. According to my church and parents, people do not get divorced, because marriages are pacts you make in front of God that can never be broken. Once that pact is broken, your entire lineage is unworthy.

Me and this boy eventually broke up because my family's passive-aggressive comments became unbearable. I realized that the church was making the decision on who I was supposed to end up with, so I began to resent these rules. In this type of upbringing, boys are born men and girls are never women. Girls only become mothers and their husbands' ayuda idónea.

In that statement alone, my role was defined. I was to be of service to a man because I was theologically interpreted for that singular purpose. I grew up hearing "ayuda idónea" my entire life, and the propaganda got old real fast. Being a stay-at-home mom was the respectable thing; I grew up seeing this practiced in Nicaragua. All the pastors' wives were stay-at-home moms, and I was taught that this was a beautiful gift that mi papi had given mi mami. I was expected to fit into that role all of my life. I get that in a working-class context not working is a luxury, and I understand that it can feel like a gift bestowed by a man to his wife. I saw the value in it, but I saw value in having choices too. Even after we moved to the United States, I was encouraged to aspire to the honorable position of mother and wife and nothing else.

Going to college was never discussed, but marriage and children were often. I was not a good student. There was no real reward at home for being a smart girl past elementary school, and there was no real punishment for being a mediocre student, so I gave up in school. Dancing and being filled with lust were punished, but bad grades and disinterest in school were rarely acknowledged. When my teacher in junior year implied that I should go to college, I immediately reflected on my grades. I was in a bad position with barely a 2.8 grade point average. But then I took the SAT and did decently on it without much effort. It turned out that my grades were not indicative of my potential, because I was still absorbing material. I had a good enough score to apply to a few state schools, much to everyone's surprise.

By then, I had started to think differently about my future. I did not know how to dream about a career or a life without a man, but I had this sense that I could at least try. And, with little help at home, I applied to college and was accepted. When I quickly realized that college was expensive, I knew I had to go to the one place that offered a great financial-aid package: the Hispanic-Serving Institution Florida International University. This meant that I commuted to college, and while higher education had never been the plan for me, once I was in it there was no stopping what I would be exposed to. Being a college student was not something I had a framework for, but somehow I managed to figure it out.

Then I got into my head the idea that I should pursue a graduate degree, and I remember the first time I expressed the notion to my parents. We were having dinner, and my papi audibly laughed and immediately dismissed me. Smart girls were of no use to any husband. That day, mi papi took the wind out of my sails, and I knew that living at home meant that this was always going to be the case.

At twenty-three, after coming to the conclusion that I had no voice because of what I was taught in church, I wanted to run away and create a new reality, respectfully. I should have just run away, but I was too afraid. I took a few theological classes and was starting to really question the validity and value of my parents' theologies. But I still believed what I had been taught, which meant that I felt incapable of explicitly defying my parents.

So, I did what any girl growing up in a conservative, patriarchal, nondenominational charismatic church does to run away from her parents and their God: I got engaged. Or rather, I proposed to my secret boyfriend and, much to my parents' dismay, we got married. I was tired of being told I was not enough, and for some reason I thought partnering up would solve things. Instead, it proved their point.

But I needed to get away. I needed to feel like I could decide something for myself. Although, clearly, I couldn't. I ended up picking, as my ticket to supposed freedom, a God-fearing Christian man from a two-parent household. Still, marriage felt like the only way I could escape my parents' choices—through an institution that I was taught would then dictate my choices.

Eventually I ended up applying to graduate school, and I started classes at Vanderbilt University in the fall of 2011. A lot changed for me when I left my parents' rules behind. I shook off the pressures, and I began to be exposed to things I would never have imagined were possible.

When I saw my friend and colleague Rev. Yolanda Norton get ordained, I sobbed in the pews. I had accepted that other churches ordained women, but seeing it happen with my very own eyes was another story, and I was shaken by it. I did not realize how badly I needed to see a woman ordained. I did not realize how badly I needed to see a Black woman get ordained among a sea of her Black colleagues. I learned about feminist theologians. I was taught about womanism and mujerista theologies. Suddenly the possibilities became endless for me. I began to see myself differently, and I wanted to become an active participant in the things that occurred in my life.

I had a short first marriage. We were young and we changed quickly. I left my husband while in the middle of my master's program. I left my security blanket and I mourned the loss of my old self. I did not know who I was without a man. After my father, after my husband, I had never been given the chance to see what would happen if I was alone.

After my divorce, all I felt was shame. The same shame that I had heard in mi mami's voice when she told my first official boyfriend, José, that his mother's divorce meant he could never be enough. I felt all the words she said to that boy, years earlier; they were carved in my heart with a butcher knife.

I felt physical pain. I was burdened by the shame I was bringing upon myself. And I had to confess to mi mami about my separation and impending divorce. I knew I could not face her and carry her shame, all while packing up my clothes and books and the life I had created in accordance with their rules.

I remember calling my mami from my inflatable bed in a semi-completed basement. My friends had helped me move there; they had packed and then unpacked my things in my new place. After they left, I sat in a corner, barely able to make complete sentences.

When mi mami picked up the phone, I instantly began to cry because I was devastated and scared. I remember my mami screaming at me for doing what my parents had always believed to be a horrible thing, leaving la bendición de un hombre. I had broken my pact with God. I remember hanging up on her, with tears streaming down my face, while she was halfway through a tirade of insults. She was throwing back at me all of my biggest fears. I knew then that I had to release their God for good.

Releasing my marriage and my parents' God were probably the hardest things I have ever done in my life. As I picked up the pieces of my heart and my sanity from that basement floor, I stepped more confidently into this new person I was becoming. I had to. I had to survive this new reality.

I accepted what I had realized years before, that the church that I had been raised in was full of sexist theologies that placed no value in me, wed or unwed. And that same church had vicious language for a woman like me, a used woman, a divorcée, arruinada.

I realized those inner demons who were telling me I was deplorable and was going to die alone, those demons were not demons but remnants of the God I had been raised to believe in. Slowly but surely, I realized that my goal was no longer to be someone's wife. And figuring out who I would become felt freeing.

Growing up in a conservative, patriarchal fundamentalist church meant that I had learned and accepted that I was always to be defined by men. The man who raised me dictated everything about me, and when I was married that same narrative was supposed to continue. Getting divorced meant learning to become my own person, with my own thoughts, and accepting that my reputation was mine and mine alone.

Growing up in a conservative, patriarchal fundamentalist church meant that when I attended a theological school for my master's degree, I was not actually expected to bring that back home, because my church did not believe women were worthy of speaking with God. Growing up in a sexist church meant that I got to see the two most important people in my life turn their backs on me when I needed them the most.

Mi mami and I eventually reconciled, and she learned to love the new version of me, the divorcée. My relationship with my papi has never been the same. The dissolution of my marriage meant that I reflected poorly on him now, and he wanted nothing to do with me. He had no tools for parenting me anymore.

I also learned to see mi mami differently. I used to think mi mami was so weak for enjoying cleaning and cooking. I used to think she was beneath me, and I would tease her to her face about her devotion to her children and her home. I would tell her to want more, and to be more, as if she could. I was unfair. Today, my relationship with mi mami has never been stronger, and my sister and I also rely on one another significantly.

I began to realize that mi mami crawled so I could first walk and then run. Mi mami is a survivor. She, too, left a home that was toxic, and fled it all by getting married herself. I inherited that trauma. Mi mami had initially reacted to my divorce the way she was taught to. But when I demanded to be loved, not despite my "mistakes" but as her strong daughter who had made decisions for herself, she came around and embraced me.

My purity was currency in a church that values female virginity. It was guarded like it was the most definitive aspect of my personhood, and losing it meant defiling my body. I was told all these things about purity culture, and I took them to heart. I was not taught to challenge my upbringing, and it never occurred to me that my parents would ever cause me harm.

In the months after my separation and divorce, I discovered exactly how much shame I was taught around sex, and how much harm was done to me by placing value on my purity. Purity culture is a huge reason why moving out of my parents' home without a husband was so discouraged. When my little sister did move out— the only one of the siblings who was able to do so without getting married first—she was humiliated for it. Her purity was in danger, and her moving out reflected negatively on my papi and his ability to take care of his girls. It also reflected negatively on mi mami: her inability to teach us the proper amount of shame and fear around living alone. I can recall long phone calls with my little sister, who innately knew that she, too, needed to leave our parents' home. She still sobbed about that decision, because she was made to feel like she was causing a scandal. It was assumed that she wanted to be promiscuous, and my parents and my older brother abused and punished her for her sins.

I was not longer living at home when this happened, but I remembered all the rules.

When I got married, I lied and told my parents I was still a virgin. As a teenager, I had decided that if I was going to fornicate, I had to keep the number of sexual encounters at a respectable amount, and I would only fornicate within a long-term, committed relationship. Not only that, but every person I had sex with had first promised to someday marry me, and in my mind I figured that was within a socially acceptable range of fornication. That is how I went around my parents' ideals but still tried to avoid becoming the unforgivable female trope of a whore. This was key, because being a whore meant total exile from respectable, smart, worthy womanhood. I played that game smart, and I played that game well.

When I got divorced, I annihilated all semblance of respectability that I might have had. And once I accepted that I was, according to my church, ruined, respectability was out the window for me. I decided to have casual sex with as many people as I desired, and I decided to have casual sex outside the restrictions set by the male gaze.

My sexual liberation was something I aspired to. Once I divested from the male gaze, the possibilities were thrilling. I had gotten married to please everyone; now I was going to ensure that I pleased myself.

Losing the respect of my parents was one thing, but losing the respect of my peers felt overwhelming. After my divorce, I wanted to resist the social expectation of sexual gratification only within the confines of serious, headed-for-marriage relationships. I did not want what I had been told was safe and best for me.

I just wanted to figure out what I enjoyed sexually. Constantly worrying about social performance—either by hiding sex with boyfriends before I was married, or having sex while married under assumed social approval—meant that I didn't know what sexual pleasure was like outside the context of social approval. I decided it was time to become every father's worst nightmare. It was time for me to intentionally become a whore.

Even if sex was my avenue toward sexual freedom, and even if I didn't care about social stigmas, I knew the threat of physical danger still surrounded me. I was, still, a woman. I could be overpowered by someone who does not understand or does not care how consent works. I began to carry a knife. And I dropped a pin and sent my location to friends when I headed out on dates. I even sent my locations to mi mami; she became my biggest supporter, even of my promiscuity.

Tinder became my playing field, and my first messages outlined my expectations: sex, and nothing else. Because I was living in Tennessee, I vetted responders about their politics and their experiences with Brown girls, because I did not want to be anyone's fetish. I was up-front about my mission to experiment sexually with complete strangers. And I had a blast, but unfortunately I learned some very interesting things about how non-Latinx folks viewed Latinas.

Because the hypersexualized Latina trope is real, people assumed my sexual prowess was part of my culture. I had escaped a cage and was attempting to liberate myself sexually, but I was still surrounded by landmines.

I was once told, before we had even left the restaurant, that I looked like I would be "wild" in bed. I was doing no sexual posturing; I was relaxed and eating fries, not thinking I was supposed to be doing any courting, since that had already been agreed via text. But I was being read as sexual regardless.

I was once told by a lover that I should not attempt to come back to his place through the window, like his uncle's Mexican girlfriend used to do. This man said that his mother had warned him about those "Mexican women." We are all Mexican to white people in Tennessee.

I was often told that I dressed too provocatively, and therefore any negative attention I received was merited. This one was hard, because I heard it mostly from other women.

Sexism is so ubiquitous that women do a good amount of the enforcement themselves. The minute I became publicly single and a self-appointed whore, I lost the respect of women in my graduate program. I became trouble. I became a spectacle, an ethnic spectacle.

Apparently, to some of my peers, my sexual desire translated to my sexual availability. I remember going to chapel with some classmates from my program, and hearing all the whispering around me. I was eventually told I was not dressed appropriately for church. I was wearing a circle skirt, heels, and a crop top. For me, when I no longer felt I had to dress to appear pure, that meant I could start wearing clothes I actually enjoyed. Even when surrounded by some of the most progressive and advanced theological students in the country, I was now being subjected to the same shaming and policing behavior I had experienced in my small-minded childhood church. Again, I felt the same tightness in my chest, that feeling of being trapped. And I did the only thing I could: I told my peers to *shut the fuck up!*

During this time, one of the most admired and prominent scholars in my program, and a woman, told me and a group of my female peers to not wear lipstick in academia, to ensure that we were taken seriously. I remember looking down at what I was wearing and what my peers were wearing, and I understood: less feminine meant more intelligent. That day, I vowed to always wear red lipstick around that professor.

If I allowed anyone else to dictate what I wore or how I looked, then it was not my body anymore. I reclaimed myself, and it cost me a lot. But belonging to myself was the goal, and there was no stopping me.

While in my program, one particular male staffer made advances toward me. Eventually he kissed me, and I was deeply ashamed about the entire situation. I did the dance of, "Did I incite this?" Still, I pushed past my doubts and I reported him to his superior. The whole thing became a show. The Vanderbilt lawyers asked me what I had been wearing and how much I had drunk before the incident, and I was immediately reminded about the shame I had been taught. I felt like I had just begun to live, and they wanted to shove me back into my box and make me behave better. Since the men around me seemed unable to control themselves, I was the one responsible, the one who had to be controlled. The misogyny was unrelenting, and I was close to graduating anyway, so I walked away from the investigation. That is why survivors do not come forward: society will blame us for what happens to us before going after a man with seemingly uncontrollable urges. By that point, I had already lost the support of a dear female mentor and professor, and my peers suddenly saw me as entrapping. The staffer was older and had more power, but to them, I must have asked for it.

I knew that my decision to become independent would cost me. But I also knew how exhausting it was to be a respectable woman, when it meant campaigning every day to convince society that I was honorable. Being a woman is already dangerous, but it is even more so when women give up their own agency.

We are socialized to seek admiration and approval to a fault. When does the social performance end? How many of us will follow the prescribed roles—marriage, motherhood—just to be respected, heard, or legible as adults?

We cannot dismantle a system as long as we engage in collective denial about its impact on our lives.

—bell hooks

My worldview began to shift in graduate school. To fully understand the male gaze and its impact on my life, I first had to redefine what I valued within myself. I had to turn away from my church's teachings on what it meant to be a good woman, and away from its rules around modesty and morality. I began to learn that concepts of purity and protection were actually methods of social control—and methods of justifying male violence toward women. To break with the rule of modesty, I had to embody immodesty.

I had loved crop tops and short dresses. My church taught me that suitable husbands wanted modest wives. Given my background, shorter hemlines and smaller tops were my way to defy the male gaze. I truly was not trying to attract male attention; I was dressing to please myself in defiance of what was "best" for my image, the image of an honorable woman.

Having been forbidden from getting tattoos, my tattoos were an act of reclamation. I had this impulse to claim the skin that wrapped my bones. My flesh was finally mine. One of my very first tattoos was of the word LOCA, because that word had been weaponized against me many times. I had been dismissed with that word for years, by my papi, by other men, even by women. So, I reclaimed the word that mi mami used to insult me when I left my ex-husband. I reclaimed the words that were meant to stop me and keep me in line and well-behaved. I etched that word on my skin and told myself that if being free and happy meant that I was crazy, then so be it. Claiming your body back is a radical act, especially for BIWOC, whose bodies are often crucial sites of oppression.

I learned a lot in the time leading up to that ritual event in 2014. I learned that everyone wants to talk about smashing the patriarchy until it comes time to live those ideals. I learned that allies are rarer than I ever thought imaginable. I learned that there was no way that I was ever going back to being that girl who got married to just to escape a controlling household. I learned to live for myself, rather than for others. It wasn't as lonely a fate as I had feared, and I was happier with the results. But most importantly, I finally understood in my core that a husband was never the prize—I am.

If performing as a "good woman" was a daily campaign, defying male expectations also requires a daily practice. For me, I first had to acknowledge how male expectations had traumatized me and left me unable to define what womanhood could look like without male approval. I had to distance myself from harmful men: men who take up space, men who want to be the center of attention, men who feel emboldened to talk about my body without my consent. There are a lot of these men. I cannot pretend that I am free of all my gendered trauma. Instead, I embrace the skills trauma has taught me about self-preservation. And then I shut out the demands of the male gaze, and I listen to my body.

I do not position myself as palatable to male readers. I won't hold my male readers by the hand. I expect them to understand their complicity in male toxicity. Then I expect them to do the work to undo male supremacy. If society teaches men that they are naturally superior, and our systems reinforce that belief, then it is up to men to disown a system that benefits them.

Even the work I do, I do despite men. I write specifically for women, to resist the indoctrinating idea that the "universal" audience must center men. I also deliberately shield myself from the male gaze. My femme and female friendships keep me in touch with parts of myself I was taught were not valuable. Through these friendships, I have learned a new skill: running away. I had been taught to stay and work to earn male approval. And now I know what that resulted in, so I run unabashedly.

I come from women who have stayed in patriarchal marriages through cheating, public shaming, and emotional abuse, with overall shitty male partners who treated them as inferior from the minute they were wed.

I come from women who, by staying, taught their sons that this was all okay, and those sons then turned against their mothers and treated them as inferior from the minute they felt like they were "men."

I come from women who cried, packed their bags, and wrote goodbye letters, but stayed anyway because they had nowhere to go, because it was unsafe to leave. I come from women who have scorned me publicly for my independence, but who secretly smiled knowing that their nina is brave.

I come from women who have stayed in volatile situations. They did it for their kids, and for their partners, but they never stayed because they wanted to. They stayed because they felt a sense of duty to everyone but themselves.

I come from women who have kept secret bank accounts and crushed sleeping pills into homemade dinners, *just for the fantasy* of a freedom they would never actualize. I come from women who, si pudieran regresar al día que se casaron, would not marry at all.

I come from women who wanted careers but somehow ended up supporting husbands instead. I come from women who stayed because they were supposed to, because the world is cruel, and they said: "Todos los hombres son iguales."

I am a runner. I need to run, because I was taught to stay and I have seen where that has gotten us. So, I take flight, fast, because I need to, because staying means that I will inevitably pass this tradition to my future daughters.

I run, fast. I take vacations. I book next-day flights to exotic locations. I spend an entire day at the beach drinking champagne alone, or I lock myself in my room, block his number, and light candles.

But I run. I run for my own good. I run and carry the women in my line in my heart, even as they stand in shock at my behavior. I run for me and for them, and for all the women who were taught to stay.

I had to unlearn "staying," and learned to run.

I know, I know that running is a luxury. I get it. But I had to pursue this type of self-preservation. Because while running hurts—staying kills.

CHAPTER 9

WHITE FRAGILITY

Whites as a group seem unable to grasp the significance of race. They ultimately misunderstand the world they have created, shocked by the lines on the palm of their own hands.

—Cheryl E. Matias

I have a lot of feelings when I write about this topic because of my own lived experiences with white people who are filled with fear about being revealed as racist. There is a difference between racism and white fragility, because white fragility prevents white people from even having conversations around their own racism. White fragility functions to shift the blame of racism from white people to BIPOC. White fragility buffers white people in their belief that they are always good, and they consider anyone who challenges that belief to be bad.

During my penultimate year of graduate school, I went on a trip with my peers to the Mexico/Arizona border. My graduate program does this trip every other year, and I had avoided it my first year because of my aversion to white saviorism and voluntour-ists. However, when the next opportunity arose, several faculty and staff assured me that this trip was not done without careful thought and reflection. I trusted them when they said they had taken serious measures to ensure the trip was ethically conducted. After I had gone on the trip and I learned what those measures actually were, I was disillusioned with the idea that these kinds of trips can ever be ethical.

We were forbidden from taking photographs of anyone, "the lo-cal color." And the speakers, hostel hosts, and organization leaders we met with were all activist and grassroots organizers, who I was led to believe were compensated fully for their time. There was an abundance of good intentions here.

Academics have mastered the art of saying enough big words to justify some pretty heinous things. But I was still persuaded this time that these academics knew better. They convinced me to join the trip. Turns out I was wrong in that assessment, and this trip would prove all my fears and hesitations to be completely valid.

At one point, we were asked to play with pretend money and to attempt to buy groceries with the equivalent of what someone in Mexico is given as their weekly wage from a machiladora. As if the United States has a living minimum wage to begin with, as if class in the United States is somehow race neutral. These "learn-ing" moments felt more performative than I had anticipated.

And a lot of these immersion practices were still familiar re-alities for me. They were things I was still grappling with as an adult, and I felt that these exercises were playing games with vul-nerable parts of my experience as an immigrant Latina. It was an exercise in empathy and bridge building with immigrants that did not take into consideration the re-traumatization of the immigrant students also in this trip. Clearly, even a trip that purported to be about helping immigrants was designed only for the benefit of white people.

Another thing that we were asked to do was cross the US border, on foot, with our passports. I was the only noncitizen, and because of this the whole group was detained for a considerable amount of time in a separate room as they verified my identity and whatnot. Again, these moments of otherness felt inconvenient to the white students, but they were harsh realities in my life and the lives of so many of us immigrants.

This was an experience curated to show the white students in our program the plight of undocumented immigrant Latinx and Indigenous people from Latin America. Our itinerary had everything you could think of, like walking through maquiladoras, crossing the border on foot through the desert, going to an ICE detention center, and even some discussions with local undocumented artists and activists.

Of course, this class was led by a woman—a Black administrator in our program, Dean Amy Steele. I say of course because white men (who are the majority in academia) focus on more purely academic endeavors and are the ones teaching the dominant required classes and not these ethnic electives. I should also note that of the twenty or so people in our group, I was the only one who was an immigrant.

There were plenty of uncomfortable moments during this entire immersive experience for me as an immigrant, and I cannot even begin to fathom how an undocumented immigrant would have felt in these scenarios. Like the total lack of awareness about the immigration process by my supposed friends and self-identified allies. And the lack of even conversational knowledge about how visas work. Their lack of desire to inform themselves about even these basic parts of immigrant life prior to this trip was baffling.

But there were also surprising moments of significance, rare as they were.

For example, there was a stop during this trip that made it all at least manageable (if not valuable) for me: when we went to see the site where a boy named José Antonio Elena Rodríguez was murdered by a border patrol agent.

In 2012, a fifteen-year-old-boy named José Antonio Elena Rodríguez was shot and killed by a border patrol officer because he was throwing rocks from his side of the border in Nogales, Mexico. A US border patrol agent named Lonnie Swartz shot this boy with his US-government-issued gun. Swartz fired twelve shots, ten of which hit the boy in the back. Swartz was later acquitted.

In the group that traveled to Arizona and Mexico, there were a considerable number of Black students and one other Latina. And hearing this story, seeing the bullet holes on the side of the building, it all hit the Black and Brown students a little differently than the white students. This was in 2014, when the Black Lives Matter movement was gaining ground and conversations around police brutality were starting to penetrate our academic bubble.

And while we held a vigil and stood in silence around this place, one of the Black students nudged me and said, "Let's take a solidarity picture, for us."

I, of course, was happy to have this moment of deep acknowledgment of our shared grief over state-sanctioned murders within our communities. So, together, we both went and tapped the shoulders of the Black students and the other Latina, and we moved a bit away from the group to take this picture, fists in the air. These were the same students who stood up to injustices within our program, the same students who were marching at BLM rallies, the same students who knew how to show up for our communities back home. And standing together during this trip felt poignant for all those reasons.

We were making a statement to white supremacy: You will not destroy us. You will not win. We were holding our pain and finding a way to exist, despite the suffocating whiteness. These rare moments eased the knot in my stomach that I held during this entire trauma-porn-filled trip.

Needless to say, even just one moment of solidarity could not be protected from the imposition of the white gaze. Just before the picture was taken, a white student stepped into the frame. The Black students and students of color looked at one another in confusion. Even then, we had to work to manage and accommodate a white person's impositions. A few of us shrugged.

I was not going to waste energy making a situation out of this white student's blithely ignorant act. She seemed to be unaware that not one white person was standing with us, a detail that all the other white students did not miss. And she seemed unaware that this was not a typical, smiling, tourist group photograph. So, I did the next best thing to maintain the integrity of what we were all feeling. I cropped her out of the picture. I needed to both respect the effort that was made by the Black students and students of color and avoid a confrontation with a "well-meaning" white person. Any intervention was going to end poorly. I realize now that white fragility means that it is not just that white people's feelings must constantly be considered (when our feelings never are). In order to avoid a white person's meltdown and cries of victimization, the only solution is to accommodate their entitlement to always be centered.

Of course, because white fragility permeates the white experience, this student got wind of what happened and became irate. She saw herself excluded and asked to speak with me, as if she wasn't the person who had created the uncomfortable situation in the first place. A moment existed that was not meant for her, and how could something not center her?

I patiently explained to her the situation, and in so many words she told me that I was being homophobic—this white student was also queer. And because she was queer, she felt that her whiteness was invisible, or should have been. She leaned into her queerness and said nothing of her whiteness. I did not continue the conversation with her, because talking to white people about entitlement and how much space they take up is hard, but talking to a queer white person is harder. She thought her whiteness was canceled out by her queerness. Somehow she couldn't be an oppressor, because queer people were oppressed.

On that day, I just nodded and kept moving forward, because no matter what would happen next, I knew she could not see past her own feelings of being excluded. What she had done was invasive, but that did not matter to her. She then sought out solidarity with the other white students for her white pain.

When I talk about white fragility, I am talking about those moments when you encounter a white person who is incapable of having any perspective about their whiteness. They decide not to see how whiteness has harmed and killed so many of us. White fragility requires them to have a certain level of willful ignorance about white supremacy and their participation in it. White fragility means that someway and somehow you, the BIPOC, have become the aggressor and the insensitive one, regardless of the situation and the history of racism in this country. If they are white, they must be right—and who cares where BIPOC stand in that equation?

White fragility has stolen moments from me. How dare I step out from the margins and respect my own humanity? White fragility requires that we stay out of sight. Whiteness always centers itself.

Within academia, white fragility exists in every comment, every group discussion, every social hour. It is precisely the reason that students of color flock to one another and create spaces where we are safe and do not have to walk on the eggshells of whiteness. And in some ways, those spaces that we create become sacred.

I remember the first time I dealt with white fragility without the safety of my posse of radical BIWOC. These women all had a reservoir of self-preservation skills to deal with those moments of dissonance that occur in mixed company. But I was on a different trip, and didn't have their presence to protect me.

In 2016, I was dating a white man who understood my politics and the ways that I moved through the world. We were moving fast romantically and enjoying getting to know one another. Every year, his family goes to Fort Myers, Florida, to spend a week at the beach and relax. He invited me on this family vacation too soon in our relationship. But I attempted to go into that environment as open and friendly as I could be. By that point, I had grown accustomed to being in rooms where no one else looks like me, dresses like me, talks like me, laughs like me, thinks like me, dreams like me—so this all felt like a new normal I had come to accept while at my PWI.

We were relegated to the same condo as his older brother and his family, which included his wife and their one-year-old. Everything seemed fine. Even in one of the whitest parts of Florida. I just tried to focus on the significance of meeting my boyfriend's family.

During this trip, I was informed about a family tradition where each couple took turns cooking meals for the extended group, and each couple claimed an evening to host. I volunteered to make appetizers to show my gratitude at being invited on this trip. I was showing up with the goodwill I rarely bring to white spaces, but I had wrongfully assumed that my white boyfriend, and now husband, is who he is because of his upbringing, and not despite it.

While I was preparing a Pinterest-inspired recipe, my boyfriend's brother came into the kitchen and told me he could not wait to taste my food, because "all Mexican women love to cook." I was shocked, and told him immediately that I was not Mexican and was not making a Mexican dish. He shrugged it off, because to him saying racially insensitive things to a person like me was normalized, because he "did not mean it like that," or because he has been told that racism is only racist when you're wearing a white Ku Klux Klan hood. I would later learn that one of his best friends is Mexican, and that he "lovingly" calls him coconut—white on the inside, Brown on the outside. Through this friend, he had been granted permission to be racist, and he thought that permission applied across the board.

But in that moment, I did not know all the layers of their racism just yet, so I made the decision to also generously shrug that exchange off as a possible slip of the tongue.

Later that week, all the relatives congregated in one unit together, and we drank and hung out. As this was happening, I kept quiet and just listened. I have this survival instinct to make myself small when I feel unsafe. By this point, so as to avoid any confrontations or comments like the one I had received from the brother earlier, I had decided to lay low. I also knew myself, and I knew that if pushed far enough, I would react, and I knew they wouldn't handle it well. White fragility means tiptoeing around white people, a self-policing. So my silence was really to protect them, because consequences to racism is something unheard of for white people who think they are not racist.

Then, one relative was talking to her boyfriend through Face-Time, and she held up her phone to show him the room. She laughed loudly. Turns out, when her boyfriend saw me, he had asked her to inquire if I knew of any good lawn-mowing companies in Chicago. Yes, you read that correctly. I have never lived in Chicago. I had never lived in a home with a lawn that has needed mowing. Apparently, as a Latinx, I was assumed to know lawn-mowing companies across the country. I was the nonwhite person in the room, and their version of a joke.

When she said that, my boyfriend froze. I learned he wasn't going to stand up to his family in the moment. So, I knew that the next time, I would have to defend myself, because if I was going to continue this relationship, I needed to ensure that they knew that

I was not someone they could fuck with. I wouldn't be a joke just because racism was funny to them.

I waited for the next comment. The thing about tolerating racism is that when I am done tolerating racism, any small infraction will carry all the other instances when I resented my own silence and complicity.

I do not quite remember what his brother said next, but it was racist and it was vile and I told him in the calmest tone I could muster that if his employer found out that he was casually racist there was a good chance that he could lose his job. I told him I would have no problem becoming the person who carefully recorded his antagonistic behavior and dutifully informed his employer myself. Then, I got up from the couch and walked out.

I did not cry, I did not stutter when I spoke to him, and I did not curse. I just defended my humanity to people who seemed unable to see humanity in me. I did this, knowing fully the futility of it.

What happened over the next few days is where white fragility thrives. When white people get called racist because they are being racist, they figure out a way to shift the blame. This is peak white fragility, to be so fragile that they forget the actual harm they caused and focus on their own hurt feelings. No attention is paid to address my pain or heal the relationship. White fragility means that someway and somehow you, the BIPOC, are the aggressor and the insensitive one.

The next day, the wife of the brother told me, with a straight face, that I was in the wrong because I could not take a joke. To her, the whole exchange consisted of me being unfunny. Today, the relative who reported the lawn-mowing statement still thinks I am a bitch; she said that I took things "too far." She found a slew of other coded ways to police my behavior, to focus on how I spoke and her dissatisfaction with my tone, and not what caused my reaction. Because, to them, their humanity trumps mine, always. This relative and I do not even exchange glances at this point, because I will not tolerate her behavior. In fact, she has insisted that I am still the aggressor in my silence and has cried to my now husband more than once about her victimization. She has used her tears to further cement my evil intentions, and I have not taken the bait. Somehow, white fragility requires that BIPOC comfort their oppressors.

The brother apologized profusely, and we were able to have a discussion where I felt respected and heard. But those relationships got off to a horrible start, and I have put in minimal effort to repair any of them because I was not at fault. And until they accept that they are racist, I will not put myself in a vulnerable position again. Furthermore, being a person who is not white means that I am tasked with doing the work of making white people see my humanity, and that work is emotionally taxing. It is emotionally taxing to keep my own feelings controlled while white people react and do not think before they speak. We are left to pick the pieces of our humanity up off the floor, all while smiling and graciously bowing out, being the "bigger person." When in reality, I want to scream and cry and fight because that is what their words incite.

> Women of Color in America have grown up within a symphony of anguish at being silenced, at being unchosen, at knowing that when we survive, it is in spite of a whole world out there that takes for granted our lack of humanness, that hates our very existence, outside of its service. And I say "symphony" rather than "cacophony" because we have had to learn to orchestrate those furies so that they do not tear us apart.
>
> —Audre Lorde

So, I decided to not put in labor for these white people, because there was no way in hell I was going to be the "bigger person" for privileged, highly educated white people who should know better. But these white people could not fathom that anything they did or said could be racist, and because they refuse to see the damage, they have done nothing to repair it.

After this vacation, my then-boyfriend and I had a series of very intense conversations, where I questioned his ability to date someone outside his race, and I questioned my own ability to date someone white, considering the circumstance we were in. We had to devise plans for how to react the next time, and there have been plenty of reoccurrences to put those skills into practice. We had to agree on what my role is in those situations and what his role is, because doing nothing and letting me fight the dogs is not my version of a mutually beneficial relationship. And we have come a long way, but that does not mean that white fragility is not impacting us on a regular basis. We had returned to this beach vacation annually since then, and it was a stressful situation every time, for both of us. In 2020, we finally decided to not go back unless his family took serious measures to mend the relationship, a pre–COVID-19 decision. And while the impact of our absence is lost during social-distancing times, we intend on making that statement again and again and again in years to come.

If none of those stories feel familiar or clear, let me tell you about white fragility today by starting with progressive Democrat Amy Cooper. Amy Cooper instantly became a household name for all the wrong reasons. I heard about Amy Cooper from almost the first moment the Central Park video went viral. I stay online pretty consistently to track and monitor these occurrences for my own work on Latina Rebels. I did not actually watch the full video until later that evening, but even from the screenshots and comments early on, I knew exactly what was happening.

A white woman was politely being told that what she was doing was objectively wrong. She had her dog off leash in an area of Central Park where dog owners are mandated to keep their dogs on a leash. Nothing wrong was done in telling her to follow a basic rule.

The person who told Amy Cooper to leash her dog happened to be a Black man named Christian Cooper. To her, his race in and of itself was an escalation; white people view themselves as morally superior to BIPOC, and now here was a Black person who did not know his place. White people will always reject the label of racist, because calling them racist means calling them a bad person, and no white person believes themselves to be a bad person. They've always been taught that white is right, and darkness is deviance. She was innocent, by virtue of her whiteness, and he was somehow criminal and aggressive, because of his Blackness.

Amy Cooper responded to this request by attempting to frame Christian Cooper. In the video, Amy Cooper calls the police and lies; she tells them that a Black man is threatening her. She knew the police would believe and protect her. She hoped the police would frighten and arrest him. Whether intentionally or not, Amy Cooper understood that because she is white and a woman, she could weaponize her whiteness and her gender to endanger a Black man.

In this video, Amy Cooper first warns Christian Cooper that she is going to get him, in so many words. She says she is going to call the cops, and then we see her get on the phone with the police. She tells someone on the phone that she needs help because an "African American man was recording [her] and threatening [her and her] dog." In the video, we see her screaming and agitated on that call, and what seems like tears or a quivering voice in response to her imaged threat.

BIPOC have been conditioned to expect vitriol when confronting white people, and Christian Cooper took out his phone and began to record their exchange to protect himself. A normal interaction would have resulted in one person telling another that they are doing something wrong, and that person would have adjusted their behavior. But we are not talking about normal interactions when we live in a white supremacist society. In a white supremacist society, white people are unaccustomed to being talked to prescriptively by Black people. White people will react violently so as to make the argument that they are not bad people, while simultaneously embracing racist tropes to "win."

> *This defensiveness is rooted in the false but widespread belief that racial discrimination can only be intentional.*
> —Robin DiAngelo

As a woman, I have a response to women in distress. But as a woman of color, I know this woman was not in any danger. When you have positioned yourselves as the purveyors of goodness and benevolence, being told you are not being those aforementioned things feels like an attack. In a society that coddles white fragility, the result is Amy Cooper.

This act of documentation has been a relatively new phenomenon as a way to prove what BIPOC have long been saying: white people will be racist to maintain the racial status quo and then deny their racism in the same breath to maintain their moral superiority. That is white fragility. If that story had been told by Christian Cooper without video evidence, white people would not have believed it. White people would have questioned what else he did, and they would have probed and left that anecdote thinking something was left out, because to them the story makes zero sense. No one would have believed that this white woman would have lied. Because white people are good, and everyone else is bad. Without this video evidence, Christian Cooper might have even begun to doubt what he experienced.

As someone whose side of the story has been routinely disbelieved by white people, I know that too many of us begin to doubt what we experience. You doubt your feelings and recollections and you begin to think that you exaggerated the scale of the situation. I have done this many times, where I thought I was insane. I have even been called insane when I have retold stories about some of my more heated interactions with white people. I have even been told by other BIPOC that I am a liar about my interactions with white people. White people are so convinced of their goodness that we begin to believe it too. We regulate how other BIPOC react to white people's vitriol, and we take the blame for situations that we did not create.

When this ordeal went public, on Tuesday, May 26, 2020, liberal Democrat Amy Cooper released a public apology, after she was put on administrative leave from her place of employment, the investment company Franklin Templeton. She also had her dog taken from her by the rescue center, Abandoned Angels Cocker Spaniel Rescue, Inc. The dog was eventually returned. But the entire internet was upset at her behavior. Her apology had the audacity to state, "I am not a racist. I did not mean to harm that man in any way."

White women are allowed to question other peoples' humanity and are still allowed to be read as well-meaning. White women's tears stop conversations on race, class, and gender in their tracks because white women's feelings are considered sacred. White women become untouchable in a white supremacist society. They can be racist on camera and then deny their participation in their racist actions, and people will believe it. We know, and history knows, that white women are just as complicit as white men when it comes to the oppression and killing of Black people, Indigenous people, and people of color.

White progressives can be the most difficult for people of color because, to the degree that we think we have arrived, we will put our energy into making sure that others see us as having arrived. None of our

energy will go into what we need to be doing for the rest of our lives:
engaging in ongoing self-awareness, continuing education, relation-
ship building, and actual antiracist practice.

—Robin DiAngelo

We have all come into contact with a liberal Democrat Amy Cooper. I remember mine was called Sam. Sam grew up in Florida, like I did. But we grew up in different areas; I grew up in the Caribbean-immigrant-friendly Florida and she grew up in the Trump-supporting Florida. That is a clear distinction for me when we talk about Florida.

In graduate school, I was reading and writing and exploring chola subcultures with the help of Chicanx and Mexican American material. I became fascinated with the similarities that cholas had with what South Floridian Latinxs call chongas. I had identified as a chonga growing up but was shamed out of this identity.

Still, I was fascinated. I wrote about chongas often, and I reflected on this subculture because I was finally learning to make sense of my experiences growing up. In high school specifically, I had created distance from chongas because I needed to assimilate into whiteness, and because people called them cheap and ugly. Chongas were just being proud and bold in their identities and aesthetics, but still, the white gaze considered them threatening.

In graduate school I was finally learning the language around this subculture by studying chola subculture. I was finally embracing my identity and started posting about this on Facebook, when this white woman in my program privately messaged me.

We were both in the same progressive graduate program, but we were two years apart. We had been friendly toward one another, which was my first mistake. I have learned that liberal white people will be white people before they are liberal—leaning into their whiteness as is convenient, and leaning into their liberal ideals with that same strategy.

In her message to me, she said she did not like that I talked about chola subculture because she was bullied by cholas and was scared of them. She also said that their "gang affiliations" should be noted, and that I had a responsibility to not uplift such a violent group of people.

I was floored. Still, like many BIPOC, I had learned to disengage because reason is not the friend of white fragility. I told her she was being racist, and then I immediately blocked her from all my social media accounts. And when I heard how she had told others her version of the story, I was of course the aggressor and she was the victim of my aggression, despite the fact that I was minding my business and she slid into my DMs.

Understanding white fragility means self-preservation. I am not comfortable in rooms that are predominantly white, because white people have shown me that my presence is only enjoyable so long as I do not object to how they choose to interact with me. I am not comfortable in rooms that are predominantly white, because white women have shown me that I am to be grateful for their friendship, and that they enjoy our friendship only so long as they can dictate how it looks and feels. I am not comfortable in rooms that are predominantly white, because white people can be racist and the only acceptable response is to laugh it off and hide my humiliation. I am not comfortable in rooms that are predominantly white, because I have to watch what I say and how I say it, because otherwise they will assume that they can say things like, "I went to your country once with my church group, and the people are so beautiful and humble."

In these interactions, it becomes mandatory that I am receptive and positive, never to respond in anger or push back or even feel hurt. White people demand docility from us, and when that demand is not met, we are treated like social pariahs at best or, at worst—well, just look at the prison population or the latest trending hashtag.

Criminalizing Blackness means that Brown people are given the terrible option of either aligning ourselves with white people or suffering similar results. And aligning ourselves with whiteness has never saved us from anything. White adjacency just enables white supremacy. Being "one of the good ones" just turns you into a tool for white people to use to attack "the bad ones." If you do not get that, you are not paying attention.

But even so, Brown girl, whatever choices you've been backed into, I know you are trying to survive as someone Brown in a racist country. More importantly, I hope to make moments of dissonance with whiteness and white people feel less suffocating. I hope you start reframing racist interactions with fragile white people as just that. I hope that you feel free to wash your hands of their fragility and racism, but it is not about you—it is bigger than you—so do not let these moments take the wind from your wings.

Do not let them silence you or insinuate you are the aggressor. In fact, boldly pick up that phone and start recording, because most video recordings are legal with or without consent in public places. That is how we will persevere.

Keep showing them how ugly they are, keep exposing their vitriol, and keep putting them on blast.

I audio record most of my interactions with white people. The majority of states allow one-party consent, meaning you can be the one party who consents to said audio recording. Look up your state laws around audio recordings in public and private spaces. Keep those emails, screenshot those texts and download them into your laptop. They are not going to stop shifting blame, so we might as well create endless archives of these encounters for us to know who to stay away from and who to create communities alongside.

These videos, audio recordings, emails, and texts all serve as reminders that our experiences with white fragility are real. We cannot be gaslighted into believing that there was no harm done.

Whatever happens, affirm what you know to be true within yourself first. Then empower yourself to self-preserve. Set rules with the white people you choose to trust. Create boundaries for yourself, and decide when and whether you want to educate them. Do not succumb to their guilt if you need to shut someone down or cut someone out of your life for your own mental health. Do not shrink yourself for their comfort. Fight hard to find your footing and center yourself. Do what you must to protect yourself.

And find your people. You literally cannot do this alone. So find your people, push against individualism, and push toward community. Challenge yourself to be less alone by decolonizing what it means to live in a white supremacist society as a BIPOC.

CHAPTER 10

DECOLONIALITY

[Decoloniality] is a way, option, standpoint, analytic, project, practice, and praxis.

—Walter D. Mignolo and Catherine E. Walsh

Like I have said, I am the first in my family to do a lot of things, specifically in the realm of education. I longed to be seen as cerebral and rational. I knew what made women valuable in my community, and it was not their abilities or intelligence. In fact, I have never heard mi papi call a woman smart. The first time I saw a woman preach at a church, I was in my midtwenties and the men wouldn't comment on her words; they only wanted to opine on her body, clothes, and hair. I remember them talking about her untamed curly hair, and that it made her look "loca." What she said was not discussed because it was not valued. I have heard mi papi weaponize his misogyny to silence me, mi mami, and my sister. And when I have pointed this out, I have been dismissed.

As a result, all I wanted to do was run toward the very values that were dismissed in women. Once in college, I joined clubs for brainy people; I tried to situate my worth in relationship to my braininess. When I gained admission into a touted elite private university, I felt validated. And all of my accolades began to go to my head. As I saw myself rising toward the status of *intellectual*, I knew that back home I was being perceived differently.

I know I had deliberately sought out this distance, but when I did come home and saw what I had done, I didn't have the sense of accomplishment and pride I thought I would feel. Instead, I just felt distant from my own family and friends. I had transformed myself, but I did not foresee the ramifications of this change. The thing I was told was going to make me stand out became the thing that eroded my community ties.

I began to feel like I was better than the people who made it possible for me to do what I do. And when I was around the intellectuals, the ones I thought I wanted to be like, I felt alone. Because I was not like them; to be an intellectual and working-class is as ironic of a statement as it gets.

When I first read about decoloniality, I started to shift and question what I had been taught, including about superiority and intellectualism. And that work of unlearning, for me, started with how I viewed mi mami.

Up until the point that I gained the language to name and understand decoloniality, mi mami and I only had a surface-level relationship based on our shared gender and oppression due to the men in our lives. But otherwise, we lived in entirely different realities. As I shared earlier, growing up in a fundamentalist, patriarchal Christian tradition meant that I developed maladaptive skills to survive, and those maladaptive skills meant that I measured my worth through colonial concepts like the male gaze, respectability politics, and meritocracy. As I constructed this image of intelligence during college, I knew that women were not seen as intelligent, and so I was urged to downplay my femininity and align myself with the men around me. I did not have many female friendships, and I had male lovers.

My maladaptive survival skills meant that I sought male approval. I had understood that since men were the respected ones in society, winning them over was a strategy for rising above other women. I wanted to be different from other women, and in seeking male approval I did not build a real relationship with the one person who loved me more passionately than anyone else in my life. Finding my way back to mi mami was a healing decolonial practice.

I am mi mami's revolution, I am the dreams she dreamed, and I am the possibilities she spoke into my Brown body. But learning to value that type of love took time, and if I am being honest, I think it took me way too long to get here.

Mi mami is not terca, nor is she ignorant, nor is she someone I need to teach all of my academic knowledge to forcefully, or even at all. Mi mami is a fountain of knowledge and wisdom that I was taught to not respect.

I have a mami who loves me, despite how much she will try to indoctrinate me into becoming a mujer virtuosa. She is a product of her time and her societal limitations. To her, where I have been and where I am going is entirely different than what she imagined for me, and when I was younger, I resisted her and argued with her nonstop.

I felt like she suffocated me, but not because she was more aggressive than mi papi with her indoctrination. Rather, I valued her less, and therefore her guidance felt like a burden.

I have been able to do things that no one in my family has ever dreamed of doing, and I thought that made me more special than other women. I thought I was more special than other Brown immigrant women.

And then, one day, mi mami said something that I will never forget. She looked straight at me and said: "Yo no soy estúpida." Like she knew what I was internalizing and she knew what I thought about her without me uttering a word. She was right. I thought she was too emotional, too irrational, and too different. She was not like me. I created an image of myself that was as far from her as I could imagine. I reshaped myself to get away from her.

I have a mami who dreams of our mistakes before they happen. I have a mami who gets "feelings" about things and warns us, randomly, much to my embarrassment growing up as an immigrant trying to assimilate. I have a mami who has kept a part of her spirituality alive, a nonmainstream type of spirituality that is messy and unpredictable, which goes against everything within Eurocentric Christianity.

When mi papi suspected he was diabetic, it was mi mami who suggested first that he put his urine in a bowl outside. She said that if the bowl had ants in the morning, then we would know for sure. Mi mami is wickedly smart and does not devalue ancestral knowledge in the ways that modernity teaches us to do.

And somehow, I could not see her wisdom as valuable for decades. I have a mami who is strong. And still somehow, with my newly acquired book smarts, I forgot.

When mi mami read my mind on that day, and knew exactly what I was thinking without me ever saying any of it, mi mami pulled me back to reality. The veil of superiority was lifted instantly. I saw this woman fight for her daughter, and fight to see her daughter outside of these impossible colonial narratives. It is like she knew I was not meant to be included within intellectual circles, and she challenged me to see yet another space that displaced me, this time from her. I saw a mami demand respect out of someone she respected—someone she raised to be respected—and I felt embarrassed.

Mi mami is where she is today because she is a survivor.

Mi mami received the education she was given access to. She had aspirations outside of motherhood; she wanted to be a reporter or a detective. When disasters happen—floods, fires—when everyone flees, mi mami runs toward danger. Growing up, mi mami would put us all into her Kia Sorento and storm chase hurricanes with her three children in the car.

I have a vivid memory of our car almost floating because we were driving in a flooded area of town. Everything had just been ravaged by rain a few hours prior. Mi mami wanted to see the damage up close. Growing up, I would groan and complain about her escapades, but this is how she gets to fulfill that part of herself that she could never fulfill, because not everyone gets to go to good schools. Not everyone gets to go to college. Some of us have to play this game of life with no cards, and surviving is the goal, not winning. The game was rigged to begin with.

Mi mami could not become who she dreamed of becoming growing up, because of societal expectations and lack of money. Instead, she decided to love the person she became: *mi mami.*

So, the minute that my education teaches me to look down on her, I have failed her and myself. Not only that, but my education has failed to teach me how to treat people with compassion. Modernity had institutionalized me through the uninviting ivory towers, and then spit me back to my communities without the proper tools to help them. Liberation cannot come from institutions not built for us.

Mi mami disagrees with who I have become, in more ways than I can name.

Mi mami would prefer that I be a stay-at-home wife and mother, not traveling and working.

Mi mami has told me that she is scared that I do not have kids yet, because quien me va cuidar cuando sea viejita.

But mi mami also has a glow in her eye when she hears about me being flown across the United States to speak to college students. Mi mami has told my sister, when my dad has treated her poorly: "Si Priscila estuviera aquí, ella me hubiera defendido."

Mi mami knows no man will ever treat me like she is treated, like some of her friends are treated, and like some of her friends' daughters are treated. Mi mami is proud of me and shows me that in her own ways.

I am proud of her, I am proud that she has always fought. Even when she does not win arguments or decisions are made without her input, she has pataleado and screamed and never succumbed to making herself invisible, and I have seen that resistance. I have learned from her how to resist the labels, to resist shame, to resist control.

Mi mami would tell me about how a partner should treat me by sampling from her own marriage. Since I was young, I knew that men should not lay their hands on you, and male partners should not make decisions about the shared household on their own, and that a true partnership demands mutual respect. I know all this because whenever she was wronged, by our church and mi papi, she would tell me eso no es bueno. She would confide in me in moments that felt like they could sully my own perception of what is good and not. Yes, she stayed, but she imagined with her words a new reality for me. And she did small acts that showed me that sometimes outsmarting systems can be rewarding. It was mi mami who owned our home in Managua before we migrated. When all the elite Nicaraguans fled the country after our civil war, empty houses were left behind, and our president allowed the citizens to claim these empty homes. Mi mami scouted homes until she found ours and claimed it; the deed had her name in it. She was a homeowner before any other woman in her family. I had no liberative models that I could mirror, but I had words, affirmations, and her acts of bravery to guide me.

I am the product of my parents' migration and their sweat and tears, and although mi mami does not understand me, she believes in me, because she believes in herself enough to fight. And her fight is what I carry.

She has redefined what it means to raise "good" kids, because her kids defied her original definition. She has adapted and she has outsmarted the rules and the indoctrination. Mi mami, in embracing me today in all my flaws, has defied a family history of shunning kids who went against the grain. Mi mami, in embracing me today, has defied herself, and so she has reinvented herself. The mami I grew up with is different than the one I know today.

The one I know today looks at me in my eyes when she speaks to me, and she is mine as much as I am hers. The mami I know, I respect with every ounce of blood running inside of me. Decoloniality gave me that. It gave me a new appreciation for mi mami.

I am not better than mi mami, but I have opportunities at my fingertips that she could never even dream of—and I cannot forget that it is mi mami that I have to thank for my new possibilities. Because while both parents moved us here, she was the one who raised me and protected me.

When I say I am mi mami's revolution, I mean I am who she could not become. I am because of her, and everything I do, I do for her. I no longer want the approval of whiteness, the acceptance of the male gaze, the acceptance of the church, the acceptance of coloniality.

Rejecting individualism is part of that narrative. Embracing re-existence is how I can thrive despite what is force-fed to me and to our society at large. Re-existence gives me wider perspectives of our joined humanities.

> *[Re-existence] is the redefining and re-signifying of life in conditions of dignity.*
>
> —Adolfo Albán Achinte

To re-exist, we have to reimagine life outside of coloniality. We have to reject our colonizer's need to name and define us BIPOC. Decoloniality is a tool, a worldview, one that is always ready to be activated. When we divest from one colonial institution, like the assumed superiority found in elite university education, we know that there are still all the other institutions that exist right alongside it. We cannot undo centuries of colonialization, but we can resist its control over us. Recently, I was verified on Instagram. This sounds like phenomenal news through the colonial veil. Verification adds a semblance of legitimacy. A PhD also imparts legitimacy in the eyes of the empire. These may seem like accomplishments with their own color-blind merit. But status or praise or education was never the goal—legitimacy is the goal, or so we are taught.

However, legitimacy is granted by proximity to whiteness, as measured by white institutions and by white systems of power. Legitimacy means being seen by white people, being acknowledged by the white gaze.

Think of the discovery of the Americas: Even that word "discovery" implies that these lands had not already been discovered by Indigenous peoples long before colonizers came. The idea that the Americas were only discovered once whiteness arrived means centering Europeans. White people decided that their whiteness alone entitled them to the power to name and claim and discover. That is because colonizers view their reality through their eyes, and legitimacy comes with fitting ourselves within their gaze—the colonizers' agenda. Coloniality is rooted in the colonization of the Americas and beyond. White people claimed themselves as the original legitimizers.

Colonizers are the gatekeepers of legitimacy. And this continues to be the case today online. I have seen white creators get that same legitimacy with half the effort. Meanwhile, I have traveled to more than one hundred campuses to speak on racism, anti-Blackness, anti-Indigeneity, and the complexities of Latinidad since 2014. I created one of the more radical and empowering pages online for Latinxs in 2013, when there was no real representation for the vastness of Latinidad: Latina Rebels. I have been featured in countless publications online and in print, was invited to the White House in 2016 for my work, and have written more than two hundred articles that have been published online since 2015. But my audience is Black and Brown, so I went unseen. I was not legitimized year after year. Even for that White House invitation, I had been unseen by the white gaze. It was a young Latina, Dulce Ramírez, who was interning at the White House Initiative on Educational Excellence for Hispanics, who sought me out. It was she who brought my name up in conversation during her first week as an intern. Somehow, while planning the first ever "Latinas in the US" summit, hosted by the Obama administration, Dulce mentioned me. But usually we Brown and Black people do not get that kind of access.

And still it took seven years of doing this exhausting work before Instagram reached out to me in 2020. They wanted to "provide support" because they had just discovered me. The idea that people's work is not worth respect because it fails to cater to whiteness is rooted in colonialism. They will claim they discovered you—and delegitimize the years of work and blood, sweat, and tears spent on centering Brown experiences—because they have a different threshold of accomplishment for Brown folks. The problem is not that my work is not legitimate; it always has been and always will be. Understanding decoloniality is understanding that whiteness is not the ultimate source of validation, no matter how much they have screamed in our faces that we must give them that power.

Decoloniality is about taking back the power that was stolen from us. The problem is that there are not enough of us in the rooms that make these decisions about legitimacy. Additionally, the problem is in the word itself, and to re-exist means to redefine it. So, I do not feel elated or grateful that I am now "legit" through the white gaze, which in this instance is Instagram. Rather, I am happy that I have never catered to the white gaze and, somehow, I got a blue check mark. But that blue check mark is very overdue, and so long as other Black and Brown creatives continue to be shadow-banned online or otherwise ignored, we are not free. I am not free.

> *If you have come here to help me, you are wasting your time. But if you have come because your liberation is bound up with mine, then let us work together.*
>
> —Lilla Watson

When we stop trying to find validation in the eyes of our coloniz-ers, when decide not to strive and beg for cookies from them, then we will never be satisfied with their crumbs, no matter how they package them. When we shed the individualism of white suprem-acy, we can actually begin to create communities among BIPOC. We can then refuse individual incentives, and instead work toward our communal benefit.

For me, that invitation to the Obama White House in 2016 was another moment of clarity. I remember feeling conflicted because legitimacy is alluring. I loved thinking that that invitation meant I was not a fluke. Being taken seriously was and continues to be important to me, but my definitions of success have changed dras-tically since.

When I received that invitation to the White House, I immedi-ately called mi mami and papi. I had them on speaker, and I told them in my most vainglorious way that Obama had invited me to the White House, as if it was not just some committee of people. But despite all my efforts to pitch my legitimacy to them, all I re-ceived in return were crickets.

I was dismayed, because as someone who has never been able to impress her immigrant parents, all I wanted was their recognition. I often battle internally between what the white gaze would find impressive versus what my immigrant, working-class parents find impressive. And the conclusion is always that they are not the same audience. I know that I need to stop treating my colonizer's accolades like they define me, because they do not, especially not to my parents.

But still, I am a person who has to continually learn and relearn how decoloniality has impacted all aspects of my life. So on that day when I called to share with them my big news, from Obama himself, I repeated myself. Maybe they hadn't heard the first time. Then mi mami said: "Que bueno!" And then she went on to ask me about something irrelevant to the enormity of the news I had just shared. I hung up and I cried, because I could not wrap my mind around their indifference. Younger me would have chalked it up to sexism and their overall expectations of me due to my gender. But today, I know that their indifference was bigger than that. I have begun to realize that I cannot serve two gods at once; I cannot expect my parents to have the same expectations for my life as American white people. There was no reconciling these expectations.

What I mean by serving two gods is that I cannot fully embrace the white gaze when I have immigrant parents who have had to adapt differently to it. My parents accepted westernization to survive, and I have had to assimilate to potentially thrive. We are not the same people, and my accomplishments are not even on their radar because those accomplishments are not really possible for people like them. People like me—proud, immigrant, working-class BIWOC—we do not get invitations to the White House. So, re-existing for me is finding ways I can utilize my faux legitimacy to create a life of dignity for my parents and for others like them. In their flourishing, I can find real legitimacy, real validation, and healing.

What I had done was replace one colonial institution, my very conservative fundamentalist church, with another colonial institution, academia. I made the mistake of thinking one was better than the other, when in fact they function in the same ways. Both of these colonial institutions are meant to indoctrinate BIPOC for seemingly our own good, and recompense in both of these worlds is only found through total devotion, an unquestioning loyalty. Learning to reject all that I had assumed was my identity was hard, but it was necessary for me to begin to truly live.

[The oppressed] discover that without freedom they cannot exist authentically.

—Paulo Freire

My successes are nothing if they are mine alone. And my legitimacy means nothing when I earn accolades in isolation and without uplifting those around me. Decoloniality allowed me to finally understand that. I cannot claim that I can fully decolonize my mind and worldview; I'm sure that there are aspects of my life where I still cling onto colonial frameworks. But I am willing to do the work it takes to resist colonization when I do encounter it.

That is not to say that liberation is easy. In fact, it is the hardest series of awakenings that I have had to contend with. It is not fun to exist and stand firmly and proudly in the margins with both my body and my mind. It is painful to unlearn everything I had fought so hard to learn. But this is the work of liberation.

Because mi mami and papi are unimpressed with what has become of my life and my work, I have to keep rethinking why I am impressed with the work I do. I have to think about what it would take for me to no longer feel impressed by my own work.

I did not end up going to the White House that year; I took a deep look at myself and knew that accepting that invitation meant complicity. Obama deported more undocumented Latin American and Caribbean people than any other president in the history of this country. This is also not just about President Obama, but the history of the United States and how my own familial lines have been impacted by past presidents. This is about the acts of terror that US presidents have enacted on people throughout the world since the creation of the United States.

And because I began to see my legitimacy through a different lens, I knew that I could not endorse that presidency or any presidency through my presence. I intimately know what complicity can look like; I did it for the majority of my young life. By not attending, I wanted to ensure I signaled first to myself that I am ferocious, with or without them. I also wanted to inform the greater powers, through my protest, that I saw them and I knew their game. I also knew their game was rigged. But I am going to win without them.

The master's tools will never dismantle the master's house.
—Audre Lorde

I utilize my White House invitation to signal my legitimacy to white people but never to signal my legitimacy to the people whose humanities are tied to mine. Mi papi and mami taught me that, and for that I am grateful. To the people whose liberation is tantamount to and tied with my own, I show you compassion and kindness, and I wrote this book for you. I call this my love letter to BIWOC.

I do not come from people who valued their worth in relation to their education. Due to migration and colonial frameworks for what is worthy and respectable, not all degrees transfer and not all careers in our home countries become viable in the United States. Mi mami never graduated college, and mi papi's teaching degree means nothing in the United States unless he is able to go back to school to fulfill whatever arbitrary requirements are imposed by American exceptionalism. This is hard to do when you are the sole financial provider in your household and you have bought into the toxic idea that men need to work and women need to stay home to raise children. There is simply no time to transfer a degree when you are busy with surviving. So, education and degrees had no value in my household, because when you understand struggle intimately, you understand that those things are not created for your benefit.

I wrote this so we can build together, because to them we are not human, but together we can be unstoppable. Relinquish the lies they told you about yourself, and build outside their white institutions and systems of power. Let's build with our communities in mind, en masse, and shut them out. They can keep the shrinking world they created for themselves; we were never wanted there in the first place. Decoloniality is woven throughout this book: Democratizing knowledge is a decolonial practice. Storytelling used to resist Western ideals and to resist the gatekeeping of knowledge is a decolonial practice. Refusing to use academic jargon, which was designed to confuse and obscure, is a decolonial practice.

Breaking hierarchies, dismantling allegiances to whiteness, scrutinizing the concept of legitimacy, and centering nonwhite people are all acts of decoloniality. Reimagining or re-existing is a decolonial concept that attempts to create a world in which our dignity as BIWOC remains intact. The living and breathing relationship that I have with mi mami today is a decolonial practice that I live out daily. Decoloniality is about divesting from colonial concepts, structures, and institutions as much as possible, even while knowing that colonialization is here to stay. Decoloniality is a form of resisting, and decoloniality is lived and experienced daily. Decoloniality requires that we fight, and I have a reservoir of fight left in me. But it also requires us to rest and be gentle with ourselves.

Plan for this to be a lifelong fight, because it is. And ensure that you have rituals of healing and significant ways of caring for yourself, to create a reservoir. Prepare for those moments when the wind gets taken out of your sails, because this will happen. The entire system relies on our complicity, and when we step out of line, we are destined to become targets. So find what your community needs, what your community values, and you will be surprised with how much you will learn.

I aim to work as tirelessly to continue to embrace my Brownness as I used to work to fit into whiteness. I hope to redirect that energy to create spaces for us, because I do not wish my experiences on others. I do not want to prepare people for the harshness of this world; I want to change it. Freedom is not a destination, it's a communal journey.

May it heal you, may it challenge you, may it make you laugh, but most importantly, may it lead you back to you.

CONCLUSION

To gain the word
To describe the loss
I risk losing everything.
—Cherríe Moraga

I have struggled a lot with ending a book that is still being written. I believe that there is no summit when it comes to the journey toward learning and growing. Everything I learned in academia has been supplemented and expanded upon since I left, and there will always be more to learn.

It is hard to conclude something about systemic social ills, knowing that different strategies will need to be continually developed. There is no easy solution that is going to be effective at eradicating inequality forever; overcoming one injustice means having to turn to the next injustice. But since I must end this book, I will part with a few words.

Brown girl, this world does not want to see you survive it, so defy it and dare to thrive. And desahógate to stay tender and soft. Desahógate to shake them off you. Tuve que aprender new ways of existing, and desahogándome often. Self-preservation is one of my new skills that I will carry with me as I continue to heal and learn better ways to keep our communities safe.

Yo me desahogue because that is how I resist a history of silence and complicity. Me desahogue para incomodarme. Me desahogue so you can sample from my stories, and find your own.

Me desahogue to resist, because at some point, I began to create hierarchies where I devalued where I came from and chose to value intellectualism more than I valued anything else. Me desahogue to remind myself that my vulnerability and my community, not colonial institutions, will heal me.

Decoloniality helped me understand why I never felt safe in any space, and it helped me find peace in creating new spaces, for me and for us. Creating Latina Rebels was a decolonial practice. When I did not see myself represented, I did not wait for change. Rather, I made change that I could realistically do long-term. I learned to find my worth from my community, and not from white institutions. But that all took time, and it took years of unlearning colonial thinking in order to learn a new way of living: re-existing.

In my desperate attempts to assimilate and seem less different as an immigrant of color, I began to value myself through colonial terms. Colonization is about nation-states who dominate, kill, and oppress people to gain economic growth and power. In the Americas, colonialism was introduced through religion and conquest by European countries. To do decolonial work means to attempt to function outside of the social norms that exist today. Decolonial work attempts to reclaim some of the power that many Brown and Black people were killed to obtain.

If you learn anything from me, learn to desahogarte. By owning my voice, by allowing myself to desahogarme, I have found myself. I was taught that complicity and silence will save me, and doing the opposite of what I was taught is peak Brown girl self-preservation. Desahógate alone, desahógate with friends, desahógate with family, desahógate to release and to gain your footing.

As Black and Brown women, we do a lot of emotional labor for our families, friends, partners, communities. And learning to step back and actively take care of yourself, in a society that does not value your life, is the decolonial practice I want you to walk away with. Your ability to thrive is based on building a community that can carry burdens alongside you.

Desahógate to find them, because they are somewhere desahogandose solitxs, and we need to be doing that together to actually make it. Because, Brown girl, we need each other.

ACKNOWLEDGMENTS

I want to take a moment and prop up my husband. He is not only my biggest cheerleader but also my best friend. We have laughed, cried, and even panicked together about the enormous task of writing a book. Thank you for your patience, decorating my office, ensuring my writings were properly backed up, and always telling me I can do anything. I lived for thirty years with no one believing in me, and then I met you and not only did you believe in me, but you invested in me.

I do not want to pretend that writing a book is easy, or that getting a book deal is an option available to everyone—because it is not. These industries gatekeep and, for me, becoming an author required having a partner who was financially stable enough to allow me to dream. I dedicate this book to my husband because I know that racism, classism, sexism, and xenophobia would have blocked me from a writing career. He leveraged his overwhelming privilege in society to prop me up, to grant me the space to write this book. I am not unaware of the fact that it took the help of a white man to get me here, and I am still grappling with that. But I intend to do the same for those coming after me; I will use every privilege I possess to prop others up, and hopefully we can create a critical mass of people who will change entire systems.

My devotion to my craft took two people: me and my wonderful life partner. Thank you for believing in my dreams and always pushing me toward what I thought was impossible. Thank you for your kindness and your unrelenting watchfulness. For sneakily showing up to business meetings at my request and to no one else's knowledge. I laugh when I think about you hiding behind plants and menus. I can see your face smiling at me from across restaurants, your eyes always believing in me and your actions always backing that up. You have shown up for me in ways that I did not think were possible. You have seen this entire process intimately; you know how much I cried and how much I have struggled with what it means to write my trauma down for others to learn. I can never thank you enough, and I cannot wait to see where life keeps taking us. <3 gracias, amor.

Also, there are a lot of people whose shoulders I stand on. I want to thank my mentors in graduate school, Rev. Dr. Cristian De La Rosa, a professor at Boston University's School of Theology. Thank you for opening doors and utilizing institutional power to create spaces that felt safe for me and other Latinxs. I also want to thank Rev. Dr. Daisy Machado, the director of Hispanic Summer Program and a professor at Union Theological in NYC. She gave me a job working on the social media pages for HSP back in 2013, which gave me tools that helped me at the inception of Latina Rebels. She has also held me real close in her arms and shown me warmth more than anyone in academia has dared to show. I want to thank Rev. Dr. Stacey Floyd-Thomas. Without you, I would have dropped out of Vanderbilt Divinity School. Thank you for taking up space and for your unapologetic brilliance. I learned more from being around you than I did any other professor in that entire institution.

I want to thank two of my readers: Zahira Kelly-Cabrera, who is known as @bad_dominicana on Twitter, and Cassandra, who is the founder of AnFemWaves (formerly known as Xicanisma). Zahira and Cassandra have a sharpness that no one within academia possesses, and I mean that with all the admiration in the world. Their critical-thinking skills combined made me rewrite entire chapters, and I cannot thank them enough for their contributions to my book. When it comes to doing critical race theory, I have found nonacademic BIWOC to be better versed and more knowledgeable about it all. I stumbled into Zahira's tweets in 2013, and she opened a new reality for me through them. Similarly, in 2014 when Xicanisma was born, I saw someone who stood her ground and did it brilliantly, in Cassandra. These two women are foundational to why and how I do the work I do today.

I also want to thank Kristian Contreras, a PhD student at Syracuse University and overall badass who took the time to share all her resources with me (over one hundred books virtually) and read some of my chapters with care and intention. I needed your eyes, but I am always surprised to see your heart in full display. Thank you for your love and your words. I want to thank assistant professor Dr. Maria Chaves Daza at SUNY Oneonta. It was she who first introduced me to La Malinche and that entire field of study. I messaged her when I began writing this book, and she happily gave me her bibliography. I am ready for another Noche Buena together, girl!

My two main readers were former peers of mine at divinity school, Rev. Alba Onofrio and Rev. Dr. Lis Valle. You two read the entire book alongside me, helped me find areas of weakness, and pushed me to say what I needed to say rather than what I wanted to say. You honed my voice and lovingly pushed me to sharpen it.

I also want to thank my agents, Aemilia Phillips and David Patterson. It took me two years to finally finish my book proposals, and more help than I can fully explain within a few short sentences. But thank you for believing in me and seeing the vision of this book. Additionally, my editor, Emi Ikkanda, is God-sent. She understood what I was trying to say and encouraged me all along the way. When I made mistakes in my writings in the past, I was treated like an imbecile. So when selecting an editor who I wanted to work with, I asked very bluntly if any editor was accustomed to working with an author who learned English as a second language. Emi gently replied with her own family history with learning English as a second language, and ultimately that is why I picked Emi as my editor. With her, I have felt valued for the skills I do have and not devalued for my writing errors, which are simply a product of my migration. I wrote a whole book in my second language, and it was celebrated by my editor throughout.

Last but not least, I want to thank mi mami, Blanca Azucena Mojica Rodríguez. To the strongest and most beautiful mami a girl could have ever hoped for, gracias. Mi único anhelo es que tu estes orgullosa de mí, lo demás nunca ha importado. Te quiero mucho y por siempre.

I am nothing without the strong, witty, and beyond radiant Black women and Latinas who have taught me how to love myself better, and how to love others. This book is mine, but it took a group of us to get it out into the world, and for that I am eternally grateful.

NOTES

My methodology for democratizing knowledge is storytelling, but in these stories lie theory and information I am not quoting but have been informed by through and through. What that means is that I have added those notes back here specifically, but my bibliography will have more extensive readings to understand the ins and outs of all these stories.

The majority of my references are from BIPOC, because citations are political. We can give power to some voices, and often the voices that are considered experts in their fields are white. In choosing to have mostly nonwhite sources, I am rejecting the racist notion that BIPOC thinkers, theologians, and scholars bring nothing to the table. We do bring a lot, and often we are speaking from lived experiences, which hold more value to me than "experts" who have no idea what they are talking about.

NOTES FOR VOLUNTOURISM CHAPTER

I introduce this chapter with an Audre Lorde quote from "The Uses of Anger," *Women's Studies Quarterly* 25:1/2 (1997), pp. 278–285. I have found that Black liberation theologians and feminists have informed my work, largely because my theological seminary had the largest concentration of Black faculty out of all the theological schools at the time when I was enrolled. I was radicalized by Black voices, Black scholars, Black feminists, and Black writers. The particular quote about anger resonates with me because there is this understanding of anger as a negative and unproductive emotional response, which I resent because my anger informs my work constantly. I write with anger, and I create with anger. This entire chapter demonstrates my anger, and my anger is generative. I utilize that same essay as a foundational text when I talk about white guilt by the voluntourists. Lorde refers to white guilt on p. 283 and says, "Guilt is only another way of avoiding informed action, of buying time out of the pressing need to make clear choices, out of the approaching storm that can feed the earth as well as bend of trees." My indictment of voluntourists comes from reading Black thinkers like Audre Lorde who give me permission to be angry, and the language I use comes from reading Lorde extensively.

Another scholar and reference I use often to inform my work on white saviorism is that of Paulo Freire. Freire is used throughout this book, as his theories can be applied generously. The particular quote I use can be found in *Pedagogy of the Oppressed: 50th Anniversary Edition* (New York: Bloomsbury Academic, 2018), p. 79. Freire's work is a good theorical framework for how oppressed people overcome their oppression, and a lot of my own language is heavily informed by him.

I am also informed by Delores S. Williams, who makes a connection between conquered lands and conquered people, from a Black perspective but also an Indigenous one. Her work is found in *Sisters in the Wilderness: The Challenge of Womanist God-Talk* (Maryknoll, NY: Orbis Books, 1993). The particular citations I am informed by for this section come from pp. 89 and 114.

A poignant secondary read in terms of language around colonialism and conquest is Patricia Seed's *Ceremonies of Possession in Europe's Conquest of the New World, 1492–1640* (Cambridge:

Cambridge University Press, 1995). This book specifically talks about the European powers that had vested interests in the expansion of their empires. Through Seed, I understood the business side of colonialism, the greed that occurred during colonialism.

There are two poignant authors and historians that I read specifically to inform this chapter. One is Juan González's *Harvest of Empire: A History of Latinos in America*, rev. ed. (New York: Penguin Books, 2011). González has an entire chapter on Nicaragua. This is a recommended read for most of my readers. There are designated chapters on almost every Latin American country, and each chapter has exhaustive information in terms of American interventions. González is an investigative journalist and a cofounder of the Young Lords.

Through González, I found the work of Claribel Alegría and Darwin Flakoll. Their book touches on the Somoza family's reign of terrors. Through their book, which details the assassination of Tachito from the perspective of his assassins, I gained a lot of insight into who this man was to the Nicaraguan people outside just my family's perspective. *Death of Somoza* (Willimantic, CT: Curbstone Press, 1996).

Luis Rivera Pagán is a historian who writes about the political and religious conquest of the Americas with numbers and actual data like how large the population size was in certain larger Indigenous communities. Through Rivera Pagán's work, I found ways to correlate colonialism in the 1400s to colonialism within American interventions from the 1930s to 1980s. For more on colonialism in the Americas, turn to Rivera Pagán's book, *A Violent Evangelism: The Political and Religious Conquest of the Americas* (Louisville, KY: Westminster/John Knox Press, 1992).

I get the majority of my knowledge about trauma from Bessel van der Kolk's book *The Body Keeps the Score: Brain, Mind, and Body in the Healing of Trauma* (New York: Penguin Books, 2015). This book unpacks the many ways that trauma manifests. It also explores neuroscience behind what happens to your brain during traumatic experiences and posits that trauma needs to be addressed directly to heal. Your body and your brain are made to keep you alive, and if you do not address the triggers your body has recognized through trauma, then you are destined to keep repeating patterns through trauma-fueled responses. Understanding how my parents' unresolved trauma has become my own trauma has been instrumental for me, hence I weave that sentence throughout the chapter: trauma is inherited. I am writing from knowledge gained and treating that knowledge as important by centering it as matter-of-fact.

Finally, I quote Donald Trump when he referred to certain countries as shithole countries. That quote came from an article titled "President Trump Called El Salvador, Haiti 'Shithole Countries': Report," *Time*, January 11, 2018, https://time.com/5100058/donald-trump-shithole-countries/. For me, highlighting the irony of this particular statement throughout the chapter takes power away from those words that hurt so many, without making this chapter about Trump. Rather, it is about what Trump's words represent about the ignorance of the American people and their relationship to the worldwide harm they have been complicit in.

NOTES FOR COLORISM CHAPTER

I introduce this chapter with the primary text I used for research in this particular chapter, which is JeffriAnne Wilder's *Color Stories: Black Women and Colorism in the 21st Century* (Santa Barbara, CA: Praeger, 2015), p. 6. Wilder writes about colorism not being contained within the Black experience; rather, it is an insidious and prevalent part of the experiences of people of color. The second quote from Wilder is found on p. 47. The term "everyday colorism" is coined by her on p. 58. I've had extensive conversations and attended entire panels on colorism, as well as read about it as authors mention it, yet this is the only full-length book that I have read about colorism that felt exhaustive. I am sure there are other texts, but this is still my primary text and I am informed by it the most.

In terms of understanding the construction of mestizaje, and how it is rooted in the erasure of Blackness specifically in my context, I read Lowell Gudmundson's chapter "What Difference Did Color Make?: Blacks in the 'White Towns' of Western Nicaragua in the 1880s," which is found in the anthology *Blacks and Blackness in Central America: Between Race and Place*, eds. Justin Wolfe and Lowell Gudmundson (Durham, NC: Duke University Press, 2010), p. 211. On p. 210 there is a snapshot of the racial categories that were included in a census and instructions given to census takers to misidentify people for the purposes of boosting mestizaje as the preferred national identity. Nicaragua is written about as an extreme case of erasure, so, whether I know it or not, I am shaped by that reality as a Nicaragua citizen by birth. When writing about any given topic, I seek to find solid footing in readings that talk about my specific context, which can be place of birth, gender, race, sexuality, class—the list goes on. But as a *light* postmodernist, I find value in contextualization. As a reader, finding your context-specific texts will unearth a series of explanations you did not know you needed for questions you were not even asking—which is a beautiful thing. So I implore you to find what is being written about your communities, by your communities.

In terms of understanding how race-based community formations came into existence, I read Justin Wolfe's "'The Cruel Whip': Race and Place in Nineteenth-Century Nicaragua," which is also found in *Blacks and Blackness in Central America*, pp. 177–207. An understanding that the construction of mestizaje was a concerted effort of centering whiteness demands that my reader engage with that entire book.

To understand how facial features and hair types resulted in skewed racial categorization, I recommend reading Mauricio

Meléndez Obando's chapter, titled "The Slow Ascent of the Marginalized: Afro-Descendants in Costa Rica and Nicaragua," found in that same anthology (pp. 334–354). Terms like blanqueamiento are further explained, and a look into how Spanish pure blood was guarded and honored is given.

Additionally, I utilize the term eugenics in this chapter. When people think of eugenics, they think of the early twentieth century. However, eugenic beliefs have existed since before they became popularized and socially accepted, and then rejected. This is not about the contemporary understanding of eugenics. Rather, it is about a system of beliefs around who is worthy of humanity and who is inferior, and the actions that followed based on those beliefs.

This chapter, much like the voluntourism chapter, uses a lot of the knowledge gained from Juan González, specifically when he talks about the conversion of Indigenous people in *Harvest of Empire* (p. 13).

Finally, I mention Gloria Anzaldúa in this chapter, briefly. Unfortunately, Anzaldúa perpetuates the "raza cósmica" stuff that feels equally problematic to mestizaje. In an attempt to reject blanqueamiento, Anzaldúa claims Indigeneity that simply is often inaccurate and blanketed. Claiming Indigeneity, as a mixed person, erases it from those communities in our countries that are still practicing Indigenous traditions and speaking their Indigenous languages. Unless we are willing to learn the languages of our Indigenous ancestors and relearn their traditions, we have to acknowledge that there are privileges in being mestizo within our particular borders. Understanding that we can revere our Indigenous ancestors without erasing and co-opting traditions that are not ours to co-opt is the work of liberation. Anzaldúa's work has unfortunately emboldened too many mestizos who are not willing to do the work of actually divesting from mestizaje but who only claim Indigeneity in passing, as if that has been optional for actual Indigenous people in our countries and here.

Nevertheless, Anzaldúa's work planted a seed for me, when otherwise I would have not fully understood the severity of the anti-Indigenous sentiments that I experienced. I use her quote from *Borderlands/La Frontera: The New Mestiza*, 4th ed. (San Francisco: Aunt Lute Books, 2012).

NOTES FOR IMPOSTOR SYNDROME CHAPTER

The quote that opens this chapter, although not about impostor syndrome, points at the difficulties and self-silencing that students of color experience. This quote is found in Richard Delgado and Jean Stefancic's book *Critical Race Theory: An Introduction*, 3rd. ed. (New York: NYU Press, 2017), pp. 50–51. Delgado, like Freire, is a primary voice that informed this entire book, so you will see this particular text in various chapters.

I am the founder and owner of Latina Rebels, and this chapter is the first time I mention this organization. For understanding the value of creating spaces for us, by us, through the Latina Rebels perspective, read Kaitlin E. Thomas, "Latina Rebels Turn to Memes, Humor to Rethink Media on Hot-Button Issues," *The World*, April 16, 2019, www.pri.org/stories/2019-04-16/Latina-rebels-turn-memes-humor-rethink-media-hot-button-issues. Finding our communities in white spaces can be the difference between dropping out and graduating. Sometimes our communities will not be physically present but rather exclusively online, and that is our new normal.

In terms of the pervasiveness of impostor syndrome, I read Jaruwan Sakulku and James Alexander, "The Impostor Phenomenon," *International Journal of Behavioral Science* 6:1 (2011). P. 75 specifically gives statistical evidence.

A primary text I learned extensively from is Pauline Rose Clance's book, *The Impostor Phenomenon: Overcoming the Fear That Haunts Your Success* (Atlanta: Peachtree Publishers, 1985). Impostor syndrome was not understood to be an exclusively BIPOC experience, so I turned to its originator to find my footing. Racialized impostor syndrome is what I am talking about throughout this text, but in order to do that I needed to understand where it came from and what impostor syndrome originally meant. Some of these terms evolve from other terms; that is how language works and how we evolve as a society. I use a specific quote of Clance's that can be found on pp. 25–26. The next direct quote I use can be found on p. 26.

The psychology of impostor syndrome is something I write about a lot in this chapter, and it is all informed by a series of articles. One of those articles is by Jeremy Bauer-Wolf, "Feeling Like Impostors," *Inside Higher Ed*, April 6, 2017, www.insidehighered .com/news/2017/04/06/study-shows-impostor-syndromes -effect-minority-students-mental-health. In terms of how hard it is to maneuver racialized impostor syndrome, I referenced Kristin Wong's article, "Dealing with Impostor Syndrome When You're Treated as an Impostor," *New York Times*, June 12, 2018, www .nytimes.com/2018/06/12/smarter-living/dealing-with-impostor -syndrome-when-youre-treated-as-an-impostor.html. I quote Dawn X. Henderson from her article, "Why Do Students of Color Feel like an Imposter in School?," *Psychology Today*, April 11, 2017, www.psychologytoday.com/us/blog/the-trajectory-race/201704 /why-do-students-color-feel-imposter-in-school. In terms of understanding what is happening the minds of those suffering from impostor syndrome, I am informed by Sakulku and Alexander's "The Impostor Phenomenon" (p. 77).

Additionally, I was heavily informed by Mikaela Pitcan, Alice E. Marwick, and danah boyd's "Performing a Vanilla Self: Respectability Politics, Social Class, and the Digital World," *Journal of Computer-Mediated Communication* 23:3 (May 2018), pp. 163–179, doi:10.1093/jcmc/zmy008. Although this article informs my respectability chapter later, a lot of this work is intersectional by default, since I embody a lot of marginalized intersections.

I mention a series of experiences in my graduate program that made me feel inadequate. In this story, I am bringing in the pain that is mentioned in Angela P. Harris and Carmen G. González's "Introduction," in *Presumed Incompetent: The Intersections of Race and Class for Women in Academia*, eds. Gabriella Gutiérrez y Muhs et al. (Louisville, CO: Utah State University Press, 2012), pp. 1–16. This entire anthology highlights the ways that Black, Indigenous, and women of color are made to feel inferior in academia, not because they think they are incompetent but because they are assumed to be. I highly recommend getting a copy of this book if you are a BIWOC and struggling in academia.

When I say that perfectionism, meritocracy, and individualism are wrong, I am informed by Kenneth T. Wang et al., "Are Perfectionism, Individualism, and Racial Color-Blindness Associated with Less Cultural Sensitivity? Exploring Diversity Awareness in White Prospective Teachers," *Journal of Diversity in Higher Education* 7:3 (2014), p. 213, doi:10.1037/a0037337. Racism and white supremacy are the underlying factors of these ideologies, and Tema Okun has a really accessible explainer for what white supremacy is and what it includes, titled, "White Supremacy Culture," Dismantling Racism Works, last updated June 2020, www.dismantling racism.org/white-supremacy-culture.html.

When I write about the hostility of the white gaze, I am talking specifically about the ways that racism has kept Black and Latinx folks from getting loans, finding apartments in the nicer parts of town, and so on. I am informed by Richard Delgado and Jean Stefancic's *Critical Race Theory* (p. 12). I am also informed by Cheryl E. Matias, *Feeling White: Whiteness, Emotionality, and Education* (Rotterdam, The Netherlands: Sense Publishers, 2016). Referring to makeup as war paint is not my original thought, rather one that is pervasive in queer spaces and femme spaces. Julie Bettie has an entire book talking about the aesthetics of Latinas as a means of regaining autonomy. This book is titled *Women*

Without Class: Girls, Race, and Identity (Berkeley: University of California Press, 2014).

My liberation talk at the end of this chapter is informed by Freire's *Pedagogy of the Oppressed* (pp. 48 and 58).

When I talk about white people's intentions, I am referencing Robin DiAngelo's *White Fragility: Why It's So Hard for White People to Talk About Racism* (Boston: Beacon Press, 2018), specifically p. 43. DiAngelo writes about "aversive racism" as the specific type of well-intentioned racism. I do not use this term in my story when I write about it, but it is what I want my readers to understand. This type of racism is not less harmful because of its intentions, and that is what I am trying to get across in this section.

When I write about makeup and church, I am informed by my own experiences but also by a well-researched concept that links Christianity and sexism, specifically found in Marcella Althaus-Reid's *From Feminist Theology to Indecent Theology: Readings on Poverty, Sexual Identity and God* (London: SCM Press, 2004), p. 7.

Finally, the Latina myths and tropes are informed by my readings of Myra Mendible's "Introduction: Embodying Latinidad: An Overview," in *From Bananas to Buttocks: The Latina Body in Popular Film and Culture*, ed. Myra Mendible (Austin: University of Texas Press, 2007), pp. 1–28.

NOTES FOR MYTH OF MERITOCRACY CHAPTER

When I note that people seemed "American," what I am implying is the nationally constructed identity of the United States as seen in television shows like *Full House* and movies like *Home Alone* that were popular during my childhood. When I write about American national identity, I am talking about class and race. The white middle-class identity is an American identity that is purported as the representation of us all. I have not been the originator of this idea; rather, I am just writing about it without attempting to convince my audience. But you can find more about this in Shari Roberts's "'The Lady in the Tutti-Frutti Hat': Carmen Miranda, a Spectacle of Ethnicity," *Cinema Journal* 32:3 (January 1, 1993), pp. 3–23, https://doi.org/10.2307/1225876.

In this chapter, I reference Bill Keller a lot in terms of understanding class and class differences. His book *Class Matters* (New York: Times Books, 2005) is foundational for this chapter. Another primary text for this chapter is David K. Shipler's *The Working Poor: Invisible in America* (New York: Vintage, 2005). I read this book in my first Ethics in Society class in my master's program. The long quote I use from Shipler is found on pp. 5–6.

In terms of resources that helped me frame class with my own experiences, I read Julie Bettie's *Women Without Class*. That sociological study transformed me and took me to my most profound aha! moments in terms of whiteness and class performance, and I highly recommend it.

I also highly recommend the podcast by the *New York Times* with host Chana Joffe-Walt titled *Nice White Parents*. This podcast explains how school desegregation has meant segregation through gifted programs and other programs that keep the white and wealthier students in smaller classrooms with better teachers.

NOTES FOR POLITICS OF RESPECTABILITY CHAPTER

The quote after the story that begins this chapter is from Audre Lorde, found in "The Uses of Anger" (p. 284). What I am trying to do is bridge the exhaustion written about to the chapter theme around respectability politics. This quote explains the exhaustion and its root cause, which I explain for the remainder of this chapter.

An interesting thing to note is that I write that I had to justify occupying my seat, ironically due to assumptions made about affirmative action. I describe this because that is what is often explicitly stated and implicitly implied in social spaces by the white students toward the students of color, yet white women are the primary beneficiaries of affirmative action, which no one is discussing. I am aggressively addressing the affirmative action implication by naming it, but I know that it is not even the case. More about this can be found in Bettina Aptheker's "Foreword" in *Presumed Incompetent* (pp. xi–xiiii).

One of the primary texts for this chapter is Mikaela Pitcan, Alice E. Marwick, and danah boyd's "Performing a Vanilla Self." Through this article, I found the origins of the term "respectability politics" and use a direct quote from it toward the end of the chapter. The quote is by Evelyn Higginbotham.

My understanding of how respectability was used as a strategy comes from Fredrick C. Harris's article, "The Rise of Respectability Politics," *Dissent*, Winter 2014, www.dissentmagazine.org /article/the-rise-of-respectability-politics.

Understanding class performances and Latina stereotypes means reading Jillian Hernandez, "'Miss, You Look like a Bratz Doll': On Chonga Girls and Sexual-Aesthetic Excess," *NWSA Journal* 21:3 (2009), pp. 63–90, www.jstor.org/stable/20628195. In this article, Hernandez addresses the white and middle-class construction of the US identity, and with that knowledge I can name my sense of displacement that continues past my migration. I use a quote from this article within my chapter, which can be found on p. 66. Additionally, all I understand in terms of reclaiming the chonga subculture is through Hernandez. My deep understanding of this article led to me writing the chonga manifesto at the end of the chapter.

Another important text for this chapter is Cynthia Enloe's *Bananas, Beaches and Bases: Making Feminist Sense of International Politics*, 2nd ed. (Berkeley: University of California Press, 2014). On p. 99, Enloe specifically talks about respectability in relationship to invasions, in colonial times but also in in times of war. There, she discusses colonial white women imposing Victorian codes of femininity as morally superior.

The double consciousness reference is specifically to W. E. B. Du Bois's concept of "double consciousness."

I utilize terms like *civilized* intentionally, because as someone in the Indigenous diaspora I find good behavior to align with civility and the anti-Indigenous connotations that word carries. I am informed of this by Delores S. Williams in *Sisters in the Wilderness* (p. 114), where she writes that since the aim of the pioneer was to transform the wilderness into civilization, this was "the reward for his sacrifices, the definition of his achievements, and the source of his pride. He applauded his successes in terms suggestive of the high stakes he attached to the conflict." Of course, the wildness could not be transformed from "savagery" to order without destroying its natural arrangement. Transforming the wilderness not only meant dealing with the natural environment; it also meant civilizing "savage" humans associated with the wilderness. Such as the Native Americans identified with the wilderness of America and the African people allied with the "wilds" of Africa. Slavery was rationalized and argued as the proper "civilizing process" for these "savage" people. And when slavery failed—as it did with Native Americans—women and men became, for the Euro-Americans, the proper strategy for subduing wilderness people.

This book and this particular quote reflect a larger narrative of subjugation through civility.

I do mention that the Bible was used to silence and shame me in significant ways. So when I write about "God-fearing women," I am referencing that to point to a particular Bible verse that was weaponized against me to keep me in line, which is found in 1 Tim. 2:9 (KJV): "In like manner also, that women adorn themselves in modest apparel, with shamefacedness and sobriety; not with braided hair, or gold, or pearls, or costly array."

I write about theologies in a singular form, since the field of theology is seldom understood as a field of plurality—when in fact the study of theologies teaches that there is not one theology but endless amounts of theologies. Yet, we are regularly taught one and that one theology is usually antiquated and European. Marcella Althaus-Reid writes about this on p. 21 of *From Feminist Theology to Indecent Theology*. Most liberation theologians are acutely aware of the ways that mainstream Christianity disregards liberation theologies for the whiter, more dogmatic older theologies.

When I specifically write about bilingualism, I am utilizing the traditional definition of code-switching, which means to switch from one language to another as a fully bilingual or trilingual person, or anyone who is not monolingual. For this, I referenced Katja F. Cantone's *Code-Switching in Bilingual Children* (Dordrecht, The Netherlands: Springer, 2007).

I use author Juliana Delgado Lopera's quote from their article titled "Spanglish Isn't a 'Wrong' Form of English—It's How Great Stories Are Told," *Teen Vogue*, May 1, 2020, www.teenvogue.com/story/spanglish-isnt-wrong-form-of-english. I especially loved this use of bilingualism, and Delgado Lopera is also from Miami, which feels very specific to my own experiences since Miami is a such a bilingual city.

I write about mestizo briefly; for more information on that topic refer to the notes on the colorism chapter.

The tropicalization of Latinas is a particular trope that binds Latinas to bodily excess. More of this can be found in Myra Mendible's "Introduction" in *From Bananas to Buttocks*.

Because a lot of these chapters intersect, race- and racism-specific text in this chapter can be found in Robin DiAngelo's *White Fragility*. Specifically, the school-to-prison pipeline reference can be found on p. 92. Another text that supports this prison pipeline is found in Richard Delgado and Jean Stefancic's *Critical Race Theory* (p. 13).

The Celine Parreñas Shimizu quote can be found in *The Hyper-sexuality of Race: Performing Asian/American Women on Screen and Scene* (Durham, NC: Duke University Press, 2007), p. 5.

NOTES FOR TOXIC MASCULINITY CHAPTER

In this chapter, I do not mention mi mami often, yet she was a passive participant in our terrorization. This chapter is not about her, but that does not mean that her complicity is overlooked. Defending any abuser is violent, and her participation in it is not ignored—rather, it is too complex and nuanced for this particular book. I do hope to write about that entire relationship in its own full-length book.

I want to contextualize my church upbringing, because framing it as conservative does not do it justice, since conservatism casts a wide net. My particular home church taught that virginity is to be protected, though only in women, and it hosted purity balls for daughters and dads. My family in Nicaragua goes to this home church also, and my uncle did not allow his daughters to cut their hair or shave unwanted body hair well into their puberty years, until they individually rebelled. Women often were discouraged from dressing in ways that would be considered sexy, so form-fitting clothing was looked down upon. We attended church four times a week, regularly. Once for Sunday, which was a daylong activity. Then Saturday for youth group, Wednesdays for small groups, and random days in the week for the worship team to practice, as well as the dance team, and any performances like plays. Men ran the church as the appointed leaders, and their wives cleaned and cooked for the congregants. When I am talking about strict binary expectations based on assumed gender, this is what I mean. There was an assumed superiority of manhood that was bred into this particular type of conservative Christian church.

My primary texts of reference for this chapter are bell hooks's *All About Love: New Visions* (New York: Harper Perennial, 2001) and *The Will to Change: Men, Masculinity, and Love* (New York: Washington Square Press, 2004). In terms of my definition of patriarchy, I suggest hooks's article "Understanding Patriarchy" (available online through Imagine No Borders, https://imagineno borders.org/pdf/zines/UnderstandingPatriarchy.pdf). hooks is the most profound author, personally, for understanding what it means to deal with toxic, violent men.

When writing about girls and dads, I am supported through hooks's *The Will to Change*. Throughout the chapter, I explicitly state that being a daddy's girl is a status that we are socialized to desire. Daddy's girl is one of the first respectable feminine categories that girls are inducted into, if their home has a present father. When I refer to my dad as a provider, I am drawing from p. 2, where hooks writes, "Patriarchal culture has always taught girls and boys that Dad's love is more valuable than mother love." I do not create theories as much as I learn from them and re-tell theories in my own stories, explaining the theory through experiences.

When I write about my father's pride, I am informed by Elizabeth E. Brusco's *The Reformation of Machismo: Evangelical Conversion and Gender in Colombia* (Austin: University of Texas Press, 2004). This particular text is rather helpful in terms of understanding that the term machismo is not the same as patriarchy—rather, it is closer to toxic masculinity by definition. Machismo is about the power and violence within a patriarchal society and as a result of that society. I opted to not use the word machismo intentionally, since there is an assumption that machismo is a Latin American problem, and that American men know better. To avoid that misunderstanding, I used the closest word to machismo I could find, toxic masculinity, so as to not absolve US-born men from blame. The quote I use toward the end of this chapter is from Brusco's *The Reformation of Machismo* (p. 80).

My main concentration while obtaining my master of divinity was in liberation ethics. So, when I am talking about "good" and "bad," I am doing so with the knowledge that Americans define good within a limited, Judeo-Christian understanding, which is what I mean by a narrow definition of good and bad. Within liberation ethics, we attempt to imagine new spaces outside the Christian binaries of good and bad, which has been an overall exclusive framework rather than an inclusive and thus neutrally ethical one. What the binaries generally exclude are female autonomy and acceptance of LGBTQIA+ folks.

There is something to be said about obtaining a theological degree from an elite institution as a Brown Latina immigrant from a fundamentalist context, and that is that while at school I spent my entire time defending my communities. Churches like the one I was raised in are considered low church, and the more progressive churches not-so-coincidentally are generally known as high churches (not counting Catholicism, which is known generally as high church). As someone from a low church, I have resented this labeling due to the hierarchy that it implies about our "uneducated" theologians and pastors—who also happen to be Black and Brown. Yet, when I returned home, I spent my time defending myself and my decision to study theology as a woman and was able to do so based on the education I had received. Knowing that I was always fighting for myself and my communities, at every juncture, is something I have not fully been able to reconcile—and you can sense that tension within this chapter. I leave that tension there, because maybe the readers will find some ways of making sense of this chaos that results simply because of all the intersections I embody.

I switch my tone toward my dad; it is a matter of distance for me. I refer to him as *mi papi* and then as *my father* or *my dad*, real quick, as I attempt to shield myself from him. Mi papi would never harm me, but my father and my dad did, often.

I utilize Cynthia Enloe's *Bananas, Beaches and Bases* quote, which can be found on p. 108. Enloe writes about gender and militarization, the connections between war and the subjugation of women. I write about this book with reverence because it gives back humanity to communities that are already dehumanized by virtue of being nonwhite. I highly recommend this text.

The final hooks quote is found on p. 14 of *The Will to Change*.

Finally, in terms of understanding emotional abuse, I recommend reading Marti Tamm Loring's *Emotional Abuse: The Trauma and the Treatment* (San Francisco: Jossey-Bass, 1998). And in terms of summing up the tales of La Malinche, I recommend the anthology edited by Ana Castillo, *Goddess of the Americas/La Diosa de las Américas: Writings on the Virgin of Guadalupe* (New York: Riverhead Books, 1997) and the anthology edited by Cherríe Moraga and Gloria Anzaldúa, *This Bridge Called My Back: Writings by Radical Women of Color*, 4th ed. (Albany: SUNY Press, 2015). I have more references in my bibliography, and for those references I have Dr. Maria Paula Chaves Daza, who teaches at Bard College, to thank. She was the first person who introduced me to the Malinche texts and who I reached out to for sources on it all, and she sent me numerous sources that were instrumental.

NOTES FOR INTERSECTIONALITY CHAPTER

I dedicate this chapter to Monique. Monique is a girl I met as a teenager. Monique joined our youth group when we took a trip to the local Christmas fair. It was nighttime when she arrived, and the senior pastor's son thought she was beautiful. I remember they spent the whole night chatting and flirting, and everyone was buzzing about it in the way that only people who value pastors and their children do. The next morning, at church, she showed up with her mom and dad. In the daylight, Monique had a five-o'clock shadow, as hairy girls sometimes do if they do decide to shave their faces. The senior pastor's son never spoke to her again, and the entire youth group whispered about this for years. Everyone made fun of Monique behind her back, but she had never done anything to us but be friendly. Monique's only crime was that she was a hairy girl. I wrote this chapter for her, and for all the hairy girls with equally gut-wrenching stories of being unchosen.

Kimberlé Crenshaw is the first person to come up with the term intersectionality, and introducing this chapter with a quote from one of her writings felt like a good way to position the entire chapter. This particular quote can be found in her article "The Intersection of Race and Gender," in *Critical Race Theory: The Key Writings That Formed the Movement*, ed. Kimberlé Crenshaw et al. (New York: New Press, 2010), p. 375.

A primary source for this chapter is a book by Rebecca M. Herzig, *Plucked: A History of Hair Removal* (New York: NYU Press, 2016). The first quote I use from this source can be found on p. 130 of her book. This text unveils the history of hair removal throughout time, including the presumption of inferior status of Indigenous people by the hairier Europeans and the torture of Brown men in Guantanamo by removing their hair. It is a dense read but a necessary one, in terms of understanding how we got to a place of valuing female hairlessness. The second quote I use of Herzig comes from pp. 9–10. I found this text when it was recommended by gender-nonconforming author, performer, speaker, and fashionist@ Alok Vaid-Menon and quickly purchased my own copy. I learn a lot outside of academia through public scholars like Alok who make accessibility their brand.

I am also heavily informed by Patricia Hill Collins's book *Intersectionality as Critical Social Theory* (Durham, NC: Duke University Press, 2019). That book is a great accompanying piece of theory that will complement a lot of what I write about for any reader interested in further unpacking intersectionality.

When I write about the ways that my intersections work to privilege me, that specifically comes from Richard Delgado and Jean Stefancic's *Critical Race Theory* (p. 58).

Gringo is a colloquial term utilized matter-of-factly to speak about white people in my community. However, the minor intonations can add a lot of context for the word. I am utilizing "-ito," which is a diminutive of the word and asserts care and love.

Myra Mendible's "Introduction," in *From Bananas to Buttocks* (p. 7), provides the in-betweenness quote.

When it comes to intersections, I became aware of my own through other storytellers. A wonderful series of essays I was inspired by comes from the anthology *Presumed Incompetent*. Through these essays, I found my own voice. A particular essay I love, on feeling special as a Black woman, is written by Serena Easton and titled "On Being Special," in *Presumed Incompetent* (pp. 153–154): "Racial interruptions were everywhere—constant reminders that I was different and unequal, and didn't belong."

When I say that I had a reckoning with whiteness, it does not mean that I ever identified as white. Rather, I had passively allowed whiteness to tell me that Indigeneity was not worthy by rejecting that part of my family line, much like everyone else in my family did. It meant that I functioned within the limited notions of meritocracy and individualism, both by-products of a white-supremacist and capitalist society. Investing in whiteness was how I ended up buying bootleg colored contacts. It has nothing to do with being white, but rather aspiring to be accepted into whiteness.

I write about conditional acceptance in this chapter as proximity to whiteness—and I name it as an illusion. A recent example can be seen through COVID-19. East Asian communities experienced a blanketed assumption of their culpability for the virus, and various think pieces that came from the Asian community described feeling the white gaze in a way that was dangerous and dehumanizing. Frank Meng, "Asians Under COVID-19: 'Yellow Peril' or 'Model Minority'? Neither," *The Spectator*, May 7, 2020, https://spec.hamilton.edu/asians-under-covid-19-yellow-peril-or-model-minority-neither-79d2969a0bc. This puts into question the model minority label since it is obviously conditional.

NOTES FOR THE MALE GAZE CHAPTER

The first quote I use in this chapter is from Paulo Freire's *Pedagogy of the Oppressed* (p. 51). As I have said, this entire book utilizes Freire as a foundational text, and it is written reflecting that.

When I write about rebelling against the status quo of respectable womanhood, I am aware of the risk in that rebellion because of my lived experiences, but I am also informed by Mikaela Pitcan, Alice E. Marwick, and danah boyd's "Performing a Vanilla Self." Explicitly, in this article we see that women have to maintain their social and economic capital through good behavior, otherwise we risk more than just friends—we risk everything.

The Bible reference on tattoos is found in Lev. 19:26–28 (NIV). Another Biblical reference I utilize, related to the terms ayuda idónea, can be found in Gen. 2:18: "Y el SEÑOR Dios dijo: No es bueno que el hombre esté solo; le haré una ayuda idónea."

A great reference and book I used to back up my own stories is Elizabeth E. Brusco's *The Reformation of Machismo*. If you also grew up in a conversative Christian Latinx household, this book will be very insightful, and might invite you to look into a new argument around machismo and Christianity that I know I had not considered. Not everything I recommend is in agreement with what I write about, but still informs it regardless.

bell hooks is one of the more relatable authors I have read in terms of interpersonal experiences with the patriarchy. The two quotes I use are from "Understanding Patriarchy." I live from this quote from this text: "Patriarchy is the single most life-threatening social disease assaulting the male body and spirit in our nation."

Two Latina theo-ethicists I am heavily informed by, whose theologies impact my own work, are Marcella Althaus-Reid and Ada María Isasi-Díaz. This includes Isasi-Díaz's book, *En La Lucha/In the Struggle: Elaborating a Mujerista Theology* (Minneapolis: Fortress Press, 2004). Whenever I am pushing against traditional theologies, I am using the knowledge of Latina theologians who have written extensively to undo toxic patriarchal theologies from hurting more Latinas.

The line about "ethnic spectacle" is informed by a cinematic journal that talks about Carmen Miranda. I have learned that a lot of the spicy Latina stereotypes are a product of interventions, and Carmen Miranda was used as a means to that end. I recommend Shari Roberts's "The Lady in the Tutti-Frutti Hat."

The idea that intellectual womanhood must be stripped of feminine markers has a long-documented history, and this comment is bigger than me—it comes from a deep understanding that women are not given proper attention and respect in academia. And for that particular professor, gaining respect meant complicity, which is my main critique of white women's survival strategy: complicity. Angela P. Harris and Carmen G. González, "Introduction," in *Presumed Incompetent*, pp. 4–5:

Among researchers and scholars, the romance of the brilliant, lonely genius in pursuit of Truth—even if the heavens should fall— still lingers around promotion reviews. These revered characteristics, however, are not only associated with the hard sciences. They are also traditionally linked with masculinity and are understood as the opposite of femininity. For instance, rationality is prized at the expense of recognizing—or being able to deal with—emotion (Harris and Shultz 1993). On every campus, tasks associated with femininity—such as teaching—are valued less than those associated with masculinity, and the most prestigious disciplines are those with the fewest women. This means . . . that people with female bodies or feminine self-presentation are likely to be excluded from certain disciplines or understood as inferior.

NOTES FOR WHITE FRAGILITY CHAPTER

This chapter's primary texts are Cheryl E. Matias's *Feeling White*, Robin DiAngelo's *White Fragility*, and Richard Delgado and Jean Stefancic's *Critical Race Theory*. The quote I open the chapter with is from Matias, *Feeling White* (p. xiii). The other quote I use from Matias can be found on p. 43. But all the aforementioned authors can be used as reference for just about everything I state in this chapter.

The quote I use from Audre Lorde can be found in "The Uses of Anger," p. 282. The symphony of anguish in this article can be found throughout the entire book, and this chapter highlights it while summarizing it all.

The assumption about Amy Cooper's political affiliation can be found online easily. I found some information on this in *The Root*. That is not to say it is an indisputable fact, rather that I am not the only person pointing out that her seemingly liberal politics do not match her actions, and with that logic and my own experiences I build on the argument against the anti-racist liberal white person.

I should note that when I talk about "immigrant friendly" South Florida, I do not want to idealize South Florida, but I do agree that white supremacy is most dangerous when white people are the ones enacting the violence. Although BIPOC can still subscribe to white supremacists' ideals, the violence they enact is on a different scale, although dangerous still.

I utilize a quote by Amy Cooper, which can be found in a CNN article, "White Woman Who Called Police on a Black Man Bird-Watching in Central Park Has Been Fired," CNN, May 26, 2020, https://edition.cnn.com/2020/05/26/us/central-park-video -dog-video-african-american-trnd/index.html.

The final quote I use is from DiAngelo and can be found on p. 5 of *White Fragility*.

NOTES FOR DECOLONIALITY CHAPTER

The primary source for this chapter is a book by Walter D. Mignolo and Catherine E. Walsh, *On Decoloniality: Concepts, Analytics, Praxis* (Durham, NC: Duke University Press, 2018). To fully understand decoloniality, and make your own assessments of it, I implore my readers to pick up a copy of this book. It is dense, but it is great for this type of work. The first quote I use to open the chapter can be found on p. 5. The second quote can be found on p. 3.

The story of my mami I first wrote for the Latina-owned publication *BoldLatina*.

When I talk about intellectualism and its distance from so many people, I am not the first to come to that conclusion. Dr. Constance G. Anthony said it best in her article "The Port Hueneme of My Mind: The Geography of Working-Class Consciousness in One Academic Career," in *Presumed Incompetent* (pp. 300–312): "In a certain respect, being working-class and becoming an academic is an oxymoron. Academics aspire to genteel, professional success; working-class life rejects the genteel for the overt—at times even rude—acknowledgement that life is difficult. Academics revel in a world of carefully chosen words and phrases; subtlety and indirection are prized. A well-delivered, witty repartee at a party is always rewarded. At a working-class party, it would be much safer to say exactly what you mean in a direct way." This sentiment is felt by academics of color, BIAOC, throughout.

When I talk about mi mami's spirituality, I am heavily informed by the "Introduction" in *Voices from the Ancestors: Xicanx and Latinx Spiritual Expressions and Healing Practices*, ed. Lara Medina and Martha R. Gonzales (Tucson: University of Arizona Press, 2019), pp. 3–20, specifically pp. 4–10. The put-your-pee-outside trick rests on the idea that sweet-smelling pee meant that there was sugar in your pee and therefore your body was not doing what it needed to do to regulate that. Rural and poor people have always found ways to keep one another alive when vital medical supplies and doctors were not around or did not exist, and this is just one of those strategies.

I use the word "modernity" because it is a word within the decolonial field that signals developing. It is a coded word used to imply improvement, though that is contested throughout this chapter.

Again, this chapter is informed by Paulo Freire's *Pedagogy of the Oppressed*, because this entire book is a pedagogy of the oppressed through storytelling.

BIBLIOGRAPHY

Alegría, Claribel, and Darwin Flakoll. *Death of Somoza*. Willimantic, CT: Curbstone Press, 1996.

Althaus-Reid, Marcella. *From Feminist Theology to Indecent Theology: Readings on Poverty, Sexual Identity and God*. London: SCM Press, 2004.

Alvarado, Elvia. *Don't Be Afraid, Gringo: A Honduran Woman Speaks from the Heart: The Story of Elvia Alvarado*. Translated by Medea Benjamin. San Francisco: Institute for Food and Development Policy, 1987.

Anonymous. "I Was Taught to Be Proud of My Tight Asian P*ssy—Here's Why I Wish I Hadn't Been." *Everyday Feminism*, July 20, 2016. https://everydayfeminism.com/2016/07/be-proud-tight-asian-pssy/.

Ansari, Mahreen. "What Is BIPOC and Why You Should Use It." *Her Campus*, February 18, 2020. www.hercampus.com/school/umkc/what-bipoc-and-why-you-should-use-it.

Anzaldúa, Gloria. *Borderlands/La Frontera: The New Mestiza*. 4th ed. San Francisco: Aunt Lute Books, 2012.

Asante, Janet. "6 Ways Women of Color Can Overcome Imposter Syndrome." *mater mea*, October 13, 2020. https://www.matermea.com/blog/diversity-in-workplace-advice-for-black-women.

Bates, Kelly. "Racial Imposter Syndrome." Interaction Institute for Social Change, October 11, 2019. https://interactioninstitute.org/racial-imposter-syndrome/.

Beckwith, Ryan Teague. "President Trump Called El Salvador, Haiti 'Shithole Countries': Report." *Time*, January 11, 2018. https://time.com/5100058/donald-trump-shithole-countries/.

Bettie, Julie. *Women Without Class: Girls, Race, and Identity*. Berkeley: University of California Press, 2014.

Browdy de Hernandez, Jennifer, ed. *Women Writing Resistance: Essays on Latin America and the Caribbean*. Boston: South End Press, 2003.

Brusco, Elizabeth E. *The Reformation of Machismo: Evangelical Conversion and Gender in Colombia*. Austin: University of Texas Press, 2004.

Butler, Judith. *Gender Trouble: Feminism and the Subversion of Identity*. New York: Routledge, 2006.

Butler, Octavia E. *Parable of the Sower*. New York: Grand Central Publishing, 2019.

Cantone, Katja F. *Code-Switching in Bilingual Children*. Dordrecht, The Netherlands: Springer, 2007.

Castillo, Ana, ed. *Goddess of the Americas/La Diosa de Las Américas: Writings on the Virgin of Guadalupe*. New York: Riverhead Books, 1997.

Cavanaugh, William T. *Being Consumed: Economics and Christian Desire*. Grand Rapids, MI: Eerdmans, 2008.

Chomsky, Aviva. *Undocumented: How Immigration Became Illegal*. Boston: Beacon Press, 2014.

Clance, Pauline Rose. *The Impostor Phenomenon: Overcoming the Fear That Haunts Your Success*. Atlanta: Peachtree Publishers, 1985.

Clifford, Anne M. *Introducing Feminist Theology*. Maryknoll, NY: Orbis Books, 2001.

Collins, Patricia Hill. *Intersectionality as Critical Social Theory*. Durham, NC: Duke University Press, 2019.

Crenshaw, Kimberlé, Neil T. Gotanda, Gary Peller, and Kendall Thomas, eds. *Critical Race Theory: The Key Writings That Formed the Movement*. New York: New Press, 1995.

Cypess, Sandra Messinger. *La Malinche in Mexican Literature: From History to Myth*. Austin: University of Texas Press, 1991.

Del Castillo, Adelaida R., ed. *Between Borders: Essays on Mexicana/Chicana History*. Mountain View, CA: Floricanto Press, 2005.

Delgado, Richard, and Jean Stefancic. *Critical Race Theory: An Introduction*. 3rd ed. New York: NYU Press, 2017.

Delgado Lopera, Juliana. "Spanglish Isn't a 'Wrong' Form of English—It's How Great Stories Are Told." *Teen Vogue*, May 1, 2020. www.teenvogue.com/story/spanglish-isnt-wrong-form-of-english.

DiAngelo, Robin. *White Fragility: Why It's So Hard for White People to Talk About Racism*. Boston: Beacon Press, 2018.

Dooner, Caroline. *The F*ck It Diet: Eating Should Be Easy*. New York: Harper Wave, 2019.

Durham, Aisha S. *Home with Hip Hop Feminism: Performances in Communication and Culture*. New York: Peter Lang, 2014.

Eady, Cornelius. *Brutal Imagination: Poems*. New York: G. P. Putnam's Sons, 2001.

Enloe, Cynthia. *Bananas, Beaches and Bases: Making Feminist Sense of International Politics*. 2nd ed. Berkeley: University of California Press, 2014.

Fischer-Mirkin, Toby. *Dress Code: Understanding the Hidden Meanings of Women's Clothes*. New York: Clarkson Potter, 1995.

Floyd-Thomas, Stacey M., ed. *Deeper Shades of Purple: Womanism in Religion and Society*. New York: NYU Press, 2006.

Freire, Paulo. *Pedagogy of the Oppressed: 50th Anniversary Edition*. New York: Bloomsbury Academic, 2018.

González, Juan. *Harvest of Empire: A History of Latinos in America*. Rev. ed. New York: Penguin Books, 2011.

Gutiérrez y Muhs, Gabriella, Yolanda Flores Niemann, Carmen G. González, and Angela P. Harris, eds. *Presumed Incompetent: The Intersections of Race and Class for Women in Academia*. Louisville, CO: Utah State University Press, 2012.

Harris, Fredrick C. "The Rise of Respectability Politics." Dissent, Winter 2014. www.dissentmagazine.org/article/the-rise-of-respectability -politics.

Hedges, Chris. *War Is a Force That Gives Us Meaning*. New York: Anchor, 2003.

Henderson, Dawn X. "Why Do Students of Color Feel like an Imposter in School?" *Psychology Today*, April 11, 2017. www.psychologytoday.com /blog/the-trajectory-race/201704/why-do-students-color-feel-imposter -in-school.

Hernandez, Jillian. "'Miss, You Look like a Bratz Doll': On Chonga Girls and Sexual-Aesthetic Excess." *NWSA Journal* 21, no. 3 (2009): 63–90.

Herzig, Rebecca M. *Plucked: A History of Hair Removal*. New York: NYU Press, 2016.

hooks, bell. *All About Love: New Visions*. New York: Harper Perennial, 2001.

———. *Teaching to Transgress: Education as the Practice of Freedom*. New York: Routledge, 1994.

———. "Understanding Patriarchy." Available online through Imagine No Borders, https://imaginenoborders.org/pdf/zines/Understanding Patriarchy.pdf.

———. *The Will to Change: Men, Masculinity, and Love*. New York: Washington Square Press, 2004.

Hull, Gloria T., Patricia Bell Scott, and Barbara Smith, eds. *All the Women Are White, All the Blacks Are Men, but Some of Us Are Brave: Black Women's Studies*. 2nd ed. New York: The Feminist Press at the City University of New York, 2015.

Isasi-Díaz, Ada María. *En La Lucha/In the Struggle: Elaborating a Mujerista Theology*. Minneapolis: Fortress Press, 2004.

Joffe-Walt, Chana. *Nice White Parents*. Produced by Julie Snyder. Podcast series, 2020. https://podcasts.apple.com/us/podcast/nice-white-parents/id1524080195.

Keller, Bill. *Class Matters*. New York: Times Books, 2005.

Kushner, Jacob. "The Voluntourist's Dilemma." *New York Times Magazine*, March 22, 2016. www.nytimes.com/2016/03/22/magazine/the-voluntourists-dilemma.html.

Lira, Natalie, and Nicole L. Novak. "Forced Sterilization Programs in California Once Harmed Thousands—Particularly Latinas." *The Conversation*, March 22, 2018. http://theconversation.com/forced-sterilization-programs-in-california-once-harmed-thousands-particularly-latinas-92324.

Lo, Imi. "Get to the Roots of Your Anxiety and Perfectionism." *Psychology Today*, March 5, 2019. www.psychologytoday.com/blog/living-emotional-intensity/201903/get-the-roots-your-anxiety-and-perfectionism.

Lorde, Audre. "The Uses of Anger." *Women's Studies Quarterly* 25, no. 1/2 (1997): 278–285.

Loring, Marti Tamm. *Emotional Abuse: The Trauma and the Treatment*. San Francisco: Jossey-Bass, 1998.

Matias, Cheryl E. *Feeling White: Whiteness, Emotionality, and Education*. Rotterdam, The Netherlands: Sense Publishers, 2016.

Medina, Lara, and Martha R. Gonzales, eds. *Voices from the Ancestors: Xicanx and Latinx Spiritual Expressions and Healing Practices*. Tucson: University of Arizona Press, 2019.

Mendible, Myra, ed. *From Bananas to Buttocks: The Latina Body in Popular Film and Culture*. Austin: University of Texas Press, 2007.

Meng, Frank. "Asians Under COVID-19: 'Yellow Peril' or 'Model Minority'? Neither." *The Spectator*, May 7, 2020. https://spec.hamilton.edu/asians-under-covid-19-yellow-peril-or-model-minority-neither-79d2969a0bc.

Mignolo, Walter D., and Catherine E. Walsh. *On Decoloniality: Concepts, Analytics, Praxis*. Durham, NC: Duke University Press, 2018.

Mills, Charles W. *The Racial Contract*. Ithaca, NY: Cornell University Press, 2011.

Mojica Rodríguez, Prisca Dorcas. "I Am Not Better Than Mi Mami." *BoldLatina*, October 18, 2108. https://boldlatina.com/i-am-not-better-than-mi-mami-by-prisca/.

Moraga, Cherríe. *Loving in the War Years: Lo que nunca pasó por sus labios*. Boston: South End Press, 1983.

Moraga, Cherríe, and Gloria Anzaldúa, eds. *This Bridge Called My Back: Writings by Radical Women of Color*. 4th ed. Albany: SUNY Press, 2015.

Musarra, Casey. "Imposter Syndrome Can Take a Heavy Toll on People of Color, Particularly African Americans." *DiversityInc*, October 11, 2019. www.diversityinc.com/imposter-syndrome-can-take-a-heavy-toll-on-people-of-color-particularly-african-americans/.

Naylor, Gloria. *The Women of Brewster Place*. New York: Penguin Books, 1983.

Peiss, Kathy. *Hope in a Jar: The Making of America's Beauty Culture*. Philadelphia: University of Pennsylvania Press, 2011.

Pérez, Laura E. *Chicana Art: The Politics of Spiritual and Aesthetic Altarities*. Durham, NC: Duke University Press, 2007.

Pitcan, Mikaela, Alice E. Marwick, and danah boyd. "Performing a Vanilla Self: Respectability Politics, Social Class, and the Digital World." *Journal of Computer-Mediated Communication* 23, no. 3 (May 1, 2018): 163–179. https://doi.org/10.1093/jcmc/zmy008.

Popham, Gabriel. "Boom in 'Voluntourism' Sparks Concerns over Whether the Industry Is Doing Good." Reuters, June 29, 2015. www.reuters.com/article/us-travel-volunteers-charities-idUSKCN0P91AX20150629.

Quinney, Richard. *Class, State, and Crime*. 2nd ed. New York: Longman, 1980.

Randall, Margaret. *Sandino's Daughters: Testimonies of Nicaraguan Women in Struggle*. Rev. ed. New Brunswick, NJ: Rutgers University Press, 1995.

Reed-Danahay, Deborah, ed. *Auto/Ethnography: Rewriting the Self and the Social*. Oxford: Berg, 1997.

Rios, Victor M. *Punished: Policing the Lives of Black and Latino Boys*. New York: NYU Press, 2011.

Rivera Pagán, Luis. *A Violent Evangelism: The Political and Religious Conquest of the Americas*. Louisville, KY: Westminster/John Knox Press, 1992.

Roberts, Shari. "'The Lady in the Tutti-Frutti Hat': Carmen Miranda, a Spectacle of Ethnicity." *Cinema Journal* 32, no. 3 (January 1, 1993): 3–23. https://doi.org/10.2307/1225876.

Romero, Rolando, and Amanda Nolacea Harris, eds. *Feminism, Nation and Myth: La Malinche*. Houston: Arte Público Press, 2005.

Roy, Arundhati. *An Ordinary Person's Guide to Empire*. Boston: South End Press, 2004.

Sakulku, Jaruwan, and James Alexander. "The Impostor Phenomenon." *International Journal of Behavioral Science* 6, no. 1 (2011).

Seed, Patricia. *Ceremonies of Possession in Europe's Conquest of the New World, 1492–1640*. Cambridge: Cambridge University Press, 1995.

Shange, Ntozake. *For Colored Girls Who Have Considered Suicide/When the Rainbow Is Enuf: A Choreopoem*. New York: Scribner, 1997.

Shimizu, Celine Parreñas. *The Hypersexuality of Race: Performing Asian/American Women on Screen and Scene*. Durham, NC: Duke University Press, 2007.

Shipler, David K. *The Working Poor: Invisible in America*. New York: Vintage Books, 2005.

Strings, Sabrina. *Fearing the Black Body: The Racial Origins of Fat Phobia*. New York: NYU Press, 2019.

Troyano, Alina. *I, Carmelita Tropicana: Performing Between Cultures*. Boston: Beacon Press, 2000.

Van der Kolk, Bessel. *The Body Keeps the Score: Brain, Mind, and Body in the Healing of Trauma*. New York: Penguin Books, 2015.

Vasquez, Jessica M. *Mexican Americans Across Generations: Immigrant Families, Racial Realities*. New York: NYU Press, 2011.

Venzo, Paul, and Kristy Hess. "'Honk Against Homophobia': Rethinking Relations Between Media and Sexual Minorities." *Journal of Homosexuality* 60, no. 11 (November 2013): 1539–1556. https://doi.org/10.1080/00918369.2013.824318.

Walker, Alice. *The Color Purple*. Orlando, FL: Harcourt, 2003.

West, Traci C. *Disruptive Christian Ethics: When Racism and Women's Lives Matter*. Louisville, KY: Westminster/John Knox Press, 2006.

Wilder, JeffriAnne. *Color Stories: Black Women and Colorism in the 21st Century*. Santa Barbara, CA: Praeger, 2015.

Williams, Delores S. *Sisters in the Wilderness: The Challenge of Womanist God-Talk*. Maryknoll, NY: Orbis Books, 1993.

Wolfe, Justin, and Lowell Gudmundson, eds. *Blacks and Blackness in Central America: Between Race and Place*. Durham, NC: Duke University Press, 2010.

Wolynn, Mark. *It Didn't Start with You: How Inherited Family Trauma Shapes Who We Are and How to End the Cycle*. New York: Penguin Books, 2017.

Wong, Kristin. "Dealing with Impostor Syndrome When You're Treated as an Impostor." *New York Times*, June 12, 2018. www.nytimes.com/2018/06/12/smarter-living/dealing-with-impostor-syndrome-when-youre-treated-as-an-impostor.html.

Yosso, Tara J. *Critical Race Counterstories Along the Chicana/Chicano Educational Pipeline*. New York: Routledge, 2006.

Zuckerberg, Donna. *Not All Dead White Men: Classics and Misogyny in the Digital Age*. Cambridge, MA: Harvard University Press, 2019.

Prisca Dorcas Mojica Rodríguez is a writer and activist working to shift the national conversation on race. She is the founder of Latina Rebels, which boasts over 350,000 followers across social media platforms, and she has appeared on NPR, *Teen Vogue*, *Cosmopolitan*, *Huffington Post* Latino Voices, Telemundo, and Univision. She was invited to the Obama White House in 2016 and has spoken at over one hundred universities in the past four years, including Princeton, Dartmouth, and Wesleyan. She earned her master of divinity from Vanderbilt University and lives in Nashville, Tennessee.